FOREWORD
by
Mansell Wallace Chairman of Chelmsford City FC

I am delighted to be invited by my cousin Steve to write a Foreword for this his new book '*Living the Claret Dream*' chronicling the exciting years from 1958 to 1968.

Many years ago when he and I stood on the terraces at New Writtle Street I never envisaged that some 50 years later he would be writing this book and I would be Chairman of the club. It delights me to know that Steve, myself and two brothers still share the same passion for City as we did 50 years ago.

The book has brought back many memories that I had completely forgotten about. I will certainly endeavour to make sure the club does not make the same mistakes as it did back then.

I like the idea of it being written through the eyes of people who also believed they were living the dream only for it all to come down to earth with a big bang.

It is through my involvement with City that I have renewed my acquaintance with Steve who moved away from Chelmsford many years ago and now has become a successful author.

I recommend that all supporters, even those too young to remember those times, read this book as it goes beyond what was contained in '*So You Think You Want to be a Director of a Football Club?*' by Peter Mallinger, and gives far more detail of the events that happened to cause the wrong decisions to be made at our club, which eventually were to push us towards a slippery slope.

The publishing of this book coincides with the 75th anniversary of the forming of our wonderful club and would make a great souvenir for any supporter.

It is a book produced by long standing supporters. Steve of course has done the research and most of the writing but with contributions from past players, supporters, administrators and even the local football correspondent from that time. Thanks must also go to Peter Symonds and Alan Berris from *The Printing Place*, who undertake all the club's printing and have worked with Steve to produce this wonderful book. Peter and Alan are not only great supporters of the club from a commercial aspect but they are fans too and have been since the 1960s.

I would also like to thank Steve for kindly agreeing that all profits from the sale of the book be passed to the club.

LIVING THE CLARET DREAM

The Glory Years of Chelmsford City FC

by

Steve Little

Born and educated in Chelmsford Steve has remained a lifelong supporter of City, rarely missing a game during his early teenage years in the 1960s before himself playing locally for Christy Sports, Westlea United and E.C.C. Staff before a more lengthy period at Old Chelmsfordians. With his career in financial services then taking him to Norfolk and Surrey he played extensively there too. Wishing to mark the current club's 75th anniversary Steve has devoted part of his retirement researching and putting together this story of City's glory years, whilst also writing a novel set in World War One and producing a light-hearted book of stories about his teenage years in and around Chelmsford. More details can be seen on his website – www.stevelittlebooks.com

ISBN 978-0-9576894-0-4

First published in the UK in 2013 by
Medehollow Productions
3 Crabtree Drive, Leatherhead, Surrey, KT22 8LW
Telephone: 0044 1372 375574

Printed and bound by
The Printing Place, Chelmsford

CONTENTS

This book is dedicated to my wife, Chris, for her patience and help.

The whole exercise has been a labour of love and I would also like to dedicate the book to all those players, managers and staff at the club who gave us, the fans, so much pleasure and yet, at times, too many moments of despair during the 10 years this story covers. Especially I would like to thank the late John Coward who took us on his journey to live his dream – so sad it never came true.

Other books by Steve Little:

More Than Just A Life – a hard hitting story of a young footballer sent to the trenches in World War One.

Days We'll Remember All Our Lives – a light hearted collection of true stories of teenage years set in and around Chelmsford in the 1950s and 1960s

Soon to be published:

Joining Forces – the sequel to *More Than Just A Life* and a fictional adventure story much of which is set in the Chelmsford area.

Full details of Steve's work can be found at:

www.stevelittlebooks.com

INTRODUCTION

This is the story of a time during the long history of one football club – a club I have supported for most of my life – when its players, officials and supporters lived the dream of reaching the 'Promised Land' of the Football League. For reasons this story will tell, that dream was shattered more than once during the ten year period from 1958 to 1968; the golden era of the 'Clarets' – Chelmsford City FC.

Chelmsford was not the only club to experience this disappointment but some like Peterborough, Oxford and later Cambridge United, Wimbledon, Yeovil and Hereford fulfilled their dream. We missed out. Why? After all, we were the best non-league team in England in 1968, so what conspired against us? Perhaps this story will explain why, but 'Living the Claret Dream' is not a statistical hike through years of matches. Steve Garner in "Wheel 'Em In' The Official History of Chelmsford City Football Club' has already produced a marvellously detailed wealth of information on each City match up to 2001 with some background information on every season and provides all the statistics one could need.

My story goes deeper and more behind the scenes with a different perspective on, without doubt, the most glorious ten years in the City's history. From 1958 to 1968 we lived our dream, with thousands flocking to games to watch our team containing, at times, many players

 1

who had, in the previous season, been playing in the old First Division! The dream was to reach that 'Promised Land' on the coat tails of the visionary Club Chairman, John Coward, a devoted City fan and local businessman. For most of those ten years it was 'Coward's Empire' and it mirrored what was happening at many clubs with one man backing and, in most cases, bankrolling the club. Sounds familiar? You don't have to look far to see it is still happening throughout football today.

History tells us that every great Empire will rise and fall; here was no exception. John Coward drove himself on so hard that it made him ill and he had to stand down, but his 'Empire' had already begun to crumble before that. It's a sad tale of 'what might have been' with some decisions made which, in hindsight, were injudicious but perhaps it all came down to 'luck' or not being in the 'right place' at the 'right time'. Prior to 1987 non-league clubs had to be elected by the current League members from within the four divisions and they were competing with the bottom four teams in Division Four who were seeking re-election. The members always seemed to vote for their 'friends' and no non-league club came close, except when a club already in the League folded and then it was common for the Southern League champions to be elected. So, winning the Southern League meant everything, but when we sensationally achieved this in season 67/68 no one dropped out of the Football League and that was that.

'Living the Claret Dream' is told from the perspective of the supporters, the players, the administrators and directors of the club from that time. I have tried to write it as if it is a journal of events, a diary or, as someone has dubbed it, a 'retrospective fly-on-the-wall documentary'. To achieve this I have had to introduce two fictional characters in young Ron and our director friend to convey the story. However, I can assure you that the facts are true to the best of my knowledge, but certain incidents have been introduced to put over these facts in a more interesting way.

As City celebrates its 75th the club is hopefully entering an exciting new era that will see the dream of us being a League club fulfilled in my lifetime.

I would like to acknowledge the help and not inconsiderable contributions from Peter Gillott, Martin Rogers, Len Menhinick, David Selby, Tony Butcher, Brian Terry and David Billings.

Ollie Hopkins, Terry and Rob Ketley, Steve Cawley, Clive Haworth, Mick Butcher, Alan Dann, Trevor Smith and many others have kindly provided me with anecdotes and stories, photographs and memories to add to the various chapters.

Editions of The Essex Chronicle were put on microfiche some years ago and this has been a great help as I trawled through over 500 copies of the weekly newspaper for background to the stories of each season. Chelmsford Library staff have kindly made me comfortable and welcome throughout the many months of research. I would like to thank those who have allowed me to reproduce photographs and memorabilia.

I would like to thank the printers for their help and hard work. If I have forgotten anyone then 'thank you' too!

Finally my thanks to my cousin, Mansell Wallace, for his support for this book and all he does for our club.

The chapters in this book will I'm sure bring back memories for the older supporters but also give the younger ones an insight into the past glories of the club.

I hope you enjoy it!

'Up the City – Wheel 'em in' – Steve Little: June 2013

PROLOGUE

Thursday 2nd June 1938 saw the birth of the current professional Chelmsford City Football Club (although it was to have certain reincarnations, it has ostensibly remained the same club). A group of local businessmen had met regularly over the previous two years to set the financial and structural boundaries in place. The new company had decided to invite share ownership from the Chelmsford public and this had been well received in the town. These men had already agreed to take over the New Writtle Street ground from the present amateur club and passage into the regionalised Southern League (the top non-league competition in England) had been agreed.

Legend has it that this group of men, including Freddie Langton and Horace Phillp, met at the Lion and Lamb in Duke Street one evening: the drinks flowed as discussion resolved all the minor sticking points, but by the end of the evening only one remained and that was the club's title – should it be Town, Athletic, Wanderers, Rovers or perhaps just Chelmsford FC? They agreed 'City' was not an option as, even in their well-oiled stupor, they were pretty sure Chelmsford was not a city.

'But we have a Cathedral!' said one, 'so we must be.' Chelmsford City we became.

So, 2013 sees the club reaching its 75th anniversary and what a turbulent life the club has had. From being one of the leading non-league teams in the UK it transcended into near obscurity with no ground of its own and not even playing home games in Chelmsford. Now a renaissance has seen the club rise phoenix-like from the ashes of despair. Those sad, largely unfulfilling years of the late seventies, eighties and nineties have given way to seasons where there is genuine expectation that Football League status is within reach and, perhaps, we are only a short free kick away from living our dream.

However, twenty years after its formation, the year of 1958 saw the dawn of an exciting era for the club. The austere post-war years began to give way to a new prosperity – a time of 'You've never had it so good' according to Prime Minister Harold Macmillan! Modern methods of coaching, training, fitness and organisation saw a steady change in how the game was played. The fledgling European Cup, as well as the World Cup, began to broaden our horizons. Even at non-league level fans flocked to support their local clubs and, for Chelmsford, attendances ranged regularly in the mid-fifties from 3,000 to 7,000.

So by 1958 the supporters who flocked to The Stadium in New Writtle Street did so with an air of expectation. Soon local businessman John Coward was to step forward with his vision to take the club into the Football League. As a (very) young fan I started to regularly attend home games just ahead of Mr Coward's era and for the next ten years rarely missed a game as the club rose to be Southern League champions in the 1967-68 season. This should have brought us Football League status, but for reasons that this book will cover this did not materialise. Other clubs were to succeed where we failed.

These ten years from 1958 to 1968 really were the golden years for 'The City' and in 1958 we were truly about to enjoy 'Living the Claret Dream'.

1

THE FIRST STEPS TOWARDS A NEW ERA

It's 1958 and young Ron has just left school and is looking for some work for a year before he and his family start a new life in Australia. His father works for one of the directors and hears City require an extra pair of hands at the club. Frank Grice, the current Secretary/Manager, needs help with the paper work and with certain tasks on match days, whilst the Social Club and the Groundsman were always looking for a volunteer. Ron, an avid supporter, is taken on for the new season and this is his inside story of how the season unfolds.

MY FIRST DAY

New Writtle Street is quiet this Monday morning. I have to stop to let a van pull out of the road leading down to Chelmsford Cricket Club, but past that turning and beyond French's yard the newly painted white walls of the football ground stretch before me. Immediately behind these the main stand looms impressively above with its glass sides reflecting the bright July sun. Set in the white walls are the wooden doors leading to the turnstiles. These have also been painted in the close season and are rich, dark claret. Above them are signs, no more than a foot square with white lettering on claret metal, advertising the admission prices for the new season, still 1/9d but 9d for Juniors and OAPs.

The Stadium – Main stand in New Writtle Street – foreground; The Barn opposite; French's Yard to the right; Wolseley Road end to the left

This is 'The Stadium' – the home of Chelmsford City Football Club, a professional club formed as recently as 1938 taking over the old club that had existed for years and adding 'City' – despite the fact that we still remain a town with a cathedral!

This is my club and like every other supporter I can't wait for the season to start next month. This time I'll be part of it – only a small part and only for a short time, but I'm so excited to be involved in a club I've supported for nearly ten years. For the new season the First Team will play in the regional Southern League with the Reserves in the Eastern Counties League and the 'A' team, largely made up of young local talent, in the Essex and Suffolk Border League.

Having secured this post through my father's connection with one of the directors, the job description was 'clerical assistant' but I got the impression at my interview that 'general dogs' body' would be more accurate! Still, a half decent job at age 17 is all I want and just for this one season. Of course, I'd love to play for 'City' but, whilst having some footballing skills, they're nowhere near adequate enough to play even semi-professionally. So a supporter I'll remain but still play the odd game for Great Baddow when my duties at the club allow but, as I'll be committed on most Saturdays, these will probably be limited.

On this warm summer morning I'm working up a sweat in my unfamiliar collar, tie and woollen suit. I've no suit of my own and my father's is far too large so I've been given my Grandad's demob one. It has the whiff of mothballs and is a brown pinstripe but I only have old light tan school shoes, which do not really go with the dark brown suit. Also, I must have grown since I last wore the shirt, as the collar is tight. Dad has lent me his tie but Mum had to sponge off a stain before I left home this morning.

Immediately behind the middle of the stand, one turnstile is open for the staff to use. I halt at this narrow entrance to the small walkway at the back of the stand and take a deep breath. This is my first proper job and I feel a little nervous but ready for the challenge.

***

Once through the entrance and into the darkness of the corridor under the stand, there's a door to the tunnel leading onto the pitch. Above my head is a sign pointing to the dressing rooms to the left, so I head right towards the club's offices. Through the frosted window I can see a figure at a desk so I knock on the door before being called in. There sits Frank Grice the Secretary/Manager. He recognises me from my interview and is most friendly, pouring me a cup of tea.

'I'm a bit busy this morning, being a Monday, so I'm sending you to Jimmy Broad, the groundsman, as he needs some help; you'll find him on the pitch.'

I head for the tunnel and the light at its end. I have dreamt of this moment, to be trotting out onto the pitch following my heroes and cheered by the fans. It doesn't feel quite the same in my pin striped suit and with the stadium empty, apart from Jimmy setting out pieces of string attached to metal spikes along the near touchline. He has one of those retractable measures to help him get the dimensions right. Like Mr Grice he is very welcoming. I'd last seen him as steward in the supporter's club bar – apparently he has two jobs at the club!

'Oh dear,' he says, looking me up and down, 'we're marking out the pitch today with the white lime so that's not going to do your suit a lot of good so you'd better go over to my hut and find a boiler suit – you can wear that. But first I'll show you round the ground.'

Having supported the team since I was seven or eight, I know the ground well but normally only from the terraces behind the goal at each end. One is open with the gardens of the houses in Wolseley Road behind. The opposite end, backing onto French's yard and the Chelmsford Cricket Club, has banked terracing with a raised green sign about forty feet wide and ten feet high supported by posts at its back: the sign itself sits about three feet above the heads of the crowd. The top of the sign carries an advertisement for the East Anglian Daily Times (EADT) and beneath is a series of letters in alphabetical order and in two rows with two hooks underneath each letter. It's to show the half time scores of Football League matches with the letters matching fixtures shown in the match day programme. I always thought this was an excellent idea as it made supporters buy the programmes to keep up to date with the scores of their favourites. Someone climbs up a ladder at half time and hooks the painted metal numbers on the appropriate hooks to the cheers or groans of the supporters.

At the end of the games, no update is given on the scores but the EADT will produce an evening paper at about 7pm on a Saturday called the 'Green Un' and this can be picked up at the railway station and will have all the day's League results and a front page report of the Ipswich and Colchester games with reports of the City, Norwich and a few non-league games on its back page. Inside there will be mainly football related articles. Hundreds flock to get their copy each week and more do so when City are playing away. The Football League results can be obtained earlier at about 5pm when they appear in the Stop Press of the London Evening Standard or Evening News, a copy of which can be obtained at the bus station. However, with the City games ending at about twenty to five most of us can still get home in time for Sports Report on the radio when we can write down the scores to reflect on later and check the pools coupons!

Looking now at the empty terracing, I can visualise the match day scene. The more vociferous fans stand behind the goals with one end normally more populated than the other as it contains the City fans, taking over that terrace behind the goal towards which City attack in the first half before moving to the other end for the second.

On the long side opposite the main stand is 'The Barn' a long covered corrugated iron structure that stretches most of the length of this side. It only covers the back half of the terracing with most fans standing in the uncovered front section unless it is raining when they huddle under the cover. A sudden downpour will see the amusing spectacle of a lemming-like rush for shelter by a thousand people or more!

I was seven when I first came to games and stood on that terrace with my Dad or Grandad but usually I'd get bored after about an hour and would run around in the crowd with a friend playing 'chase'!

Common to most grounds the pitch is surrounded by a low wall about waist high to a grown man. This July it is pristine white with nothing covering it whatsoever. Between the pitch and the wall is a narrow red/orange cinder track. There had been plans to create a greyhound track around the pitch edge and a trial event was held, but the Council refused permission and the idea was shelved. As I walk with Jimmy across the pitch I'm most impressed at how good it looks and feels. He tells me he cut it yesterday and it has those stripes that you only normally saw on TV at Wembley for the Cup Final.

'Do you know, lad, this is the best surface in the South of England except the one at Ipswich and they've got several full time staff working on it!' growled Jimmy.

Just then Bill Parry walks out of the tunnel and comes over. He's the Club Trainer and I've met him before. He knows my Dad from Christy's where Bill works when not on City duty. They play cricket for the works' team and I sometimes help out if they're short. At first Bill doesn't recognise me out of my cricket whites but we're soon exchanging pleasantries.

Some of the players emerge onto the pitch.

'*Get off!*' shouts Jimmy, '*keep to the cinder track, I'm marking out today.*'

The players look scruffy in their faded training gear; dirty plimsolls left from May, socks rolled down to their ankles and an assortment of old shirts and shorts probably grabbed from the lost property cupboard.

Bill goes over to them looking only a little smarter with his old claret tracksuit tucked into socks; he, too, is wearing plimsolls. '*Get running slowly then,*' he shouts and the eight players reluctantly set off. Tony Butcher is at the back of the group. He's my hero, not much older than me and I know him from our days at Kings Road School. He's making his mark with the team already as an ace goal scorer. In front of him I recognise Nigel Gardiner with his shock of blond hair. He's another local lad made good, but dogged recently by injury. I've also met him before, as he knows my Dad.

At the front of the group is, as ever, Derek Tiffin, the skipper and very much the leader. 'Mr City' he's called; unruffled and elegant. Even this morning he looks smarter than everyone else, his hair neatly creamed down with a dead straight side parting.

As the group lap the ground Jimmy leads me to the tunnel, but just as we head for the dressing rooms a tall, dark figure looms in front of us. He looks dishevelled with several days' growth on his face. I recognise him straightaway, it's Arthur Adey. He has unruly black hair and fierce eyes with heavy brows. I've heard many stories about him and some are no doubt true; he is, indeed, a character.

One story is most definitely true as it came from Bill Parry. On an away train trip Arthur was in a foul mood and something innocent said by Director Mr Benge upset him. When Mr Benge left for the buffet car Arthur picked up Mr Benge's hat, took it into the train's corridor, opened the window and threw it out. Arthur returned to his seat saying '*that bloke was getting on my nerves*' – nothing was said to Mr Benge who remained bemused for the rest of the journey wondering where his hat had gone.

The mercurial Arthur Adey – a brooding menace on and off the pitch. 26 goals in 44 matches in the 1958/59 season were not enough for Harry Ferrier and Arthur was released

Arthur seemed to invite trouble and not just on the field. Out with some of the players one evening he had too much to drink and had an altercation with an American serviceman from Wethersfield. He laid out the Yank and the police were called. Another serviceman claimed Tony Butcher was also involved in the attack. The incident went to court. The Yank stood there at well over six feet tall with huge biceps but across the courtroom there was Tony in the dock – all five feet nine and ten stone.

Tony's defence (and he was not involved in the fight at all) was to tell the Bench: *'Can you really expect a measly bloke like me to stand up to this colossus?'* The case against him was dismissed. Arthur was fined.

Bill Parry also told how big Arthur had so impressed Arsenal when playing against them for Bedford in an FA Cup match that they were on the point of offering him top level football but when someone at Highbury looked into Arthur's disciplinary record on and off the pitch, the club's interest in him quickly came to an end.

Arthur brushes past us and we enter the home dressing room. Jimmy turns on the light but it's still quite dark. I've always imagined this inner sanctum would be huge and luxurious, so I'm more than a little disappointed. There is a massage table in the middle of the room but it has seen better days. Through a doorway is the sunken bath with its white tiles gleaming clean. A single toilet cubicle is set to one side.

Suddenly, the dressing room door opens and in comes a small, bald man in a jumper and tracksuit bottoms.

'Ah, this is Benny Welham, he's the man with the healing hands!' laughs Jimmy. Benny looks at me, nods and as he passes I get that familiar whiff of horse liniment.

Back out in the corridor we move into the small gymnasium, containing mats, wall bars, climbing ropes, a vaulting box and pommel horse. Weights are laid out on the mats.

The Essex Chronicle has already quoted Mr Grice promising his players would be fitter and stronger for the coming season with a lot of work using weights to be overseen by Bill Parry who was using a former Olympic weightlifter to help him.

Behind us we hear shouting. The latecomers arrive to get changed and I can hear Bill's familiar voice berating them from behind the dressing room door. Jimmy shrugs and smiles. We move out to the back of the stand and climb the stairs. I've never been up here before. Black, backless rows of seats with small, painted white numbers stretch along its length. There is a 'Home' and 'Away' section blocked off for the directors and guests with seven or eight steps leading down towards the pitch to the left of the tunnel.

There is a small area at the back of the stand for the press with some reserved seats. Lower down and to the left and right of the tunnel is a standing area called 'The Enclosure' where it costs an extra threepence to stand, compared with the rest of the ground. This is where Dad and his mates usually meet.

From the Directors' seats I can see the terracing to either side of the stand and backing onto New Writtle Street. Not many supporters stand in these areas unless there is a near capacity crowd, which is not very often. The Supporters' Club has its office and social area against the perimeter wall to the street and Jimmy's storage hut is there too. He leads me to it and finds the boiler suit before I re-join him on the pitch. He does the careful marking whilst I hold the marker posts and top up the white lime mix for his spreader.

For the next hour the players continue their pre-season training. It is nearly all running either round the pitch or up and down the terracing. Some peel away to be sick. Bill bellows out a mixture of criticism and praise, his shouts echoing around the empty ground. To think nearly twenty thousand fans could be squeezed in here! The whole time they train a football is never in evidence. Mr Grice came out and watched for a time but soon returned to his office.

We break just after twelve and I take my pack of sandwiches under the stand into the cool shade, heading to the gym where I hope it will be quiet, but the players are now there lifting weights supervised by a man I later learn is the weightlifter, Bill Watson. I watch for a while and the players ignore me. Goalkeeper Jack Parry is sitting on a mat and Bill Parry is throwing a small medicine ball either side for him to dive and catch; some sort of conditioning, apparently. Jack winces a few times and when Bill isn't looking massages his shoulder, the one that has given him trouble in the past. Not all the playing staff are there as some are not even part-time and, I assume, work all day. Soon after, I leave them to it and sit on the steps up to the stand and eat what Mum has prepared.

At one o'clock I report back to Jimmy who is sitting smoking outside one of his huts.

'Well done this morning. Now, as you're in work gear, I want you to help paint the crash barriers around the terraces. I've got some young lads coming in to do it and you can give them a hand; you can go home when you're finished.'

I wait for these lads to turn up and look round the ground, there are loads of these barriers so I hope there are plenty of painters or we'll be here all night!

By two o'clock only three have arrived and we start to paint. It's heavy-duty gloss and takes an age to put on because it's so thick; Jimmy said not to drop too much on the concrete and we have to make sure it doesn't run.

Exhausted we finish at seven. I can't be bothered to change into my suit, deciding instead to leave it in Jimmy's hut overnight. What a day. Not quite what I thought being an 'administrative assistant' would entail, but I've been told I'll be working with Mr Grice tomorrow.

THE START OF THE SEASON

J C Chaplin, the football correspondent of the Essex Chronicle, confidently expects City to finish in the top 11 of their division to ensure participation next season in the Premier Division of the

Southern League once the current two regional divisions are merged.

Mr Grice was quoted as saying that 'the season bids fair' – a typical way he understates most things!

I'm not needed for the first match, which is away at Trowbridge and ends in a 2-2 draw. We have had a few friendlies but with small crowds there has not been much to do. On match days I have to help with the turnstile count and total up the cash in Mr Grice's office where I have my own small desk. I have to be around to answer the telephone during the matches but this has an alarm ring on the stairs to the stand, so I position myself there watching the play and listen out for any ringing. I normally get to see the second half of most games.

Despite some new signings the side has a familiar look – Parry – Doherty, Jones – Bolton, Tiffin, Lawler – Dicker, Adey, Stroud, Butcher, Walker.

Roy Stroud is a pleasant chap and always asks how I'm getting on. He's a bit of a Nat Lofthouse in my eyes in the way he plays but since Lofthouse bundled Manchester United's goalkeeper Harry Gregg into the net in May's cup final win, many of us have gone off the England and Bolton striker, everyone having a soft spot for United after that awful plane crash in February.

I've found Mr Grice to be very helpful but I only see him when he is carrying out his secretarial work, normally on Mondays and Thursdays; the rest of the time he is with the players.

It's now the end of August and our first home game against Cambridge City. Same team as last week I was told, so I could pass this on to the programme printers yesterday.

Cambridge bring a large number of supporters and, despite still being holiday time, the crowd is nearly four thousand. Stroud, Adey and Butcher score the goals in a 3-1 win and so we are up and running.

***

The good form continues in the league with only one defeat up to the end of October. Now in November we have a run of away games coming up but when I arrive at work on Monday 10th Mr Grice is at his desk looking very gloomy. I'd heard we'd drawn at Yiewsley 3-3 on Saturday, which I thought a good result.

'Hello, Mr Grice; are you alright?'

'Stroud broke his leg on Saturday,' he tells me, *'a bad one and he will miss the rest of the season.'*

I'm not exactly sure what a broken leg is but it must be serious to miss months of the season and, with Roy Stroud averaging a goal a game, he will be badly missed.

When I arrive home in the evening I tell Dad about Stroud but he'd already heard at work. I ask him to explain what you do when you break a leg and after he tells me I feel a little queasy.

It's Saturday 15th November and we have a home game against our nemesis, Worcester City, who we always seem to get drawn against, and then lose to, in various cup competitions. This is the first round of the FA Cup after we had laboured to beat Harwich and Parkeston at the beginning of the month.

I no longer have to check the gate money and answer the phone as we have a Mrs Black who comes in to do just that on match days. I am responsible now for seeing to the needs of the visiting team and their officials plus the referee and linesmen. This means I can now watch most of the game.

Mr Grice has put John McCorkindale at centre forward to replace Roy. John joined in the summer from Gillingham but he's not really in the same class as the other forwards.

As the Worcester game progresses it is clear our visitors are settling for a draw. We huff and puff and the crowd get on the backs of some of the players particularly Butcher who always seems to be the butt of their criticism. Many sitting around me are not happy with Mr Grice's tactics. In the summer Brazil won the World Cup in Sweden and like the Hungarians in 1953 did not seem to play with wing halves and inside forwards but with four defenders and four forwards with just two in the middle helped by the two wide men from the front four. Mr Grice was sticking to convention. I also heard some of the players saying they were not happy with the way the team was set up plus they were fed up with the continual weight training and running.

I was asked to leave the office one day last week when Derek Tiffin came in, having asked for a chat with Mr Grice. I waited in the outer office and could hear the raised level of their voices in animated conversation but I couldn't hear what they were saying. Perhaps it was about the team's concerns.

Mr Grice seemed very down after Derek left especially as this came on top of Roy's injury.

The Worcester game ended 0-0 with a replay due next Thursday and when I arrive on Monday I see a note of the gate from Saturday – over five thousand, the best this season by far.

Later I receive the news that I'm to go to the replay, my first official away game! The coach trip takes forever on a cold and foggy day. When Mr Grice announces the team just before we arrive at Worcester's ground, Butcher is dropped and Eddie Smith, who we signed from QPR in the summer, is in. There were a few murmurings at the back of the coach near me but out of the hearing of Mr Grice.

Waiting for the game to start I thumb through a less than impressive Worcester programme full of adverts. It does contain the usual pen pictures of the City, something I'm very familiar with – as I prepared them! I noted one thing when helping with the programme for Saturday's game in that Worcester's captain is Roy Paul; the same Roy Paul who captained Manchester City to FA Cup glory in 1956 when they beat Birmingham City 3-1 and Bert Trautmann broke his neck! This is a bit of a comedown for Paul but apparently Worcester is his home city.

For an afternoon kick off on a Thursday, the crowd is huge and very noisy – maybe it's early closing day. We're not in the game but at least Eddie Smith scores; however, Worcester score three and again knock us out of a cup competition. On the coach home Mr Grice looks more down than ever. The players, seated towards the back of the coach, mostly sleep for a good part of the journey, but I end up playing whist with Tony Butcher, Bill Parry and Benny Welham. The journey home is a bit quicker but it's midnight when I get to bed.

On Saturday the 22nd I am at the club in the afternoon to help with the Reserve game. The first team are on the long trip to Yeovil and I feel pleased not be asked to go this time.

At ten to five I take the call from Yeovil and hear we've won 2-1 with Adey and Walker scoring but the bad news is Jack Parry has broken his arm for about the third time since he's been at City and with reserve keeper Stan Evans already injured we're in a bit of a mess! Perhaps Jack's strenuous arm and shoulder work in the gym has weakened something.

***

As we reach the end of December I'm pleased to say we're doing well in the League. We'll almost certainly be in the top division next season when the Southern Leagues are merged.

We lost at home to Gravesend during the month with local man Eric Milburn in goal but beat them in a replayed League Cup game. Following that, a very one-sided 8-0 win over Trowbridge in December with a hat-trick for Arthur Adey is the highlight plus a very rare appearance for everyone's favourite, Nigel Gardiner, but, unfortunately for the fans, in the away game on the day after Boxing Day at Poole!

***

Looking back at the first month of 1959, I've been very busy watching all this month's games both home and away at Mr Grice's request. However, we've only had two league games, losing at Cambridge City and drawing at home to Weymouth. The Southern League Inter Zone Competition has kicked in and we are in a mini-league with Cambridge United, Kettering, Bedford and Clacton but in January we only win once when Lyall Bolton scores a rare goal – the winner, at Clacton.

I had to endure my worst ever City match on January 10th at Cambridge United. Poor Eric Milburn had a nightmare and let in SEVEN as we lost 7-2 – it was a dispirited display and I travelled in Mr Grice's car but he said very little on the way back. The rumblings of discontent remain amongst some of the players with so many injuries and a dip in form. Roy Stroud now has pleurisy and will definitely miss the rest of the season. Stan Evans is, at least, back playing and has relieved young Eric from his torment.

In four days we're knocked out of TWO cup competitions. First, Dartford win 2-1 at The Stadium on a rotten Wednesday afternoon on January 21st – we were awful and there were so few at the game that I actually counted the crowd from my seat! I made it 442 but officially it was 489! There has been more talk around the club about floodlights but the Chairman, Alderman Langton, always says it would be too costly for us.

On the Saturday we lose at home to Clacton 1-0 in the Essex Professional Cup with another crowd of fewer than 2,000. The goals seem to have dried up and there were shouts in the crowd to bring back McCorkindale, or even local lad Tommy Mingay, to supply the firepower and to get rid of Butcher! Adey was also being criticised for his aggression on the pitch as he, too, has been having a lean spell.

In his New Year message J C Chaplin had said, '*The Southern League will become the most important and most all-embracing non-league organisation in the country'* – with the dross we have mainly seen this month that did not look quite so likely now!

***

Looking back on February, what a month this has been! Frank Grice has resigned! It was formerly announced in the Chronicle on the 27th but we at the club had known about it for a little while. I knew Mr Grice was under pressure but I was surprised when I heard as we had only recently chatted about Romford, just up the A12, deciding to turn professional and how Mr Grice was looking forward to some fierce local rivalry in the years to come.

At the beginning of the month Mr Grice had told the Chronicle he was looking to improve the team. The paper carried the story of a rumour that Mr Grice might sign Johnny Crossan who had played for Coleraine, but due to certain 'irregularities' in his transfer to Bristol City was 'banned for life' – however, he was able to play abroad or outside of the Football league. Crossan had been at Sparta Rotterdam and then Standard Liege. It was frightening to contemplate Adey and Crossan in attack, with their reputations.

Mr Grice had been at the club since 1955 and at 49 was still young enough to progress. He had played for Notts County and Spurs, but his greatest success was when managing Northern Irish club, Glentoran, where he unearthed and developed the talents of internationals Billy Bingham (Everton), Danny Blanchflower (Spurs) and Jimmy McIlroy (Burnley) – so he clearly knows a good player when he sees one! Mr

Langton paid tribute to Mr Grice's efforts in seeing the club through such a difficult time with the near bankruptcy just after he arrived and then moving the club forward now that it was part time professional.

I could see Mr Grice was not happy in the short time I had known him. There were the disagreements with some of the players and with the Chairman. However, his leaving was still a shock and a disappointment for me. There was now word that the Chairman, Mr Langton, was also thinking of standing down, having been at the head of things from the start in 1938.

Rumours abound about Mr Grice's successor. One name mentioned is Arthur Rowe, currently the Crystal Palace manager, who had been at City before his great success managing Spurs with their 'push and run' tactics that brought them League success in the early 50s with players like Alf Ramsey and Bill Nicholson.

Mr Grice works out his notice and the last game he sees is at home to Exeter City Reserves on the 28th when the team excels with a 5-1 win with goals from McCorkindale (2), Butcher, Adey and Walker. This win pretty much secures our place in the top division next season. However, a midweek draw at home to Bedford in the League Cup competition means we will not progress to the knockout stage when a win would have been good enough.

I have been charged with preparing the manager's job advertisement, which I have been told to send to the 'Sporting Record' – the final version is as follows, *'Chelmsford City Football Club requires an experienced Manager or Player-Manager. House if required. Good salary for the right man.'*

***

March is drawing to a close and has been another month of excitement! I was surprised to read in a Sunday newspaper that our manager's wage was in the region of £30 a week, I assumed it would be more, but then it does include accommodation.

The Chronicle announces that Arthur Rowe will not be returning but another name being linked to us is Alec Stock – it amazes me where they get this information from as nothing has been said about this at the club!

I help sift through the letters and applications. I recognise some of the names but have been sworn to secrecy. I help set up the interviews with Mr Langton and some other Board members. All these are finished by the 20th and the Board meets to discuss whom they wish to take the club forward.

I'm finally given the details of the chosen one and release this to the press. It is to be a 38-year-old Scot, Harry Ferrier, currently Secretary/Manager at Gloucester City. He had an excellent playing pedigree as a left back in the highly successful Portsmouth team of the late 1940s and early 1950s, which included two First Division championship-winning medals. He often captained the side.

I was told to put a quote from him in the press release, part of which stated that his first job at City was '… *to do some sorting out, introduce some strict discipline and get the players fitter than they had ever been.*' Mr Chaplin writing in the Chronicle described him as '… *a big man with a determination to get things done*'.

Mr Ferrier watches the two games at home against Yeovil and King's Lynn before taking over. These are won by 2-0 and 8-2, with Butcher, McCorkindale and Adey now forming our spearhead and in the goals once again.

The Essex Weekly News carries a pen picture of Mr Ferrier. He joined Barnsley when he was 16 and was soon offered professional terms. After war broke out he returned to Scotland to play for Stirling Albion and then Celtic before moving with the army back to England where he played for Middlesbrough and then moved to the Woolwich Depot in London. There were a large number of wartime friendlies and he guested for every London club except Charlton.

He once turned out for Portsmouth in 1945 and when the war ended they signed him from Barnsley. He had nine seasons there and was a first team regular winning two first division medals and getting to the semi-final of the FA Cup. Having already won the League they were favourites to lift the cup and become the first club for nearly fifty years to win the much coveted double, but they lost to Leicester who went on to lose to Wolves in the final.

In 1954 he became player manager at Gloucester City where he stayed for over four years before coming to us.

***

We have just completed our last game and are sixth in the league. I have not been happy since Mr Ferrier joined and have just handed in my notice. Essex Cricket Club advertised a clerk's job in early April and after a couple of interviews they have offered me a post with a much better salary and conditions. It will last until the end of the cricket season in September and then in October the family leaves for Australia.

Looking back, Mr Ferrier has certainly had a dramatic effect. He clearly doesn't fancy Arthur Adey as a long term asset despite his twenty-six goals this season. The FA suspends Adey for 14 days following his sending off against Cambridge United for a seemingly trivial offence and the Chronicle suggests victimisation by referees against poor old Arthur! The retained list is issued and twelve of the pros are being released including Arthur and Roy Stroud, who, it is rumoured, may not play again. Jack Parry, Doherty, McCorkindale, Jimmy Jones and Jimmy Brennan are also released and this has caused quite a stir in the town!

Ferrier says that he wants to introduce a younger element to his team for next season. As the season draws to a close, long servants Derek Tiffin (since 1950) and Nigel Gardiner (since 1952) both have testimonials. There is now a rumour that young Geoff Hurst, son of former player Charlie, may take a step down from West Ham, where he lingers in the youth team, and join us. However, the Chronicle reported that he had an excellent game at left half for West Ham Colts against Arsenal that finished 1-1, so perhaps he has a future at West Ham after all.

On my last day Mr Ferrier leaves for what he calls a scouting trip/holiday in Scotland with his wife and young son, 8-year-old Harry Junior. He wishes me good luck and I say the same to him. He's not my cup of tea but in him I can see someone with a lot of drive and ambition. Hearing him on the phone he clearly has an awful lot of contacts in the game and I expect many new signings especially with twelve being released. Next season the Southern League will contain twenty two teams in its top division and, so, with many more games, a larger squad of players will be required.

With my time at City at an end I feel proud to have been part of the club even though just for the one season. I can see changes are afoot. Mr Ferrier is ruthless and ambitious supported it seems by director, Mr Coward, who I am sure will take over from Mr Langton, if and when he decides to stand down. The club is on the cusp of change and so is football. The Brazilians in Sweden last summer showed to the world how there is a shift in the balance of power in football. The British game is in a rut; stuck almost in its pre-war style. The Hungarians showed us in 1953 a new dimension to the game but few clubs or international sides appear to have learnt from it.

Now we seem to be coming out of the post war blues a new footballing era is perhaps about to dawn and none more so than at New Writtle Street. I shall follow the club's fortunes with great interest even from the other side of the world!

2

BUILDING THE DREAM TEAM

A Yorkshire man to his core Peter Gillott was THE signing in 1959 to kick-start the golden era of the club. An England Youth International with some experience in the second tier of English football yet still in his early twenties, he came to Chelmsford and stayed. A stalwart at left back, who never gave less than 100%, he remained a crowd favourite throughout all his years at the club. Released to Margate for a while he returned to successfully steer the Reserves, as player-coach, to the Metropolitan League and Cup triumph in 1968 and played a few games in the championship winning First Team that season. He remains a true City legend and still lives in Chelmsford. He has been known to don the number 3 shirt for the Old Chelmsfordians even in his 70s! This is his story of how he prepared for the 1959-1960 season at Barnsley but ended up as the star turn at City.

With the summer of 1959 seeing my National Service finally over, I'm at last back home with wife Sylvia in Barnsley and ready to get on with my career with the local club; we have also talked of starting a family.

I have to come clean that my National Service did involve playing a fair amount of football which got me out of many hours of drill and other boring army stuff, much to the annoyance of my mates! But what an experience for a simple South Yorkshire lad to play in the company of top division players and internationals like Trevor Smith from Birmingham City and Ray Pointer from Burnley. I do believe this has brought my game on and, when we spent some time in Egypt, I actually captained the 'British Army' team in some exhibition matches. I dare say my somewhat brash Yorkshireness and loud voice marked me out as a leader on the pitch much the same as a sergeant-major on a parade ground. On a more serious note I am looking forward to putting this experience to good use in the new season at Oakwell and becoming established in the Division Two side as Barnsley's left back.

On the other hand I do know my limitations. To play for England Youth was an enormous honour and I would like to believe I could move on to greater things but football is a precarious game. I might not even make it into Barnsley's team and, even before my National Service, I always felt the need to have something to fall back on. There has always been this nagging possibility that I'll not make a career out of professional football or might have to pack up due to a serious injury or something like that. My father has always encouraged me with my football but also made sure I learnt a trade, so I have trained as a cobbler and should my football career quickly come to an end I can always turn to that if necessary.

***

Bob Shotton is assisting manager Vic Ward with the running of Barnsley and we get on well. Out of the blue he tells me Chelmsford City are interested in signing me. This comes as something of a shock at first with me barely knowing who they are or even where Chelmsford is! What I do know is that they are prepared to match what Barnsley pay me (the maximum possible is £20 a week) and would allow me to be part time. This is tempting as I would earn almost the same from the football but be able continue my trade as a cobbler. Chelmsford confirm in writing that they'll offer £20 a week for the first team, £17 in the Reserves and £14 in the close season. I'm given a couple of days to consider their offer.

Being one of a large family Sylvia, like me, knows it will be a wrench to leave South Yorkshire but from a financial standpoint it makes sense, particularly as part of the Chelmsford deal will be to have a club-owned house for us to immediately move into. This would settle us down nicely and we can look to start that family!

I take my time and talk to my father and brother about it. They encourage me to take up the offer, adding that it will be handy to have me close to the races, especially the Gold Cup. This flummoxes me for a moment until I realise they thought I was going to Cheltenham and not Chelmsford!

Back at Oakwell, Harry Ferrier, the new manager of Chelmsford, who is scouring the country for new players, has contacted Bob again and is waiting for my answer. I know of Ferrier who played a big part in the success of Portsmouth after the war. He was stationed in the Barnsley area during part of his wartime service and 'guested' for the club in some friendly matches, so he knows a lot of the locals and, in his search to strengthen Chelmsford, has sought out some old friends for help and this is where Bob comes in. It is he who recommended me.

I weigh up what to do. The lure of Second Division regular football is considerable but in the end I tell Bob I'll take up Mr Ferrier's offer. I know it's a bold step by dropping down a couple of rungs but I'm realistic enough to know that I'll not make it right at the top of the game as that has become plain from those Army matches and seeing those top pros at close quarters.

***

The move goes smoothly and we are soon settled into our new home, with neighbours and people in the town very welcoming when they find out I've signed for the local team. The local paper is full of Harry Ferrier's success in recruiting a whole new batch of players with the most dramatic and well-known being wing-half Len Phillips, with whom Harry had played at Portsmouth. Len played for England less than five years ago, actually earning three caps; all in winning matches. At home I have the programme of the match he played in against Wales in November 1954 and I can't wait to meet him – what experiences he must have! Inside forward Mike Barnard has also signed; in fact, straight from the Portsmouth first team currently playing in the First Division – quite a coup by Harry because, due to some oversight, Pompey failed to register Barnard and, like me, with the money being the same, he decides to join up with Harry.

I meet them both at the first training session in the middle of July. Len is a typical plain speaking Eastender born in Shoreditch and has been brought in by the boss to pass on so much of his experience to us all. Quiet and friendly off the pitch he is known to be volatile on it, often upsetting referees who, of course, know of his pedigree! Henry Michael Barnard is not only a professional footballer but also plays cricket for Hampshire – City's offer of part time suits this doubling up of sports where one overlaps the other. Perhaps due to mixing in the more upper class cricket circles Mike is always smartly dressed and so well spoken, unlike the rest of us; yet he is a damn good footballer! He is of Jewish extraction, which is unusual in a footballer. Alec Eisentrager, an ex-German POW born in Hamburg, is also brought in. He was only 18 when captured during the war. He comes to us from Merthyr Tydfil, having been at Bristol City previously after he stayed on after the war and, like Bert Trautmann at Manchester City, decided to make his home here, with Alec marrying a girl from Wales. Despite his background and with the war only ending fourteen years ago, the Chronicle reports he's proved very popular at his previous clubs and I'm sure it will be no different here. A small, balding inside forward he's apparently quiet on and off the pitch and I'm sure he'll win many friends in Chelmsford during his time at the club.

The Chronicle reports on the other signings with Les Brown coming down from Dumbarton and so showing how far Harry is stretching his net using his various connections. Les is described as a fast and direct right-winger, a quality crosser of a football. Right back Terry Hayward makes the short trip from West Ham having impressed when City beat them in the Essex Professional Cup in May. Forward Jimmy Mason arrives from Chester. There are two new goalkeepers in George Longridge and Reg Newton, who are already playing non-league football. Soon the very experienced Ken Birch joins from Southampton.

When I meet up with Harry ahead of pre-season training he tells me he's coming to the end of his search but moans about the League clubs who continually go back on their word: *'You think you've got a player then find you haven't'* he told me, yet we both know that clubs will try to hold out for a fee from a League club because under the current transfer rules non-league clubs are not required to pay a fee for a player who drops out of the Football League.

New friends I meet up with and other fans I chat to are astounded at this influx of players, most with a considerable pedigree and even known through national newspapers and radio.

The players who have been at the club for a while are not at all resentful with Harry's new broom. Long standing captain, Derek Tiffin, plus Les Dicker, Geoff Walker and Tony Butcher are some of those remaining and will be mixed with the new guard to form the nucleus of Harry's team.

So we get into the pre-season training. I spend a lot of time trying to get people to call me Gillott as in 'Jill Lott' like it is pronounced up north but eventually I give up, only Butch continues with the correct pronunciation. Just like at Barnsley the training involves an awful lot of running. Round and round the track at The Stadium and up and down the terracing followed by 'The Killer' – the long run. We head out to the south of the town along the A12 towards Ingatestone then cut off to the left and onto Galleywood Common, then down Wood Street, Longstomps Avenue, London Road and into New Writtle Street. Agony! This is all under the supervision of ex Olympian, Bill Watson, who was brought in by the previous manager to condition the team using weights. Harry is having none of this and wants a different approach, looking to generally condition the players rather than have specific weight training. Bill relishes his new task and is expert at it, combining work here with his more permanent role at Tottenham. Living locally he agrees to help City in his spare time, normally in the evening training sessions.

I'm surprised and delighted to find such a professional approach at a non-league club, more than matching what I saw in my time at Barnsley. The whole City staff feels we are part of something special. Chairman Mr Langton tells us we are embarking on a new era for the club in the hope that we can bring success to the point that we are voted into the Football League, following in the footsteps of Spurs and Colchester who have already progressed through the Southern League.

We train on Tuesdays and Thursdays. Some of the squad are good trainers but others are not and look to avoid the harder parts of training, feigning injury or even work commitments to miss some sessions. We spend some time in the gym but far less, so Butch tells me, than under the previous management. Even when the dark evenings come we still pound round the cinder track and then go into the gym.

Reporter J C Chaplin watches some of the training and in his column writes: *'It's stricter and harder than I have ever seen before!'*

The team is bonding well. The so-called stars are down to earth and far from being 'up themselves'; Harry is such a character and has the right influence on the lads. Great player he might have been but his life style is not what you might expect from an ex-professional footballer as he smokes heavily, drinks quite a lot and is now putting on some weight, but he remains so likeable and has this wealth of knowledge about the game which can only benefit players and supporters alike. He passes on some of his defensive experience to me at training with some positioning tips, but it's former player and now coach, Bill Parry, who deals with most of the footballing side of things – not that we see much of a football during 'pre-season' but as the friendlies come and the start of the season looms, he becomes more and more influential as we work on tactics and a few free kick and corner routines.

Len Phillips helps with some of the tactics too, this being one of the reasons Harry has brought him to the club.

I'm really impressed with the ground and facilities here. They are comparable with Oakwell and many of the grounds in the lower divisions. However, playing for Barnsley Reserves in the Central League has one redeeming feature in that we get to play at grounds like Old Trafford, Goodison Park, Villa Park and Hillsborough against those clubs' reserve teams, but it looks to me that City has the capacity to expand the ground when we get into the Football League to be not far short of what these Division One grounds offer.

I've read in the Chronicle that there has been a meeting at Kettering of fourteen non-league clubs, including us apparently, to investigate the possibility of a fifth division. If that were to happen, the City dream of League football could soon become a reality.

***

Harry has been frustrated in his search for a new centre forward but eventually tells us one evening at training that Bert Stokes is coming. He has experience at Grimsby and Scunthorpe and Harry says this signing is the final piece of his jigsaw.

Alderman Langton, the Chairman, invites all the new players to the Supporters' Club Annual General Meeting. The team is aware of the huge sums the Supporters Club has given over the years and how the main Club could not possibly survive without them.

The Alderman gives a stirring speech: *'We are looking forward to a champion season. A new era has come. We have a new manager and many new players. All the new players are in their 20s and with first rate experience. Will they blend? There is every reason why they should. They are good class players and we are paying them good class wages. We have every reason to be optimistic.'*

Very positive words indeed and I see a smile on the faces of Phillips and Eisentrager when the Alderman talked of the new players in their 20s!

Some of the supporters at the meeting were upset by the increase in admission from 1/9d to 2s on the terraces and to 2/6d in the enclosure in front of the main stand, where to sit remains at 3/6d. However, the disgruntled have to back down when they hear City's profit for last season was only just over £16 12s (less than one week of my wages!), so indicating how important this price rise is to increase the gate revenue.

Excitement seems high in the town with good attendances at the practice matches and none of us can wait for the season to start.

Our first league game is against Worcester City at the Stadium on August 22nd. Despite it being 'work's week', with many of the factory people away on holiday, nearly four thousand turn up to watch, more than double the crowd for the last game of the previous season. I have a decent debut sharing the full back duties with Hayward in front of George Longridge. The half back line is Birch, Tiffin and Mason with wingers Dicker and Walker keeping their places from last year along with Butcher but with Eisentrager and Phillips, who both scored in a 2-2 draw, playing as inside forwards. Chaplin wrote the following Friday that: *'Peter Gillott should challenge his man earlier than he did on Saturday.'* So that was me told!

31

By the end of September we've completed ten league games, winning six, drawing two and losing two and are one of the league's front runners. However, throughout October and most of November we win two but lose five games in a row. We've twice played Headington United in the League, drawing away and losing narrowly at home – we are also due to play them in the Southern League Cup – all these games are within ten days in September! By the end of them we are sick of the sight of Ron Atkinson and his younger brother Graham; both huge blokes with attitudes to match. Ron is the better player but full of himself and scored all their goals against us in those games, which made him worse than ever!

Len Phillips is finding it hard to settle and is out of the team for a time in September. He has moved back to wing half to replace Birch and Barnard has come in as inside forward with Brown replacing Dicker on the wing. Perhaps the fans are not used to the more precise, measured approach of an old international like Len as he will never just hoof the ball forward, preferring to keep the ball until the right pass can be made. Frustrated, the fans shout 'Get rid of it Phillips' which, more or less, has become his nickname!

The big match of the season for us comes when we are drawn away in the First Round of the FA Cup against Crystal Palace at Selhurst Park, having disposed of Grays Athletic in the previous round. With an eye on getting support for our cause to be elected to the Football League, it's imperative to have a good cup run and hopefully beat some league clubs. Peterborough United have already made a name for themselves by drawing at First Division Fulham last season before losing by the odd goal in the replay.

For some of the older pros in our team or those, like me, who have played in the higher leagues, a trip to a well-supported club like Palace is welcomed but not that daunting – Len had, after all, played before nearly 90,000 at Wembley in 1954!

In the lead up to the game there is great excitement in the town. The Essex Chronicle is full of predictions and the latest odds. Chaplin considers us good enough for a 2-2 draw but Bernard Webber believes we'll lose 5-1! Webber always seems to have a bias for Colchester and rarely has anything good to say about us, unlike Chaplin who is far more balanced. The odds were Palace 1/4 on, City 5/1 against and 4/1 the draw. Harry fancies the 4/1; that I do know!

Webber is critical of Les Dicker playing centre forward and bemoans the loss of free-scoring Roy Stroud, still struggling away from City to recover from last season's broken leg and subsequent illness. The Chronicle has been carrying stories, confirmed by Harry, that: *'two or three players are being tapped up by League clubs'* but none of us know who these players were, except Jimmy Mason who's been told he is being watched by Crystal Palace!

Coaches galore leave the town and swell the Selhurst crowd to over 17,000. Butch is troubled with an ankle and not available, so again we have to play Les Dicker out of position at centre forward because Albert Stokes, who promised so much as a goalscorer, has largely failed to deliver. We are doing well in the first half on an awful quagmire of a pitch and are holding them at 1-1 with Mike Barnard scoring but then, in the second half, we run out of steam, when young Johnny 'Budgie' Byrne, tipped for great things, shows a lot of class and takes the game away from us.

Captain Tiffin surprises me by moving me up front in the middle of the second half, changing the team around – something he'd often done in the past so I've been told. As I've not scored a goal for over two years it seems an odd decision, but Derek said I was to put myself about to disrupt their defence and let the other forwards play around me. Harry appears livid when he sees this happen and lets rip in the changing room afterwards. The plan didn't work either and we concede two more goals from Byrne and Dave Sexton.

We were never overwhelmed in the game and the great Arthur Rowe is most complimentary afterwards but we shouldn't have lost to a team in the Fourth Division by such a score and this is not helping us get a reputation like Peterborough did with their good Cup run.

Chaplin says in his report: *'Gillott and Hayward met speed with speed with tremendous guts and determination'* which pleases us both!

But still we can't win over some of the fans, a Mr G. Smith from Braintree writes to the Chronicle: 'What has happened to the City Manager's policy of 100% effort from every player?' Harry has to be stopped from giving an abrupt reply!

Never mind; the Palace game kick-starts our season and we enter an amazing run by drawing one and winning seven of our league games from the end of November, when we were only seventh, until the end of January by which time we have moved into the top three. However, during that time there are hints of our fragility and perhaps displayed all too clearly when in December we play Colchester at Layer Road in the Essex Professional Cup, losing a bizarre match 6-5! We are 4-1 down at one stage but fight back to 5-4 before succumbing – we leave out a few players for that match but Butch returns and nets a couple and Gordon Barker (the Essex cricketer), in a rare outing, scores two and the equally untried Springett the other. Poor old George Longridge in goal has an absolute stinker. Some of our supporters really get on his back and to think he was man-of-the-match at Palace! In his column Chaplin condemns the fans for their appalling behaviour. Harry feels George has had his confidence blown away and turns to Reg Newton, but I fear George might be on the way out of the door.

Chaplin gives me some stick after the Colchester game for: *'being given the run around by winger Williams for the early part of the first half'* which upsets me but he does also say that *'as the game went on Hayward and Gillott were outstanding at full back'* – such is life, but generally I've been happy with my form.

J C Chaplin is quite a character. Old school but still relates to the younger players. He mixes well with us and doesn't expose any indiscretions in his column, not that there are many. He does like a drink and will hold court in any pub in town. Apparently, on the day of one home match a few years back, he rather over imbibed at lunchtime and sent a minion to report on a game but filed his column based on a large amount of erroneous information, much to his consternation. Fortunately, his editor forgave him!

The Chronicle carries stories over the winter about changes or decisions that might help or hinder the City's ambition to get into the League. There has, as I have already mentioned, been talk in the past of making a fifth division and, with this now pooh-poohed, there is talk that the Fourth Division might be extended from 22 to 26 clubs, which at least might give us a chance.

Being as negative as ever, Bernard Webber doesn't rate our chances and is convinced Peterborough will make the League this close season, if not the next. He points out one other problem in that something like

£15,000 would have to then be paid to league clubs for me, Les Brown and Mike Barnard under FA rules if we're elected. Bearing in mind we only had that small profit last year this might be difficult to find.

Having had a bad run of three defeats in February, we do win our last game of the month and then have a great result away at Bedford on March 5th but now face Bath City at home – they are riding high in the league but if we can win then catching them is still a possibility.

They are a good side with some money behind them, so they have a selection of really good players from some top clubs. There is a much larger crowd than normal after Chaplin talked up the match's importance. It is dubbed the 'game of the season' and for the wrong reasons it comes to be so! We are soon 3-0 down but Bath's tactics inflame our crowd. Bath have Ted Purdon up front and he's as hard as they come – he was a big name at Sunderland playing alongside the likes of Len Shackleton and Billy Bingham but was punished along with some team mates for some illegal payments and then moved on to Workington and Barrow. I'm not sure what Purdon did but I hope it was not part of some betting scam. Rumours currently abound of some strange goings on at all levels of the game!

Anyway, Bath know Len Phillips is a big influence and work on his short fuse when they do their best to upset him with some harsh tackling especially by Purdon. Infamously Purdon once challenged the West Brom goalie in his Sunderland days with such venom that the poor chap never played again, so badly was his back injured when barged from behind!

It's blood and thunder stuff on this March day at The Stadium and I love it; it's my sort of game. Not for the first time Purdon crunches into Len with his boot above the ball and scything down Len's shin. Finally our man flips, lashes out and is sent packing by the ref. The City crowd normally doesn't like any rough stuff or dissent to the referee from its team, but on this occasion they applaud Len as he exits down the tunnel. For a short while I fear some of the crowd might run onto the pitch such is their anger at the Bath players and Purdon in particular. We eventually lose 4-2 and I have to say Bath's tactics were shocking but perhaps that's what you need to win this league. They are now thirteen points ahead of us and unlikely to be caught by anyone.

The whole team is upset with the way we finish the League season with only five wins, four draws and NINE defeats in our final eighteen matches.

***

During this first season with the City I've been keen to obtain a cobbling job or even start my own business, as this is what Sylvia and I agree remains important to our future plans and, of course, partly the reason for coming to Chelmsford in the first place. I start to believe that my own shoe repairing business is the way forward and recently spoke to supporter and director, John Coward, about it. Local successful businessman that he is, he strongly advises me to work for someone else first, build up a reputation and, through the football, get my name more widely known, especially if I intend to stay in Chelmsford for the foreseeable future. He knows the manager of the Co-op store and recommends me to him as a candidate for a job in their shoe-repairing outlet. They kindly offer me a position and I start there with this welcome supplement to my income. At last we feel at home and I will forever be thankful to John for his help.

***

The season is not quite over. We have a great run in the Southern League Cup, normally played on midweek afternoons before small crowds. Chairman Langton seems to have had a change of heart and is now determined to bring floodlights but the expense remains a problem, despite the club pocketing £1,000 from the Palace cup-tie. A Wednesday afternoon gate of 513 for a game against a top side like Headington United is not the future.

We get through to the League Cup final to be played over two legs in April against Worcester City, apparently an old cup adversary. We play first at their ground and win 2-1 with goals from Barnard and Walker. I'm pleased for Geoff Walker as we play well in tandem, with him on the left wing and me behind him at left back. I like to forage forward and he always covers for me. He has great touch and expertly controls my rather over or under hit passes.

Nearly 5,000 turn out at the Stadium for the second leg, as it's Easter Saturday and not midweek. It's a close game at 1-1 then little Alec scores and we've won the cup with Derek Tiffin proudly receiving the trophy as the crowd spill onto the pitch at the end.

***

Back in early March there was talk of changes at the top. Freddie Langton and Archie Draper have been involved as directors of the club right through from 1938 but are now old men and are reported to be on the point of standing down. It's eventually announced that Mr Freddie is continuing as Chairman but is looking to hand the reins over to John Coward in the near future. John is younger and seen as something of a visionary. He has a successful heating and plumbing business in the town and has invested in shops and even an up-market hotel. He has grand designs for the club, the aim being to virtually 'walk' into the Football League, with a top quality ground and team to go with it, all it needs is a good FA Cup run and, more importantly, for us to win the Southern League. Peterborough have won the Midland League for the past few seasons and have had yet another good FA Cup run and, as Bernard Webber predicted, have been given Gateshead's place in the Fourth Division. Sadly, we poll only three votes from the League teams at the AGM when you need over thirty, so we seem some way down the pecking order.

So, my first season draws to a close and I've played in every competitive game – that's 55 for the season. Despite my foraging forward at every opportunity and auxiliary centre forward at Crystal Palace, I've not managed a goal; even full back mate Terry Hayward got three but they were all penalties! We have the Southern League Cup and the memory of a great day out at Crystal Palace (apart from the result!) but end up a disappointing sixth in the league after such a good first half of the season.

It was good to see my old Army team mate, Ray Pointer, finish as leading goalscorer for Burnley when they snatched the Division One title from under Wolves' nose by winning away at Manchester City to end up top when they had not been there all season. So, a least a great end of 1959/60 for one team of 'Clarets'!

Sylvia and I have been welcomed warmly by the locals and the Co-op is very pleased with me, happy to let me to take time off for the occasional afternoon game. I'm still interested in starting up on my own but will wait for a while. I'm determined to keep my Yorkshireness and my accent but at times some of my phrases have been misinterpreted or folk have just not understood my thick accent. Different words also mean different things. For example, I was pounding round the cinder track at the ground on my own one early closing day when an elderly gent came over to the perimeter wall. As I stopped near him to catch my breath he called out: *'I hear you're a bit of a snob.'* I thought I'd misheard him at first and I might be many things, but no one could accuse me of being a snob.

'Sorry, what did you say?' I asked, a little brusquely.

'I said, I hear you're a snob, you know … you repair shoes, that's what we old 'uns call it around here.'

I was relieved not to be accused of being stuck up.

'Up north, sir, I'm a cobbler!' I explain.

'Well that's as maybe, lad.' And off he went.

So what of Harry in this his first season? At least a trophy after a lot of changes to the playing staff, but perhaps it's what has occurred off the pitch that will be seen as the turning point in the history of the club.

Harry remains a character. He loves greyhound racing and often visits the Romford track. On one occasion during the season I went with him when my father was down from Barnsley with one of my brothers. Harry had a sizeable bet on the favourite in trap six on the outside. It was going well maintaining its place out wide when the dog starting in trap two suddenly veered out to the right as the two came round the last bend and caught the back end of Harry's dog that had a clear run in to win. Harry's dog stumbled a little and the other dog went past to win. Well, Harry was apoplectic with rage. The trainer of the winner was congratulating his dog when Harry was over the fence and onto the track ready to lynch both dog and trainer for costing him his valuable win. We had to get after him and calm him down. When we got him back to the terracing my father said: *'And this is your boss?'*

In one home game I received a nasty blow on the head and it split my forehead, so I had blood pouring down my face. It happened right in front of the stand and I was led straight down the tunnel to the changing room by Bill Parry and Benny Welham. It was nearly half time and they had about fifteen minutes to get me fixed up and back on the pitch. Benny said I needed stitches and quite a few. Bill sent someone off to fetch the doctor who lived about a mile away. Just as the lads and Harry came in at the interval the doctor arrived. Benny didn't want me to go back on but Harry insisted, as he didn't want to play the second half with ten men.

I was on the treatment table and the doc put in eight stitches wrapping my head in a bandage so I looked like an extra from Emergency Ward Ten! Harry told Benny to get a brandy from the bar. Bill Parry said: *'You do look a bit groggy Gil.'* I felt OK but Harry looked shaken and pale; I found out later that he didn't like the sight of blood! Anyway Benny turns up with the double brandy and puts it down on the cupboard next to me: *'Here, Gil, this'll set you up to carry on.'* I reached out for the glass but Harry picked it up, drank the brandy in one, shuddered and left the room muttering: *'That's better'*. There was no time to get another brandy and I was soon out on the pitch ready to start the second half.

3

JOHN COWARD EMBARKS ON HIS CLARET DREAM

Imagine what it must have been like to be a director of such a well-run club as City, particularly when two of the founder directors of the new club in 1938 decide to retire. Suddenly a wealthy local businessman steps up to become Chairman – he has a vision, a dream but also the drive and determination to make City a club that will not just be a member of the Football League but also compete in its higher divisions. 1960 saw this change at the top and with it the start of an era the club had not seen before nor has seen since. However, it was not all a bed of roses and became something of two steps forward and one back BUT it was exciting – the facts as reported have been recorded from that time and the following is how a director might have viewed the start of this pivotal era for the club from his position on the Board, in this the season of 1960/61.

Looking back now in the summer of 1960 at the previous season, it has truly been a time of change with the arrival of the likes of Gillott and Phillips and the last few months have been as traumatic as any I can remember for the club.

By the end of February 1960 we on the Board knew Freddie Langton was about to stand down as Chairman, but stay on as a director, at least for a while. He felt he could not fully commit himself to the club as he approached his 77th birthday. Archie Draper, like Freddie, was here in 1938 when the new club was formed, but he told us he too would stand down at the end of the season, which he duly did.

Freddie announced that John Coward, who we all knew very well, was willing to step in as Chairman. John has only been with us on the Board for a short while but has already made his mark and we know John, with comparative youth and enthusiasm also on his side, has a wealth of ideas to take us into the Football League.

He has built up a reputation as a successful and popular local businessman. He has always shown loyalty and generosity to those who work around him, often paying for weekends away for his staff. Whilst he rarely attends these events, the stories coming from them are legendary. John likes a drink and a good time but he embraces the work hard/play hard philosophy.

Despite John's elevation we were all upset when Freddie told us he was calling it a day, yet we were not surprised but just sad to see him go after so many years. He said he felt tired and was certainly not looking well. When I drove him home after the Board meeting at which he made his announcement he was very down.

The press release announcing the changes was issued in early March and John took his first meeting later in the month, outlining his plans in more detail. He wanted the floodlights installed as a matter of urgency and through his local contacts had spoken to the Christy family and subsequent to that Christy Bros quoted us a very competitive price. They can immediately start putting up the pylons, as a prominent League club, believed to be Charlton Athletic, cannot now afford the lights they had ordered. John has negotiated a knock down price of about £10,000, with the work to be carried out in the summer. We approve this at the next Board meeting after John guaranteed the funds would be made available, but he was intending to submit more plans to raise additional monies for further development of the ground. John immediately sets in motion this raising of funds and wants £5,000, on top of the £10,000 for the lights, to carry out other work on the ground. About three-quarters of the original shares issued in 1938 remain unsold so we are all encouraged to buy some and many of us do. The Supporters' Club has been fantastic in raising funds over the years and they also help to sell the additional shares, soon enough money is raised to give Christy Bros the go ahead. The floodlights are intended to be a defining addition to improve the image of the club and boost its income in the years ahead. Remember, even Wembley does not have lights and nor do a large number of League clubs; certainly very few outside the Football League.

John is indeed a breath of fresh air. Freddie is a wonderful man who has given so much but we are entering a new era in the football world. There is already talk of removing the maximum wage and the Professional Footballers' Association is preparing their case and will probably put it to the test in the near future.

The game itself will eventually move on. The Hungarians taught us a lesson in 1953 but we've been slow to learn from it and adapt the way we play, sticking with the old team set-ups. This is vulnerable to a more flexible type of play such as Brazil showed when winning the World Cup in 1958.

With the austerity of the post war years now behind us and industry picking up, more wealthy businessmen are interested in getting involved in their local clubs, such as 'Master Butcher' Bob Lord at Burnley, Jack Hayward at Wolves and Louis Edwards at Manchester United at the very top of the game. They will be needed if the maximum wage goes and it becomes a free for all. Attendances are rising but well below those before the war, but the floodlighting should soon pay dividends with poorly attended afternoon midweek games becoming a thing of the past. Most professional clubs are now looking into floodlights with most committing themselves as they all see them as a money-spinner. For the Football League clubs a new League Cup competition is muted just for those in the four divisions but only played during the week and under floodlights. In the Non-League we are already discussing some form of similar competition but the floodlight commitment from clubs is less certain at this lower level with funds so restricted.

John Coward's vision is for League status. We have a great ground and better than many in Division Two of the League. Chelmsford with its industrial base and closeness to London will continue to grow quickly in the post war boom – we are already seeing signs of this. All we need is to get into the League but when the League's AGM takes place in July we only poll a paltry three votes and Peterborough have taken Gateshead's place. Clearly we have a long way to go!

***

Gordon Barker, Ken Birch, Lyall Bolton, Les Dicker, Albert Stokes and goalkeepers Longridge and Newton are not being retained for the 60/61 season. Good servants all and we wish them well. Jimmy Lawler is off to the United States to further his career and Jimmy Mason has been signed by Crystal Palace so we have made room for an expected influx of new players, helped by three of our houses being freed up; a useful bargaining tool to attract a few star names.

At the May Board meeting John reiterates his plan to sell more shares in the club and to make the ground improvements in addition to the floodlights. These improvements include work on the offices, boardroom, the pitch and the installation of some refreshment bars around the ground to increase our income. We are already well on our way towards this figure.

John also wants to look into the securing of the land behind The Barn as far as the river and also the land between the cricket ground and us. He sees no reason why we should not look to have a full sports complex adjacent to the ground and even talks of a hotel being put in. I'm not sure many of the Board members believe this viable, but for now at least John's enthusiasm and the breadth of his ideas carry us along.

At the end of the meeting John announces that Harry Ferrier will be given licence to strengthen our team drawing top players away from leading League clubs like we have already done with Gillott, Brown and Barnard. We will match the new players' wages of course and their other benefits as far as possible. If we did not believe it before we all know now we are in a very different era!

***

With the summer of 1960 in full swing, Harry has left with his wife and son for a 'holiday' in Scotland but this is more a scouting mission. I have to spend time in the office at the ground in case Harry should call with a proposition to sign a player. One afternoon he rings and sounds tired. He has interviewed three players so far with the main one in Middlesbrough. These are a goalkeeper, centre forward and a winger. I know one is Harry Taylor who played sixteen games for the Newcastle first team last season and can play on either wing or centre forward. This certainly looks promising and Harry F is also impressed by the other two.

A few days later I get another call. Harry's made it to Scotland and has interviewed another TWELVE players. He was disappointed in all of them bar one, a wing half.

Out of the blue I take a call from John Chaplin and what a bombshell! He's been to see Derek Tiffin for a routine interview and reads out what Derek has said:

'If the City club will let me I have definitely made up my mind to go elsewhere.'

Tiffin has also told Chaplin that perhaps the fans might have seen too much of him in City colours. Chaplin also tells me Derek is upset about comments made *'from a certain quarter'*, but none of us knows who he is referring to. Chaplin will publish in the Chronicle on Friday and thought he would give us a chance to respond. I decide to get hold of Harry who is now in Stoke and he confirms Derek has said nothing to him. I pass this on to Chaplin who accurately writes up a piece for the paper.

The fans are as stunned as we all are. Derek has been with us since the late 40s and a fixture at the club. He has a very good job at Plessey so chose the part time professional route when he could so easily have made it to the top level.

Harry tells me he has had some success in Stoke and has lined up a young lad called Eddie Rayner, a strong wing half.

I'm getting excited with these likely signings from top clubs to add to what we have here already. I can't wait for the season to start but have reservations about the terms we might be offering albeit still within the maximum £20 a week. Are these players likely to be migratory and only stay for a short time? They might simply take the benefit of the same wage as in the League but with the addition of another job, something they could not have done at most League clubs at the higher level.

We soon resolve the Tiffin issue and he agrees to stay – a relief to us all. Perhaps he felt he needed to make a point.

***

Visiting The Stadium one day in July I find the groundsman watering the goalmouth at the Wolseley Road end. He's re-seeded and put down new turf where necessary. He's worried that if we get a wet autumn the pitch might not be able to cope with the wear and tear with so much of it being new.

One floodlight pylon is in place and another is being unloaded from a lorry in New Writtle Street behind the main stand. We are looking to have the lights available in September and it is proposed there will be an official opening in early October with Norwich City having confirmed they will be willing to come; at present we do have other irons in the fire. John Coward has come up with the idea of a celebrity match under the new lights as a trial run with money raised going to charity; we all agree this to be an excellent idea and this is being progressed.

***

At the recent Board meeting Harry is there. He wants to sign Denis Hatsell from Preston and confirms Harry Taylor will come from Newcastle; both were regular Division One players last season. We can match their maximum £20 per week but it is the fringe benefits he wants to run past us. John agrees to underwrite any extra cost if the increased gate revenue we hope to obtain does not cover it. Hatsell is valued at £10,000 and Taylor at £7,000 and we will have to pay these sums should we get into the League. With teams like Accrington Stanley reportedly close to being wound up, our chance might come sooner rather than later and these fees may become a reality.

I have my reservations about the terms being offered to these players and the fact we are signing them at all. The League clubs are up in arms about it all, as they are not seeing any money coming in when their player leaves to join a non-league club. I am not sure how long before the Football League and the FA put a stop to it all. Jimmy Hill and his PFA have confirmed they will push for the removal of the maximum wage by legal means if necessary during the coming season and that may well spell the end of this transfer system.

However, the Board approves the players' terms against my better judgement.

***

Bernard Webber in the Chronicle sees the new season as *'A history making one of progress'*. He hopes the much vaunted new floodlights will give a lift to the club and believes the cost is justified. He also sees John Coward as: *'… a man of great drive that means business.'*

When we sign Hatsell it is a sensational story – a highly rated player dropping from the top league to, effectively, the fifth tier. We even get coverage in the National Press but I sense trouble ahead from the League clubs who remain unimpressed at not receiving what they consider to be a justifiable fee. I hear some are getting together to use their influence to force the FA into a change to its rules on these transfers. I am also concerned that the League clubs might brand us with an unfavourable iron by never voting for us to join the Football League. After all, we only received support from three clubs in this year's election vote, but John brushes this aside confident we can meet this problem head on and cope with it.

Harry Taylor is duly signed along with Eddie Rayner (valued at £3,000) from Stoke; a wing half with 'exceptional speed and skill' – in all we have a team that would have cost about £40,000 if we had to pay the quoted fees.

At a Supporters' Club meeting I'm amazed at the fans' excitement at the prospect of watching players coming here from top clubs; players they've actually heard of adding to those who came last year.

***

After the players have been training one evening I bump into Peter Gillott and he tells me he knows Hatsell and Taylor from his Barnsley days and believes they will be great acquisitions. However, we both heard earlier in the day that Hatsell has to have a knee operation and may not play until January next year, which is extremely disappointing. We were certainly not told of this at the last Board meeting when we approved the signing-on terms!

That same evening our new goalkeeper Dave Evans (valued at £1,500) joins Peter and me for a drink in the social club and we rib him about his one and only visit to White Hart Lane. It was only last February when he was playing in goal for Crewe Alexandra in an FA Cup replay against the Spurs, after a 2-2 draw on the Saturday. I ask him what the half time team talk was like when they found themselves losing 10-1. He says there wasn't one! However, he points out that it was only 3-1 in the second half and maintains he was man of the match despite Les Allen scoring five goals! He has a good word to say about both sets of supporters that night. Over three thousand Crewe fans went along helped by the fact that they all worked on the railways and had free travel! The home crowd gave the Crewe players an ovation at the end for their plucky second half performance especially as Crewe went a whole 23 minutes without conceding a goal. The Spurs' fans started a chant in Dave's favour enquiring about his sore back from bending to pick the ball out of the net thirteen times!

****

Harry also signs Roy Hollis from Southend and we know quite a bit about him, being fairly local. Wally Bellett returns to us from Chelsea via Plymouth Argyle. He was in the Chelsea youth set up with the likes of Jimmy Greaves but has not quite made the grade at the highest level. I like the look of Eddie Rayner who I watched yesterday in training, he's quick and sharp in the tackle.

If we can match the start from last season, but maintain it this time, we have a chance of the league title. However, as before, a run in the FA Cup will really help give impetus to John's vision. We are exempt in the Cup until the fourth qualifying round so let's hope we get lucky with the draw.

****

We've improved the pitch and the floodlights are going up. With a motor room required for the lighting, we have also added a pressroom next to the boardroom. We have also re-sited and rebuilt the refreshment bars with everything in the ground already getting a good lick of paint.

John wants to extend the main stand and then cover all sides of the ground in stages, starting with behind the goal at the Wolseley Road end. We have the facilities of a Football League club and all that is required now is to somehow get there.

***

What a start to the season! Seven wins, a draw and one defeat (away at Bath, so no disgrace) sees us top of the table at the beginning of October and this without Denis Hatsell and we're also unbeaten in the Southern League Cup. Could this be our year to lift the Southern League title? It would be most welcome now that it is no longer regional and has much greater prestige?

The team from September 1960 before the 4-1 win against Cambridge City
Back Row Left to Right: Bill Parry (Trainer); Terry Hayward; Wally Bellett; Len Phillips; Dave Evans; Derek Tiffin; Eddie Rayner; Harry Ferrier (Manager)
Front Row Left to Right: Mascot; Les Brown; Alec Eisentrager; Roy Hollis; Harry Taylor; Geoff Walker

Harry, assisted by Ossie Willsher, has spent more time with the team because trainer Bill Parry has been in hospital with peritonitis during September. He was seriously ill for a while but seems to have pulled through.

I've been working on the special opening of the floodlights due to be finished by mid-September. Christy Bros have done marvellously well in getting them finished despite some appalling summer weather. John still wants a charity match as the first use followed by a game against good league opposition.

Harry has been using his contacts in our search for top opposition for the official opening and we do still have Norwich as a fall back. Harry receives many promises but then we suddenly hit a snag because the Football League, for some unknown reason, now only allow their teams to play FOUR friendlies per season, two at home and two away. Most teams are already committed including West Ham, our main target. It would have been nice to see Geoffrey Hurst playing at The Stadium; perhaps we could have persuaded his Dad, former City man Charlie, to put on his boots on this special occasion.

Harry is in a dark mood about the League rules and we are running out of time. Joe Anderson, a friend of mine, works at Norwich as Assistant Secretary. I call him up and he has a word with Archie Macaulay, their manager, and they agree to come down on Monday 3rd October. Norwich are doing well in the Second Division having had a good start to the season and are best remembered for their great FA Cup run in 1959 when, as a Third Division club, they narrowly lost to Luton in the semi-final.

Having the charity game as a dry run for the Norwich night, we leave nothing to chance. The TV Stars XI put on a good show against a local R.A.F.A. XI and the lights are wonderful. As Christy's have erected these pylon lights at much bigger grounds than ours, their experience has helped create a very impressive effect. For the thousands who turned up it was a unique experience and good to have so many youngsters and ladies along, all to see someone they hear on the radio or watch on their TV screens. Mike and Bernie Winters had the crowd in stitches with their antics on and off the pitch. Mike isn't a bad player but as for Bernie …!

Ahead of the official opening with Norwich in October we decide to hold two other games under lights. A youth team game and a league match against Wisbech Town; with the latter on a Wednesday. The atmosphere seems much better than when a match takes place in the afternoon and the win against Wisbech was well received but the game itself was pretty dire. However, what disappointed me most was the crowd. We only had two hundred more for this game than the previous home game on the Saturday afternoon. This is, most definitely, not part of John's 'vision'. Perhaps Wednesday is a bad evening for the fans and, as a result, we have decided to opt for Monday nights for our floodlit games in the future.

The brilliant lights shine down on the pitch and the packed terraces as City defend a corner at the Wolseley Road end against Wisbech

Norwich, to their credit, put out their strongest team and secure a narrow 3-2 victory but with a bumper gate of 7,505 we now know, if we didn't before, that a new era for the club has arrived, so let's hope a good number of them return on a regular basis. At the next Board Meeting the optimism is such that some are getting over excited about the potential increase of income, especially as a series of floodlit matches against strong League opposition have been arranged for the end of the season.

***

It's the New Year – January 1961, and we're fifth in the league. Oxford are top and we are 8 points behind with two games in hand but we'll do well to catch them.

Good heavens, the pitch – what has gone wrong? On November 5th we had a plum tie at home to Port Vale in the first round of the FA Cup having disposed of Wisbech after a replay and it's fireworks indeed on the day. The gate is over 9,000 – what a payday for us and a chance to show we can compete with League opposition, but the pitch beats both teams – awful thick mud – and the match came close to being abandoned. We deserve a replay but the referee disallows Harry Taylor's goal that would have made it 3-3 with not long left. Same old story; we play well against better opposition, on paper at least, but lose – a replay would also have given us a welcome financial boost.

Tony Butcher challenges the Port Vale goalkeeper in the FA Cup on a quagmire of a pitch in front of 9,000 fans

All we're left with is a pitch that we need to sort out and by Christmas we've paid out over £2,000 to have tons of mud taken off, a new base added and then over 18,000 turfs put in place. A group of supporters have banded together to raise most of the cost; what a fantastic gesture!

In the wider world the bumper Christmas purchase, for adults at least, was *Lady Chatterley's Lover* by D.H. Lawrence. There has been huge furore over the book but it was finally given the go-ahead for wider publication in November. I know the lads in the changing room have been passing it around and there's been a fair bit of sniggering and a few *'Have you read this?'* comments. I once read an under the counter copy when I was at university many years ago and found it a bit boring – perhaps Peter Gillott understood it better with the heavy use of the Yorkshire accent!

The expected removal of the maximum wage arrives in January. We're worried we might not be able to compete now with bigger, wealthier clubs or continue to be able to sign players like Taylor, Gillott and Hatsell in the future. The rest of the directors are downcast about it but, at our meeting later in the month, I raise the point that surely league clubs will have to cut back on their playing staffs due to the rise in wages. This could mean many more players coming into non-league football with the Southern League attracting the better players. Time will tell if I'm right!

***

When we went ahead with the floodlights our long-term plan has always been to arrange friendlies at The Stadium, attracting some League teams, even from the top League in England or Scotland. We know clubs often come down for the Cup Final or Internationals at Wembley and we could fit in a game against them. We have decided to run a few more of these special friendlies next season as well as those already arranged for this April and May.

Harry is apoplectic with rage at the Board meeting on April 11th in between the two legs of the Southern League Cup Final with Yeovil and his mood is not helped by the fact that after the first leg we find ourselves 3-0 down. The reason for Harry's ire is that he has read the comments in the Chronicle by 'City Man', actually the less than supportive Bernard Webber, who claims the City fans are being over-fed with football this season and are unimpressed by the team's performances on the pitch.

Once we have calmed Harry down we review where we are. In fact, second to Oxford and still with a chance of winning the League. We are seven points adrift but with two games in hand and, if we secure four points from those games, anything can happen. The last two home games have seen gates of 4,700 and 3,500. So, all this rather refutes Webber's views but, with the friendlies arranged for April coinciding with our Southern League cup success, there will be a large number of games at The Stadium in a short space of time and perhaps Bernard does have a point. However, he should look at the wider picture. We have only lost three games so far in the League in 1961 and two of them were to Oxford. In fact, the match of the season was against them on March 6th – if we had won there was a chance of us catching them and the double of league and cup would still have been a reality. However, they are a strong team with more funds than us and thus able to afford five full timers whereas we have none. Their 2-0 win at The Stadium makes them clear favourites for the title but we still do have those two games in hand and we still have that second leg against Yeovil to come.

Harry tells the meeting he is confident we can retrieve the situation against Yeovil and wants to take serious issue with Webber. He shows the directors the draft of the response he wishes to include in his programme notes for the Yeovil second leg. To say they were strong words would be an understatement, so the next day I have to sit in Harry's office and help him re-draft these notes. In response to Webber the controversial part now reads:

'I see in the local paper I am again reminded that you, the public, have been over-fed with football this season. I fail to see this, as our gates at all games have been proved most encouraging. On the blank Mondays when we have had no match, the telephone has always been busy with enquirers making sure this was so. I see also the 'City Man' suggests we retain only two of the Reserve team for next season! When will reporters realise that the general public like to read a report of the game in detail and not what Mr Webber or 'City Man' thinks is best for

Chelmsford City or you – the over-fed public! I would be very interested to hear what you the public think of the games we have staged at 'The Stadium', as you are the people we want to satisfy, and we are trying to do this. I know we have had some poor games at home, this happens to all clubs.'

***

Harry is looking at his retained list candidates and having seen the latest Reserve game (after which Webber made his comments) also puts in his notes:

'The least said about the Reserve games versus Newmarket and March Town the better and I'm afraid that we will be very lucky to finish in the first four, as the in-and-out form of most of the Reserve players is just too bad to bear thinking about. I hope some of them realise that the time of assessment is near.'

Strong words indeed but we know Harry wants a clear out of players and already has some names in mind to sign for next season. He and John Coward have already had some lengthy discussions on some targets where money has been much talked about. We are not sure quite what effect this will have on us. We are not bound by the League rules on removing the maximum wage so it is likely we will still pay the maximum of £20 per week, but on the flip side we're not bound by the League rules on bonuses and John has already said that he wants to make extraneous payments above and beyond the contracted amounts of up to £20, including those win and draw bonuses.

What we do know about current League players is that we will still be allowed to sign these without payment of a transfer fee as long as we remain outside the four divisions. Harry suspects that most league players are not going to get much more than the previous maximum, except at the top level, and John is confident we can match what some of the lesser players want. Some lower League players would still welcome our part time deal, which requires training just two evenings a week and so allowing them to also have a full time job.

***

55

The overnight hotel stay before the first Yeovil cup match brought one of the lighter moments with John. He has a marvellous relationship with the players and they all enjoy his company and generosity. John does like a drink and after somewhat over imbibing all that evening stumbles upstairs and heads for his room. It takes him some time to locate the correct corridor and when he arrives at the right one he spends several minutes pacing up and down trying to find the number on the door corresponding to that on the piece of wood attached to his key. There are doors with the number before his and the one after but a tall cabinet filled with books stands between the two and where he believes his door should be. By now he is totally confused and befuddled. Out of the corner of his eye and further along the corridor he spots two players' faces in the doorway of their room roaring their heads off.

'*What have you done you b******s?*' Cue more laughter. The players led by Tony Butcher and Peter Gillott had moved the cupboard to cover John's door!

***

The second leg against Yeovil is amazing as Hatsell with two and one from Butcher make it 3-3 on aggregate. Denis scores four minutes from the end of normal time to draw us level. The crowd goes wild and one or two run on the pitch. There are no further goals in extra time but we lose the toss to host the play off, so it's at Yeovil and is set for Friday April 28th before the home league game against Folkestone the next day. That will mean the boys will have played ten games in four weeks.

In the bar after the win I have a chat with Yeovil's Ernie Taylor. Ernie was a special signing for Manchester United immediately after the Munich disaster and played in the 1958 cup final against Bolton. He gave me a remarkable insight into what it was like at Old Trafford in the aftermath of the disaster – the desolation, the sadness and the mourning for the loss of so many from their team and their backroom staff. Yet he felt there always remained hope, fuelled by the reaction of football fans not only at Old Trafford but across the world. He thought it nothing short of a miracle that the club could keep going and, but for Nat Lofthouse's awful 'foul' on goalie Harry Gregg, might have lifted the FA Cup only three months after the tragedy. I still find it remarkable that despite losing those seven players they have rebuilt their team to such an extent that they managed seventh in the First Division last season and look like finishing in a similar position this time round.

***

Some relief from the league and cup were the two friendlies in April – as if ten competitive matches that month were not enough.

Firstly and as a result of Denis Hatsell coming down from Preston, former England international and Preston stalwart, Tom Finney, brought a team along for Des Brewer's testimonial. Des deserved a good turn out and duly receives one. He was a star of that local half back line of him, Tiffin and Gardiner – one of the youngest and best in the league in the mid-fifties.

Finney at 39 shows us all his magical skills that graced the international scene for so long – many have described him as the most complete forward player this country has seen in that he could have been selected for England in any of the five forward positions. The All Star XI wins 3-2 in front of an appreciative crowd with several well known league players joining Tom, including Bovington from West Ham and Doherty and Bacuzzi from Fulham. Harry asked the All Stars to include some players he was looking to sign for next season, but no one stood out for me; however, you can never guess what Harry made of them.

The following Monday sees another friendly and this has been arranged for some time. Harry with his Scottish connections has persuaded Third Lanark to pay us a visit and it's quite a coup. They are riding high behind Kilmarnock and Rangers in the Scottish First Division and ahead of Celtic, and are down for the England/Scotland game at Wembley on the Saturday. They promised to play this friendly on their way back from London as part of our celebration of the new floodlights and to help raise the money to pay for them.

I had been in contact with Bill Hiddleston at Third Lanark for some time to make the arrangements, as Harry was really busy with all the matches taking place in such a short period of time.

⚽ 57 ⚽

The Sunday and Monday papers were full of Scotland's humiliation at Wembley – 9-3 to England! I was worried before this game that the Lanark team might take this weekend off in London to live it up and might be hung over when they arrive in Chelmsford. They surely would have been if they had been out on the town celebrating a victory but perhaps they just drowned their sorrows instead!

When I met Bill at The Stadium on the late Monday afternoon he looked bleary eyed and it did seem that for most of the Sunday many from the club had been out in London.

'*Ah ... but not the team,*' he said, but I was not convinced.

'*What about the match, then?*' I asked mischievously. '*More like a rugby score?*'

'*Aye, very nearly, but we had that clot Haffey in goal; he kept dropping the ball or letting it through his hands; my ma could have done better.*'

'*They can't all have been his fault – I mean we had Haynes, Greaves, Smith, Charlton, Robson ... much better than your lot.*'

He laughed: '*Yes and we had Mackay, Law, McNeill and St John BUT you didn't have Haffey, that was the difference, he's been told to stay in England and not come home. Some of our fans were apparently burning effigies of him in Soho on Saturday night.*'

'*Anyway, what a season you're having,*' I suggest, '*ahead of Celtic too. Who should we look out for then?*'

'*Oh we have the best forward in Scotland in Alex Harley; he's already scored over 30 goals in the League already and he'll get 40 before he's finished. Then there's Dave Hilley, already represented the Scottish League, cultured, intelligent. Beyond them there's Goodfellow, McInnes and Gray; they're called the 'scarlet' goal machine! You'll do well to stop them.*'

I pass this on to Harry but he knew about them already.

There was a lot of banter between our boys and their lads before the game. Our Les Brown played up there for Dumbarton of course and he's been getting his leg pulled from all quarters about the 9-3. Harry, with his Scottish connections, came in for the most stick from the Englishmen in our dressing room and he didn't take it very well, laying into the team before the match somewhat unnecessarily given this is an end of season friendly. He did make one good point to the team in that a win was important to enhance our reputation and proving we are good enough for the League; another step to help our dream become a reality.

What happened during the evening was quite unbelievable. Dorothy, our Football Queen, had the privilege of 'kicking off'. The Dagenham Girl Pipers added to the drama especially with their Scottish music to honour our visitors, performing before the game and at half time. Amazingly 9,564 turned up and saw a terrific performance from our boys

Third Lanark came out of the blocks as if they were seeking revenge for their compatriots' defeat on Saturday and, further back in history, the drubbing at Culloden! I caught part of their team talk before the match as I passed their dressing room door. The language was most certainly ripe yet strangely stirring and I'm sure I heard Bannockburn and Robert the Bruce mentioned more than once!

Les Brown notched a rare goal and Butch and Hatsell scored the others. Lanark missed a penalty but certainly did not take it easy nor look as they had over imbibed at the weekend. It was a hard, fast match well controlled by the referee, a Mr Partridge, of whom great things have been predicted.

Hiddleston and their other directors were full of praise for the City. Hatsell showed his class by outshining Harley and Hilley – I had been waiting to see this from Denis – perhaps his talents are better suited against opposition with a higher technical ability than we are used to in our league.

We had quite a few drinks in the bar with the Lanark boys. John Coward brought in some single malt and that went down very well indeed.

***

Returning to the more serious business of league and cup, John Coward announces we'll fly down to Yeovil on the Friday and return that evening ready for the game against Folkestone the following day. We need to be down at Rochford early in the day for the flight on Channel Airways from Southend Airport. Most of the players haven't flown before and nor have some of the directors and pressmen. Two or three flyers are airsick but none of the players, although many looked pale and apprehensive. I'm not so sure this is as relaxing as John would have wanted it!

We play poorly and lose 2-0 – after such a tough game the boys force themselves back into action the next day but look jaded and drop points with a draw against Folkestone having lost to them away ten days before.

One bright note is that Hatsell continues to prove me wrong. I initially thought him a waste of money, as he was not fit to play until well into the season, but he is now in double figures for goals since November.

He's popular with the team and the supporters with an abundance of skill, but I still think he's coasting a little towards retirement. He's protecting his knee, he knows another injury to it will probably spell the end and probably, without intending to, he's not quite giving 100%. Harry Taylor on the other hand has been superb. He's gritty, determined and always gives 100% – one of our best ever signings along with Len Phillips: poor old Len … and Butch to a lesser degree. The crowd cannot get used to Len's controlled game of never willingly giving the ball away. He's careful, studious … class – but most in the crowd want him to smash it forward. As for Butch, the local boy, he always has the crowd on his back but by the end of April he's scored nearly 30 goals – what more do they want?

***

With the money from these friendlies plus a staggering £1,950 from the Supporters' Club and £200 a week from the City Pool competition, we have paid off nearly £5,000 of the debt for the floodlights and the other improvements.

All through the winter I've been helping John put together a brochure to be sent to all the League clubs. It's very glossy and impressive by the time we are ready to send it out. If only we could have had a better FA Cup run and got closer to Oxford, who have now pretty well sown up the league, our case would be even better. I still feel we have upset one or two clubs and I'm not sure local Essex and London clubs want another from their area, competing for the fans.

Conversely, the northern clubs tend to vote for their own; however, whatever Peterborough can do so can we, or so we believe.

Now at the end of April and looking back, this is our record for the month:

April 1st – Dartford – Home – Win 6-1 – League
April 3rd – Cheltenham – Away – Win 4-2 – League
April 8th – Yeovil – Away – Lose 3-0 –League Cup Final First Leg
April 10th – Star FA XI – Home – Lose 3-2 – Friendly
April 15th – Yeovil – Home – Win 3-0 – League Cup Final Second Leg
April 17th – Third Lanark – Home – Win 3-0 – Friendly
April 18th – Folkestone – Away – Lose 1-0 – League
April 22nd – Wellington – Away – Win 2-1 – League
April 28th – Yeovil – Away – Lose 2-0 – League Cup Final play off
April 29th – Folkestone – Home – Draw 2-2 – League

TEN games and we've got three more between the 1st and 6th May, plus we also played on March 31st!

Evans, Hayward, Gillott, Phillips, Tiffin, Brown, Butcher, Taylor, Barnard and Walker have played in them all, whereas Hatsell has missed just the one. I really don't know how they've done it.

The brochure has been sent to all the League clubs and to other interested parties. Vice Chairman Fred Langton Junior will attend the League meeting for the voting and has asked me to join him.

Before that we have a Board meeting and Harry tells us he is reducing his staff. We knew Des Brewer would go but are surprised when Harry announces Geoff Walker and Eddie Rayner will not be retained – they have played for the first team throughout most of the season. Roy Hollis and Alec Eisentrager were less of a surprise having had their best years. They've been fine servants and good clubmen. Alec despite his German army background won over the locals with his 100% effort and affable nature. Local boy Tommy Mingay is also being released and I'm disappointed as I could see him doing as well as Butch, but Harry doesn't rate him at this higher level.

Harry tells us he has a top centre forward lined up but won't tell us who. He also says other star names have been approached, but I'm a little sceptical given the question of the wages they might demand. If it does happen I wouldn't wish to see us getting over committed on cost and coming a cropper! If we get into the League we might see 9,000 turn up every week but then, of course, we'd have to pay out the transfer fees for those already signed at no cost. I have warned John but he is confident we can cope. It does seem to me he's putting a lot of eggs into the one basket, but it's exciting; yet let's hope this new Coward Empire doesn't collapse before the building is finished.

Harry tells me an interesting story about one of the players who has complained he is not receiving the same salary as Hatsell, who receives £20 per week in the season and £14 per week in the summer close season, whereas the other player is on £16 a week and £11 in the summer. *'But Hatsell is a better player than you,'* Harry explained. *'Not in the summer he isn't!'* came the cheeky reply.

We have another friendly to play in May on the night before the FA Cup Final against Bradford Park Avenue who are coming down to watch the Wembley match. Unlike Third Lanark, they don't look that interested and we beat them 5-0. There is another good crowd and they see a brilliant performance in goal by Alan Collier, given a trial by Harry. Alan's at Luton and only a few years back was touted as likely to be one of the top keepers in the country. Harry says he'll move heaven and earth to sign him; perhaps bad news for Dave Evans who has played in every other game during the season.

Oxford United duly win the league and deservedly so, but if only we had maintained our early season form. The loss to them at New Writtle Street in early March pretty well cooked our goose.

After all the matches have been played I have to write up a report of the season for the Board from the playing perspective. This entails a lengthy meeting with Harry and not just an assessment of the team but one of him too.

I have watched him carefully this season. He is well liked by the players and the staff, but he does work on a short fuse as we saw with his verbal spat with Bernard Webber. Away from the club Harry spends too much time at the greyhounds and, I hear, gambles more than is good for him. He likes a drink too and I do worry about his lifestyle and tell him so.

He laughs it off as usual but knows I'm serious. We have decided to increase his wages and this has come after he told us at the end of March that he'd had an approach from Portsmouth to manage the club where he used to play. He did have an interview but told me: *'I did not really intend to accept it. I am here to get the City into the League.'*

***

Now in the summer break, we turn our attention to the Football League AGM. Hartlepools (for the fifth time!), Barrow, Chester and Exeter are up for re-election. The League has accepted nominations from Oxford, Cambridge City, Bath, Gravesend, Hereford, Bedford, Romford and us. City and Oxford are the clear favourites according to the London National Press. However, it is disappointing so many teams apply, splitting the floating voters who might just opt for the status quo instead. Oxford clearly have a chance having won the Southern League but only the City and Bedford boast good grounds AND the support.

In the Chronicle on May 26th John is quoted:

'We are looking forward to election to the League. We have quite a good chance. We have done a lot of circularizing and the club is quite well known and liked amongst the League clubs. But whatever happens we'll keep trying.'

I leave the League meeting despondent and have to telephone John to give him the bad news that we only polled three votes; one behind Bedford. Oxford got nineteen but you need over thirty. The 'old pals' act' seems to have kicked in. For us in the future it might just be a case of 'waiting for dead man's shoes', as when Gateshead folded and were replaced by Peterborough. There has been talk for some time about a feeder non-league with automatic promotion but the League clubs have, not surprisingly, always vetoed this.

John is beside himself. After all the hard work and cost of the brochure, we have fallen short by some margin, not even matching Bedford. I'm sure many League clubs have noticed the publicity given to the controversy surrounding the Hatsell-type signing and are annoyed that non-league clubs like us will sign their players avoiding the normal fee. I did hope I was wrong with my prediction on this but, if ever proof was needed that we are not as well thought of as we believed, only three votes gives the answer.

⚽ 63 ⚽

I meet up with Harry on the following Monday and we talk about it.

'I'm not surprised,' he bemoans, 'as those League AGMs are like old pals' reunions.'

Harry tells me he's signed Tom Beattie a wing half from Clacton. Not exactly one of the 'star names' he promised but it's a start as he replenishes the team. He will not divulge any of his other targets to me but confirms he has some surprises in store. However, we agree to place an advert in the 'Sporting Record' for players in all positions.

During our meeting he shows me an article from last Friday's Chronicle. It tells of Geoffrey Hurst still only 19 being invited to the World Cup training camp by Walter Winterbottom as a prospect for the Under 23s.

'I've been watching this boy,' explained Harry, 'and have approached West Ham in the past. They were not so sure he'd make it as a wing half and talked of letting him go but now this has happened they'll want to keep him. Doesn't he live in Chelmsford?'

'He does,' I confirm. 'Well at least his parents do. You must know Charlie Hurst from your playing days. He ended up in the town and has set his roots here too. Geoffrey went to school here, plays cricket for Chelmsford and is a prospect for the County too. I know Charlie and he's never been sure he'll make it as a wing half, but there's talk he's being tried as a centre forward; after all there's considerable competition at West Ham in his wing half position with this Moore lad seen as a great prospect and expected to move on to play for England. Have you seen Geoffrey play?'

'I have,' confirmed Harry. 'A bit lumbering and his touch is not as good as some but he's physically strong, maybe he'll be better as a centre forward or perhaps a centre half where he can use his bulk. I'm going to keep an eye on him and move in if he doesn't look like making it. I see him as a possible replacement for Derek Tiffin in the long run.'

Time will tell, but if Geoffrey has caught the eye of Winterbottom I suspect he will have a career at the top of the game.

We then move on to discuss what funds have been raised in the last month. A brand new Hillman Minx was put up as a fund raising prize by Lasts, thanks to our director, Bob Last. People were invited to guess how many fans watched all the Football League games on April 28th and the nearest won a new car worth nearly £800 and the draw raised a welcome £1,800.

At the Supporters' Club dinner at the Saracen's Head to which all the directors and Harry were invited it was announced that over £100,000 had been raised over the past ten years. A monumental achievement truly underpinning the football club and, if we're honest about it, keeping us afloat!

In June I receive a call from John suggesting we meet in his company offices for a change. He's having second thoughts on Harry and has heard of a few high quality managers available but won't tell me who they are or how he's heard about them. Has he been approached directly or just read something in the papers? Chaplin at the Chronicle has his ear and may have put some names forward.

John believes Harry, quite rightly, is stretched too thinly. Managing the whole club is a massive task acting as the Team Manager and Secretary plus helping with the coaching. John has in mind appointing a full time Secretary to relieve Harry, or any new Manager, of some of this work and suggests Len Menhinick to fill this role. Len and his family have been involved with the Supporters' Club for some time. He is currently Secretary of the Old Chelmsfordians' Association and also involved heavily with the local football scene, so would come with much experience. However, John foresees a problem of prising Len from his current job yet now seems determined to do so and I know Len will be a fine acquisition.

John also gives me a clear indication that he has a bee in his bonnet about Romford and sees them as a coming force. He may have some issues with Parrish, their Chairman, because there is some deep-seated ill-feeling somewhere in all this, but I'm not sure why. I get the impression that John wants to make sure we remain the local top dogs and will provide adequate finance to ensure we maintain that current position.

By the end of the meeting I'm confident John has decided to stick with Harry. I do feel John so badly wants the City to win the Southern League and progress upwards that at times he is impatient. I try to persuade him that these things take time and that he must bear in mind that not so long ago we very nearly went out of business and it will be much better if we can build a strong base for the club then move on.

He does see my point of view but, as he is putting in most of the money and not me, he has the right to want immediate results, but we all await next season with interest.

4

THE EXPANSION OF THE COWARD EMPIRE

The 1961/62 season was memorable for me as I did not miss one single home game in any competition involving the First Team or the Reserves; after all, there is not much else to do when you have just reached your teenage years. Chelmsford City was my life back then – I was despondent when we lost, elated if we won. This is how the 61/62 season unfolded, seen through my young eyes at the time – Steve Little.

My first experience of watching the City was with my grandfather on Saturday afternoons in the 1957-58 season. In those early days the players all looked so old and I suppose many were older than my father, who was himself still playing locally at that time. It was difficult for me to maintain interest for ninety minutes or more and I did find the games somewhat boring at times. Other things took my interest and the job I really wanted when I was older was to be the person walking around the perimeter of the pitch at half time with a board giving the lucky dip prize winning numbers and the lucky programme too. I religiously collected the claret and white programmes for each match living in hope that one day I might have the winning programme number and scoop that prize.

If I couldn't secure that job then the excitement of putting up the half time scores from the First and Second Division matches on the East Anglian Daily Times sign behind the goal would be an excellent alternative.

I watched more of the games as I became older and began appreciating the finer points of the beautiful game especially as I was now playing schools' football at Kings' Road by the age of eleven. Arthur Adey and Derek Tiffin were my early idols, but I always liked Tony Butcher and could never work out why the crowd disliked him so much.

My father, Norman, became Chairman at Galleywood FC, having played there when he was younger, and I cut my teeth watching them in the Mid Essex League against the likes of Mundon Vic and Kings Road Old Boys of whom I was now one.

I couldn't tell much difference in the quality of football but it certainly looked different in front of a large crowd at The Stadium. Rich claret shirts for the City men compared with the faded black and white quarters of Galleywood. City's matching white shorts and claret and white socks compared with the selection of colours worn at Galleywood – several shades of grey, some jet black and even red interspersed with the white!

At Galleywood there were the Goulds and the Perrys – local families who always supplied much of the team – Hearsall Perry was one regular – what a name and not a bad player!

Alf Lodge, as Secretary, ran the club, always seen riding his bike around the village wearing his battered cap and long brown mac whether a hot or cold day. There were no showers at the Galleywood ground, but one sink and a single tap in the cricket pavilion doubling up in the winter. Oranges were provided for the players at half time – I always hoped one or two would be left and I'd be offered one – then perhaps a cup of tea at full time. There were two kick-about balls as hard as iron – worse if it was wet – with laces pulled across where the bladder's little valve stuck out so the pump nozzle could be inserted to inflate the ball. The laces had to be tied with a special hook. My father dubbined the ball before each game. Some of the players still wore brown boots whereas at the City they were always black.

Unlike the open field at Galleywood, The Stadium was a 'proper' ground and it always looked impressive especially with a large crowd. I had no experience of larger grounds until our lodger, Mike Copps, took me to see Spurs against Wolves in 1958 at White Hart Lane – now that was a real ground holding nearly fifty thousand and soon after that I was taken to Wembley to see England play Sweden at Wembley. That was something else altogether!

The Stadium was fine though. For a start, unlike Galleywood, there was somewhere to go when it rained with The Barn almost covering the whole of one long side. The only time I sat in the main stand was to watch the final of the Mid Essex League Cup Final on an Easter Monday – Galleywood got there a couple of times. It was too expensive for my parents to pay for me to go there on my weekly visits.

With Chelmsford being the 'Clarets' I decided to support Burnley, also the 'Clarets' – they were a great team in the late fifties and I was unique at Kings Road and now equally so at the Grammar School in that no one else chose to support them. I really did hope Burnley's success would rub off on the City.

Not being a bad player myself I had hoped to get into the school Under 13s but my hopes were dashed when the team was announced in the September. The good news was that I could now watch the City throughout the winter not only on a Monday night but also on Saturdays too. Rather sadly I spent most Friday evenings pouring over the Chronicle's sports pages, absorbing everything about the City; cutting out and keeping all the articles then re-reading last week's programme. Suddenly, I was besotted!

***

Starting off with the summer break of 1961, my expectations for next season are already lifted with the news of the signing of Alan Collier, a goalie from Luton, who had played brilliantly against us in a friendly last season. We are told he is a gardener by trade and will be carrying on with this. Keith Abbiss joins from Brighton, a wing half brought in to replace the excellent Eddie Rayner who left at the end of last season. I liked Rayner. Abbiss soon proved a bit airy-fairy for my tastes but my friend Rob Ketley thought him marvellous and was always going on about 'Abi' this and 'Abi' that. But Abbiss was to find himself dropped in November and rarely played after that, much to Rob's consternation but then he was only nine, so he'd probably get over it.

As soon as the competitive matches started, we looked great up front with Tony Butcher confounding his critics, yet many fans were still not satisfied with his performances despite him scoring a dozen goals by mid-November.

Alongside Butcher is new signing Peter Harburn who came down from Workington but has played for Everton. He turned down League football to join City apparently because he benefits from a club house for his family – a wife and three children – and this helped his decision. Tall, dark and moody he looks frightening and I wouldn't like to meet him on a dark night in the town. Unusually he has a square of jet-black hair on each cheek as if his sideburns have been split in two and this makes him look even more menacing. I ask my father about this fashion and he says it's an old time thing favoured by sailors.

John Doherty is someone I've heard of. He has played for Fulham in the First Division for the last few seasons but has been out of favour recently.

Most of the other summer signings prove a little disappointing, if I'm honest. The local papers kept telling us about all these great signings to come, but we all felt those who arrived to be a motley bunch unlike the previous season when we were signing players straight out of the top English league – players I'd heard of – some even had their faces on cigarette or bubble gum cards.

Gordon Dale isn't bad – 32 and bald, he looks older than my father. He comes to us from Exeter and was at Portsmouth before that and Mr Ferrier knows him well. In 1951 Dale had been valued at £20,000 but that was ten years ago. He's a tricky left winger and brought in to replace Geoff Walker, who'd been with us for years. Dale lives near the south coast and will train there with Phillips and Barnard; they will travel together to both home and away games.

There was a big hooh-hah about the pitch after it got carved up in the wet last season and it has been re-laid – again!

Soon a problem arises over Collier. There's a legal wrangle with Luton about whether we should pay them a transfer fee. It is sorted out eventually but we seem to have upset Luton. This will probably mean another club that won't vote us into the Football League.

There have been changes under the main stand with the old gym now a social club. Apparently this is to help raise even more funds. The players can now train under the floodlights using the cinder track around the pitch.

My father attends the Supporters' Club AGM and comes home annoyed. From the start of the 1962-63 season the Supporters' Club will no longer be producing the traditional claret and white programme, the proceeds from which is added to their funds. Instead, the programme will be reduced to a black and white booklet size and the profit will go straight to the main club. I share my father's anger at the change.

The old and the new – the supporters prefer the old on the left!

The Essex Chronicle tells us the training has been stepped up to four nights a week from the usual two. Bill Parry, the trainer, has been ill and in hospital again, but has planned all the sessions from there. Apparently Mr Parry nearly died and has now been told to take it easy when he's sent home.

One item of news that has caught my eye is the restarting of a Colts' team. There are trials at Melbourne Park for any 15 to 17 year olds who might want to play. Bill Parry, when fit, and Ossie Willsher will be overseeing these and it is hoped the City can pick up some good local young players. I know of some who should go along from KEGS, Malcolm Pannell is one they should look at and maybe Paul Young or Ian Wilson.

When the curtain raiser friendlies take place the pitch is unrecognisable from the end of last season. Pristine green and nothing like the First World War battlefield it was when we played Port Vale in the FA Cup last November.

Mr Coward reiterates in the local papers his passionate vision of us getting into the Fourth Division within five years. Every supporter I've spoken to is excited by this and especially when we hear talks are taking place to extend the size of the Fourth Division and splitting it into three separate divisions, apparently geographical like North, Central and South. Surely we'd get into that and be on our way.

Mr Coward wants an average gate of 6,500 'to enable us to go further ahead' – last year we averaged 4,414 and this was the highest in the Southern League and much higher than many Fourth Division clubs, especially those in the north. We get 4,814 for our first home game, which is promising.

Mr Ferrier, according to the Essex Chronicle, is happy with the reserve strength but disappointed he couldn't add a little more quality into the First Team.

There is a move for us to have league matches on Friday evenings instead of the Saturday to attract those who work or play on Saturdays and give an extra day's rest should we have a Monday night game. This seems an excellent idea and I'm sure the team prefers the atmosphere created under the floodlights.

***

Finally the pre-season build up and excitement is over and we start off away at Merthyr and win 3-0 with goals from Hatsell and Harburn two. The team is Collier, Hayward, Gillott – Phillips, Tiffin, Abbiss – Taylor, Hatsell, Harburn, Butcher and Dale. In the first home game we win 2-

0 with Abbiss and Butcher scoring. So, with two new players already on the score sheet and Collier not letting anything in at his end, we are well on our way.

Our first loss is at Wellington and then we have a further test at home against the perennially strong team from Yeovil. Over 6,700 are there and we continue our good start winning 3-2. This was a fine result; helped by a Collier penalty save, but it also marked the first goal I ever saw left back Peter Gillott score, it was a penalty but never mind. He has now joined Tony Butcher as my joint favourite player. This followed a chance meeting with him at Melbourne Park one Sunday morning. I was with some friends having a kick about when he joined in. Afterwards we chatted with him; all feeling a little embarrassed being in the presence of one of our idols!

From the end of September until the second week of November we win every league game; all six of them, with four of the games away. Before this run we also beat Bath City 5-0. They are a shadow of what they used to be, all their money has gone and with it the 'star' players. This remains my worry for the City, could it also happen to us?

The gates are still above last year's average, better than Colchester's but short of what Mr Coward would like. He and Mr Ferrier are upset with some of the supporters. Despite the league run seeing us at the top of the Southern League and winning in the Southern League Cup and the FA Cup, there was still a minor bout of slow handclapping at one of the games. Dale doesn't seem a favourite and fans are shouting for him to be dropped. Tony Butcher gets his normal criticism and the 'Get rid of it Phillips' section of the crowd has found its voice again.

Some of us just wonder what these people want. Three supporters sent a letter to the Chronicle saying, *'clear out the dead wood before the rot sets in'* – this when we are still top of the league!

***

Now in my early teens I'm allowed to go to games on my own but often accompanied by Rob Ketley and sometimes his older brother Terry. Others from school are often there, some you link up with like Mick Newman and Roger Bird, others you avoid.

Most of my close friends are playing for the school football or hockey teams on Saturdays so unable to make many City games. Some always criticise the team anyway and succeed in winding me up, making me even more passionate in my support.

For Rob and me Saturdays have the same ritual. Catch the Number 45 bus from the Woodhall Estate to the railway station. Walk along Viaduct Road passing all the little businesses set in the arches with the bus depot on our right. From there we turn left under the railway line and into Central Park. When it's dry we have a kick about using a tennis ball making a goal with some items of clothing. Other boys join in. At half past two we head to the ground. Normally using the bridge built to enable fans to get over the river and into The Barn. If we fancy the other side of the ground, or have more time, we go over the more attractive white bridge into Wolseley Road and then into New Writtle Street. I always buy a programme. The rest of my pocket money mainly goes on a Wagon Wheel, always has to be a Wagon Wheel … such is superstition!

We stand behind the goal unless it's raining when we go under cover in The Barn. When not sheltering, we lean over the white perimeter wall and beat the advertising boards with our hands during exciting moments or when a goal is scored. Sometimes the hoarding comes away and we move off. The man on the tannoy frequently asks supporters not to do it but no one takes any notice. Occasionally the lone policeman on duty comes around and ticks us off.

The tannoy system makes us laugh. It rarely works properly, often crackling and distorted. We get the team changes before the game followed at half time by the lucky draw and programme numbers, but that's about all unless someone is parked where they shouldn't be or have left their lights on. The faceless man on the tannoy always blows into his microphone to check it's working. His standard phrase is *'Will the owner of car number … please return to it and move same immediately'*; an unusual choice of words. At one match he brings the house down when he announces that a driver has parked and left his engine running!

At half time we wait expectantly for the First Division scores to be put up on the East Anglian Daily Times sign. Our programme tells us which games correspond to the letter on the sign. The man climbs his ladder and puts up the metal numbers, but he is known to sometimes get these wrong. I am anxious for the Burnley score and Rob for that of the Villa. If Rob's older brother Terry is with us, he's a 'Spurs' man. Also at half time we walk from one end of the ground to the other, so we can stand behind the goal the City are kicking into in the second half.

Elated or disappointed at twenty to five we shuffle out of the ground. We exit via the rear of the main stand. The reason being a scribbled note of the 'gate' is left on the window ledge outside the Secretary's office. Why this is important to us I don't know – it's just one of those rituals. If we have been watching a Reserves' match and hang around outside the office for long enough someone may come out and tell us how the First Team have fared. We then head for the bus station. It is about five when we get there and I have my tuppence ready to buy the latest Evening News, the one with the final football scores stamped into the stop press column. Sometimes we have to wait and miss our first bus. A Rippon's newsagent man is in their lock-up under the railway arches just behind the public toilets at the bus station and we assume his job is to prepare the stamp having listened to the results on Sports Report. The results either add to our gloom or perk us up.

By five thirty we are home, often cold and hungry. As soon as winter arrives our feet become blocks of ice and we have to warm them up in front of the open fire. A week later we invariably have chilblains.

If I have not been told the First Team result at the ground from their away game, the Southern League results are given out at about 6.30pm on the Light programme on the wireless in a show hosted by a chap with the unusual name of Jacob (pronounced Yak Ob) De Vries, presumably of Dutch origin. Most weeks my family would all be at Nan and Grandad's house for our tea (always salad followed by trifle with Carnation milk). A hush would descend around the table as the results are read out. Often, especially if City had won, Grandad would hop into his Austin Seven and head to the railway station to pick up the 'Green 'Un', containing the match report. I would then pore over every fact of the First Team game and the shorter report of the Reserve match I had seen earlier.

***

I've known Clive Haworth from our Kings Road School days and I wouldn't call him an avid fan, but such has been City's start to the season in the League the whole town is buzzing with the excitement that this could be OUR year; Clive is no exception.

He attends most home games with David Tebbit who was with us at Kings Road. However, they always wait until half time before coming into the ground for free! In November Clive proudly shows me his new scrapbook. It's an exercise book neatly covered with a thick material to keep it clean and has 'Chelmsford City' emblazoned across its front. He is sticking in the match reports from the Essex Weekly News and that's handy for me to read as we get the Essex Chronicle at home. He says his Dad can't afford the Chronicle, which incidentally has the much better City coverage. I point out there's only a penny difference but he just shrugs it off.

On page one of his scrapbook he pastes in the report from the match against lowly Bedford Town on November 15th. His start coincides with the beginning of the end of the season for City. Things go downhill from that very day when we proudly stood at the top of the table and three points ahead of our nemesis, Oxford United. The Reserves were second behind Tottenham Hotspur 'A' with games in hand.

Both local papers remain full of City pushing hard to get into the League with the impetus from Mr Coward. On November 4th ,after a win in a replay against Wisbech Town for the second year running, we are drawn at home in the FA Cup to the bottom club in our league, Kings Lynn, who have only won three games in sixteen. The excellent Alan Collier has one of those occasions all keepers experience when late in the game he lets a soft shot trickle under his body and into the net for an unlikely 2-1 win for Lynn.

This drives a stake into our hearts. The Chronicle says we so badly needed a cup run to 'get noticed' nationally. Like most seasons recently this hope is dashed at an early hurdle.

Mr Ferrier responds to the Kings Lynn defeat by bringing in Alec Moyse from Poole Town. Hardly a Hatsell or a Taylor but, apparently, he's a proven goalscorer albeit at a lower level.

My cuttings and Clive's scrapbook now read like a tragedy, players falling short – the half back line not functioning with Barnard singled out for criticism in the 2-2 draw with Bedford. In the next few games we are awful, not helped by Dale then Taylor in successive matches pulling muscles and so becoming limping passengers for the rest of the game. There's been so much talk about replacements being used for injured players as there have been a succession of FA Cup Finals with players breaking legs or others just limping out on a wing meaning the teams often end up playing such important matches with ten men. Each season the FA promise to look into it but nothing seems to be happening.

***

One interesting piece of news caught my eye in the Chronicle. Derek Ablett, who was at KEGS until recently, scored all four goals as City Youth beat Colchester United 4-3 in the FA Youth Cup. Perhaps Derek, a centre forward, has been picked up in the trial sessions at Melbourne Park. He has very blond hair and reminds me of one of my Burnley favourites, England International Ray Pointer. Derek soon gets picked to play for the Reserves.

***

Mr Coward says in the Chronicle that he now wants average gates of 8,000 to help get us into the League:

'We CAN reach the 8,000 mark. If the fans respond – and they are already responding well – I see no reason why when the time comes we should not become members of the Football League, perhaps sooner than some expect. But so much depends on those gates.'

My City friends pick up the 'sooner than some expect' comment. Is there going to be a Fifth Division or a larger Fourth? Does Mr Coward know more about this than he's letting on or is he just having a swipe at the press? Time will tell.

Much of City's support comes from the large factories in the town. Stories true or otherwise soon get passed around about what's happening at the club and my father tells me of one he's just heard. Apparently, Mr Coward generously gives the team a 'bonus' if they beat Romford (apparently he doesn't get on with their Chairman and likes to put one over him.). After the 2-1 win at Romford in September the players apparently get a nice surprise when Mr Ferrier hands out some five-pound notes at the next training session. There is also a rumour that the three players who train down in Hampshire, Barnard, Phillips and Dale, didn't get theirs as Mr Ferrier 'forgot' to pass the £15 on and there was a suggestion that the money went on a greyhound instead. It must have won as the three duly did get their money.

These are interesting times at Romford. Mr Parrish, the Chairman, has pushed the boat out to bring in some well-known, if a little past it, players. Ted Ditchburn is the player manager who had a long career as 'Spurs' goalkeeper and played a few times for England. He has signed free scoring centre forward Len Duquemin from Spurs – a member like Ditchburn of the great Tottenham side of the late 40s and early 50s. Interestingly, Duquemin is a Channel Islander who hid from the Germans during the occupation there in the war.

In the Romford defence for one of the games they lose to City was Malcolm Allison loaned out to them by West Ham. He's big, uncompromising and probably the dirtiest player I've ever seen, but not a bad player given he had a lung removed a few years ago.

***

After the debacle in the FA Cup against Kings Lynn, there were letters sent into the Chronicle – one said *Chelmsford City RIP* which given we were still top of the league was a bit much; while others said Mr Ferrier was to blame. One mentioned that he persisted with 'dear old pals in the team' no doubt a reference to Phillips, Barnard and Dale all of whom had been with him at Portsmouth and these three have been on the receiving end of the crowd's criticism recently. In the Reserves Blake the winger who was to be a first team certainty has also been the butt of abuse from the fans.

***

I haven't missed a home First Team or Reserve game so far this season and I love the Monday night floodlit games that have a much better atmosphere than those on a Saturday. Perhaps a larger number of younger men come along especially some of the hundreds who play in local football on a Saturday and they are more prepared to join in the chants. Our lights are said to be some of the best around. On November 25th the first team loses 4-2 at a very murky Tonbridge. There had previously been complaints about the quality of their lights from the manager of Oxford United saying such clubs should be made to play all their games in daylight if they could not afford effective lighting and the Southern League should adopt a benchmark for suitable light. A very fair point as during the Tonbridge game it was reportedly almost impossible to see the ball when it went into the air.

On November 27th there are no such problems at The Stadium when we host Colchester in the Essex Professional Cup. Despite losing 2-1 after extra time the team play well and are very unlucky losing to a highly controversial penalty in the second period.

From the second half of November until Christmas we don't win in eight games, drawing four. My hero Peter Gillott is dropped only to return on Boxing Day.

If the crowd were upset when we were top of the league they are now beside themselves and a miserly home crowd of just over 3,000 see the 1-1 draw with Merthyr Tydfil in mid-December. A few seat cushions are thrown from the stand onto the pitch in disgust at the end of the game and the Chronicle stirred the pot even more by saying the wages of the whole Merthyr team amounts to only £150 a week. My father reckons our wages are more than three times that figure.

***

So, with 1961 drawing to a close and with the league title at one time in our sights, we fall away – the older supporters are not surprised, believing we were lucky to be doing so well given how poorly we were playing. There is much disquiet. Mr Coward's vision looks in tatters with yet another early exit from the FA Cup. It seems we can beat the likes of Third Lanark, Bradford and so on in friendlies creating the right impression but when the game is more competitive we fall short. The gates are nowhere near where Mr Coward wants them to be with our average by December of just over 5,000 being a long way away from the 8,000 he demands. However, ours still remain higher than most Fourth Division clubs.

The team from season 1961/62
Back Row: Left to Right: Norman Stevens: Terry Hayward: Alan Collier: Len Phillips: Derek Tiffin
Front Row: Left to Right: Brian Dellar; Harry Taylor: Tony Butcher; Alec Moyse; Denis Hatsell; Gordon Dale

Perhaps the team does need an overhaul. There's not much in the Reserves apart from Terry Eades, a centre half, but he's still only a teenager yet stands out above the rest. Perhaps instead of having the Reserves full of underperforming pros, the second string should be young players on the up. One, Malcolm Pannell, as I predicted, has been playing regularly. He is a registered player with Witham Town but they have allowed him to play for City – I'm not sure he wants to be a pro as I heard he wishes to become a teacher and play as an amateur.

The summer signings remain damp squibs. Dale is skilful but a bit slow and certainly not better than Walker. Harburn has scored ten goals like Tony Butcher but seems moody and at odds with everyone. Alec Moyse is the one bright spark and I expect great things from him in the second half of the season.

At present we have 22 professionals and this seems far too many.

We have a contingent travelling each match day from the South Coast and Blake has now joined Phillips, Barnard and Dale.

One Saturday Phillips and Blake were due to play at Lowestoft for the Reserves but were held up at Godalming in Surrey by a landslide and got no further. What motivates them to travel all that way to play in the Eastern Counties League? And to think a few years back Len Phillips was playing at Wembley for England.

Rob Ketley, a true Villan, is beside himself when it's reported that ex Villa man Stan Crowther might be coming to City. Crowther has played for England under 23s and I have him in my sweet-cigarette card collection. He played for Villa when they beat Manchester United in the 1957 Cup Final and then he was signed by United immediately after Munich in 1958 and lost in that final to Bolton. So how the mighty are fallen and he's apparently only 26. He also had three seasons at Chelsea but is now at Brighton and there is a rumour that he was only good enough for their third team and refused to play, which is why he is leaving.

Anyway Rob is disappointed when Crowther doesn't sign and the player is quoted as saying he is disillusioned with football, so drops out of the Leagues and goes to Hednesford Town of all places; a strange decision at such a young age too.

Suddenly in the New Year the club announces it will go full time next season and this will surely mean we cut down the number of professionals and make up the Reserves with amateurs. With the gates dropping to around the 3,000 mark after Christmas we are even further away from what Mr Coward wants and it begs the questions of how we can afford to go full time – the factory gossip is that it is to be financed by Mr Coward but surely we must need gates of at least 5,000 to supplement this.

A lottery competition is being started by the Supporters' Club and this will mean even more money from this quarter. If their fund raising ever stopped for any reason we would be in 'queer street'.

Still, whilst the finances might be tight, I see from Clive Haworth's Weekly News cuttings that their reporter has spoken with Mr Coward and he confirms the Wolseley Road end will be covered shortly with The Barn extended the whole length of the pitch. However, no mention is made of the development of the land around the ground.

I don't miss a game through the winter but the team remains so inconsistent. The gates are continuing to fall but from the end of January to the beginning of March we go on an unbeaten run of six games at the end of which we are just two points behind Oxford at the top and one point behind Guildford and Bath but Oxford have two games in hand on all of us.

Suddenly on March 11th Accrington Stanley fold and resign from the League with huge debts of over £40,000, thus creating a vacancy. The Daily Mail says that it is almost certain the Southern League will provide the new team. The northern clubs are in diverse leagues with most grounds not meeting League requirements and certainly not the crowds to sustain that level of football.

Mr Chaplin in the Chronicle holds the view that Oxford look certainties to take Accrington's place, especially as they secured so many votes at the last League AGM and are currently top of our league. The national dailies have reports that several other League clubs near the foot of the Fourth Division may well follow Accrington as the League is likely to clamp down on the reckless running of some of these clubs. I wonder to myself just how healthy the finances at City are when suddenly out of the blue we sell Harry Taylor to rivals Cambridge United for what is reported to be a *'four figure fee'*. Taylor came down from Newcastle and was one of my favourites – always giving his all – a tough, hard tackler and excellent goalscorer particularly in his first season last year. This season he's been in and out of the team and his goalscoring touch has deserted him a little, but his transfer does suggest we might need the money and so cash in before he loses value.

Inevitably, when he returns to play against us at the end of March he scores BOTH goals in a 2-1 win for United.

Also in March Mr Freddie Langton Senior sadly dies. He was one of the original founders of the new club in 1938 and is much praised in the local papers for all he has done for City. His death coincides with

Mr Len Menhinick being appointed by Mr Coward to act as the club secretary to relieve Mr Ferrier of this responsibility and so leaving him to concentrate on team matters: this splitting of the roles seems a good idea to me. Apparently Mr Menhinick turned down Mr Coward's initial approach but an improved offer won him over. As Secretary of the Old Chelmsfordians' Association and with a heavy involvement in local football administration, he seems an ideal choice for this role.

My father hears on the factory grapevine that Mr Menhinick has found the behind-the-scenes set up very amateurish but that Mr Coward knew it and so, with the club going full time, he wants a much more professional approach throughout. The Chronicle subsequently reports that Mr Menhinick is to be given a free rein to re-organise the administration of the whole club and so ensuring we create a professional image to ultimately improve our credentials for getting into the Football League.

On the pitch the season peters out with us losing six, drawing three and winning only three of our last twelve games. Clive Haworth's scrapbook comes to an abrupt stop six league games and a couple of friendlies from the end of the season. He says he feels disillusioned and won't support the team anymore. A little drastic, but this was perhaps reflected in the town with only 2,031 attending the last home game against Yeovil to mark the end of yet another very disappointing season.

Oxford duly take Accrington's place. They do deserve it with their league performances, but are helped by some publicity given to them on an ITV sports programme, which outrages Messrs Coward, Ferrier and Menhinick who believe this gave Oxford an unfair advantage. However, when the League AGM takes place we receive a measly four votes.

It seems to me that we have a very long way to go to fulfil the dream and perhaps our best hope is the introduction of new divisions or feeder leagues but we'd still have to win them and we seem some way off of having a team capable of achieving it.

***

Ahead of Mr Ferrier announcing his retained list for next season there is much talk in the Weekly News about the effect full time will have on some of the players, like Peter Gillott, who specifically came to us so he could be part time and have another job. The Weekly News speculates that *'the majority of the present staff will NOT be offered terms'*; however, some who do not wish to be full time may be kept on as the full time numbers may be as low as twelve, with room perhaps for six part timers.

In the event Doherty, Abbiss, Blake, Dale and Harburn are being released having been with us for just one season. Does this make sense? Does it not show that Mr Ferrier's signings were actually no good? Most of the fans think so.

Derek Tiffin is affected by this full time/part time furore but we all hope he stays. He completed his 400th Southern League game in April after 13 seasons with us. My father takes me to the Social Club for the presentation being made to Tiffin by the Supporters' Club, but there are many fans upset that the presentation was not done on the pitch in front of a few thousand fans instead of a small number squeezed into the Social Club.

On Monday April 9th we host another friendly this time against Port Vale, our conquerors in the FA Cup last season when we were robbed of a replay. Out for revenge we fail miserably and are hammered 5-0 and, but for Collier's heroics, it could have been more. So much for us showing the outside football world how good we are against League teams – it worked last season but not this. Still, as the game ended the tannoy announcer came on to say that my other team, Burnley, the other Clarets, were at Wembley for the FA Cup Final against Spurs having just beaten Fulham 2-1 in a replay that very evening. At least one Claret team has had a good season and Burnley remain on course for the 'Double' of League and FA Cup.

Sifting through my cuttings covering the season, I have to say they tell of another disappointing story of expectation dashed by reality.

But then as far as City is concerned … there's always next season … and I can't wait.

5

ARE WE DREAMING OR IS THIS REAL?

Martin Rogers first reported on Chelmsford City in 1962, and from 1964-80 was on the staff of the Essex Chronicle Series. For several years one of the country's leading speedway promoters, he has written and/or edited 19 sporting books. He and his wife Lin now live on the Gold Coast in Australia. The 1962/63 season was the most defining one to date in the history of the club and Martin was in a unique position to observe such a pivotal time for the club – this is his story of that season.

This is World Cup year, so June is all about football fever, right? Well, a few weeks into the close season maybe not quite as much as you might think.

This is June, 1962; the World Cup is being played out in Chile, 7,250 miles and several light years away from Chelmsford. They're four hours behind us so timing isn't great, radio commentaries are crackly, television coverage pretty much non-existent and national newspaper deadlines completely shot.

England travel to South America without great expectation and, as in the three other post-war tournaments, that's just as well. They don't progress beyond the quarter-finals of the 16-team tournament in which Brazil beat Czechoslovakia 3-1 in the final, Chile and Yugoslavia are the beaten semi-finalists.

Of the 31 matches, a dozen pull crowds of less than 10,000, only those played in Santiago attracting serious numbers.

West Ham's Bobby Moore, 21, and Jimmy Greaves, 22, of FA Cup winners Tottenham, are the youngest members of Walter Winterbottom's England squad in which Bobby Robson, one of three West Brom players included, is the oldest at 29.

Of the 22 top-tier clubs 14 have a representative but there's nobody from unfashionable Ipswich, still celebrating winning the First Division championship at the first attempt, five years after Alf Ramsey guided them to the Third Division (South) title.

Our lads lose 2-1 to Hungary, beat Argentina 3-1 and draw 0-0 against Bulgaria, edging into the quarters by virtue of a better goal average than the Argentines.

But despite being without Pele – injured in their second match – the boys from Brazil are just too good for our lads, winning 3-1 and refining their swagger on the way to a second successive World Cup.

Much closer to home the England cricketers are swaggering, too, showing far too much experience and quality for the Pakistan touring team. Essex are coming off a much improved June after failing to win a match in the first month of the summer and at second eleven level, pundits are talking about the promise of Geoff Hurst and Robin Hobbs and excited by the emergence of a 17-year-old Keith Fletcher.

British hopes of a drought-breaking Wimbledon are raised and then dashed, as Roger Taylor and Alan Mills fail to progress past the fourth round of the men's singles, while Ann Jones goes out in the women's semis to eventual champion Karen Susman of the US.

Petrol prices are steady at 4s 10d a gallon, a pint of beer 2s. 4d. Ray Charles is at the top of the *Billboard* hit parade for a fifth successive week, with *I Can't Stop Loving You*, a throaty, haunting refrain which could have been specially penned for recently spurned teenage paramours and City tragics alike.

Notwithstanding my job as a reporter, I can't conceal the fact I come into that category, having absorbed the claret and white into my veins as a schoolboy convert all of four and a bit years ago, my enthusiasm – like that of many others – fuelled by the exciting developments of the past two or three seasons.

Football is very much on my mind, more so than ever since joining

86

Echo Publications in March. They publish Soccer Star, the game's only weekly magazine, the monthly *World Soccer*, regarded as something of a bible by the increasing number of students of the international scene, and *Speedway Star*.

Since leaving King Edward VI Grammar School, I have had two years with Reg Hayter's Sports Reporting Agency in Fleet Street, covering (among many other things) London and South-East football; reporting on matches at all the League clubs and more besides for national, evening and regional papers.

During this period I would be much more likely to be found working at Stamford Bridge or Loftus Road, than spending time at New Writtle Street watching my club of choice. My schedule usually involved attending four or five matches a week, as diverse as a First Division derby between Arsenal and Spurs, an FA Youth Cup tie, or a Football Combination game.

It was a steep learning curve, especially on a typical Saturday afternoon at the likes of Charlton or Millwall. Depending upon the opposition, I could be doing two or three running reports – all different – for *The Star*, *News* or *Standard*, and a regional evening paper (say 50 words before kick-off, a further 50 at 3.15, 3.30, half-time, 4.10 and 4.25 with an intro and a couple of paragraphs on the final whistle).

Then a couple of the Sundays would want anything from 200-400 words wrapping up the game, to be phoned through to copy takers by 5.45 to catch early editions, and, as often as not, two or three follow-up stories to be filed on Sunday for the Monday papers.

I also sought out news items, gossip pieces and wrote previews during the week, in between attending night games, so one way and another I quickly built up my contacts and working knowledge of the players and managers across the board. Observing and learning how seasoned writers such as Albert Sewell and Dennis Signy kept themselves on top of everything was a huge education.

This body of work obviously appeals to my new employers, with the quite different requirements of magazine schedules allowing much more predictable and regular hours – and the opportunity to see rather more of the City (and my own little club, St. Margaret's) than had been the case.

If anything, my awareness of who's who and which players are doing what is heightened by moving to *Soccer Star*, who each week faithfully chronicle the line-ups and details of every match in England and Scotland and maintain contact with all the clubs. And the first few weeks of the 1962 close season are taken up with research for the *World Soccer Digest* which is a bigger, glossier rival to the long-running *News of the World* pocket annual.

***

With all this experience I'm as well positioned as anybody to evaluate summer signings, when they are made public. Chelmsford, still nursing deep disappointment after seeing erstwhile rivals Oxford United voted into the Fourth Division, are determined to ramp up their own claims. The decision to go full-time has been announced, Harry Ferrier cleared to concentrate on his managerial duties following the appointment of Len Menhinick as club secretary, but the jury is still out as to how they'll go in the upcoming season.

Save for two or three notable exceptions, close season recruits in recent times have been accompanied by no great reputation although the 1961 crop began promisingly enough, before fading away to finish fifth in the Southern League for the second year running. Clearly things are going to have to improve if League status is to be anything more than a flight of fancy.

Then on June 30, it's out with the melancholy and in with the optimistic trumpeting which presages the build-up to the start of another campaign. This is the day on which Football League contracts are up after which the managers who have done their homework can officially get their new signings to put pen to paper.

In Chelmsford, the fanfare is ramped up to almost unprecedented proportions when Harry and Chairman John Coward, like magicians triumphantly plucking rabbits from a hat, announce the end result of a stunningly audacious swoop on the market.

A year has passed since Jimmy Hill's PFA crusade triggered the historic abolition of the maximum wage and Fulham chairman Tommy Trinder noisily anointed Johnny Haynes as the first £100-a-week footballer. But for most, the promised rewards are still slow to arrive. League clubs can still place players on their retained list or the open-to-transfer list and effectively freeze their movement.

Non-league clubs, however, operate under no such strictures. We all know that, legally, they can sign listed players without having to pay a fee and it's something City have done with some success in recent times, grabbing Dennis Hatsell from Preston, then Harry Taylor from Newcastle to name but two. Yet nobody is prepared for how well they have done their homework this time.

Eight new signings include Bobby Mason, transfer-listed by Wolves at £22,000, former Chelsea starlet Tony Nicholas, who Brighton rate at £15,000, and Roy Isherwood, a diminutive winger from Blackburn who has shadowed England's Brian Douglas for half a dozen seasons at Blackburn.

All three made heads turn in the First Division while still teenagers. Mason, who was starring in the European Champions Cup as recently as 1960, racked up 54 goals in 173 senior appearances, Nicholas 40 in 124 and Roy of the Rovers Isherwood chalked up 49 outings in the top flight.

Also coming in are Peter Corthine, scorer of 24 goals in 73 matches with Southend, and Ron Smillie, 228 games in two stints with Barnsley and one at Lincoln – and the beauty of it is these aren't grey, grizzled old-timers nearing their use-by date and going out to pasture. Mason is 26, Nicholas 24, Corthine 25, Isherwood and Smillie at 28 -anything but veterans.

These are the glittering prizes, exciting attacking players, and the grapevine suggests a trio of more familiar free transfer signings in defenders Tommy Pettigrew (Stirling Albion), Mike Collins (Luton) and Tony Lowe (Aston Villa) can play a bit, too.

However, the talk of the town is all about the names enticed away from clubs many of whom are still unhappy about the end of a £20 maximum and loath to increase player wages, creating a football of unprecedented possibility for the likes of Chelmsford. Rumour suggests Mason will be paid £45 a week, while several of the others will be on wages well in excess of anything they earned in the Football League.

It's typical John Coward. The fiercely ambitious, larger than life local businessman has no qualms about paying the big bucks to the major beneficiaries of his manager's scouting raids. He dreams of a Chelmsford City side which can win the Southern League and sooner rather than later be in amongst the Oxfords, the Peterboroughs and Colchesters of this world – and that's just for starters.

As the beginning of every campaign nears, the frisson of excitement builds into something palpable. All round the country, of course, it's much the same. At the big clubs and the little ones … new faces, new ambition, the hope that this will be THE year.

City faithful, like supporters in many another centre, have seen it all before, and yet, this time, the reasons to be optimistic seem entirely valid. Everybody is talking about the new players, confident they will provide fresh impetus to drive the club forward. It is years since there was quite such a buzz of anticipation.

***

Six games and 16 days into the season proper, however, the much-vaunted strike force has failed to hit the target in four matches, three of them on the road. Bobby Mason impresses with his guile, a sure first touch, dexterity of foot and mind but the supporting players are yet to tune in on the same wavelength. City have drawn four and lost two, and it's not quite the explosion from the blocks we had been primed to expect.

That's not to say the opening matches have been short of incident or interest. Despite a 2-0 first-day defeat at Bedford, a healthy 7,029 turn up at The Stadium on the Monday night to see Chelmsford and Romford do battle. It finishes 1-1 and contains much of the best elements of the rivalry between the clubs.

Fans, opposing managers and chairmen all have their particular reasons for wanting to see their teams do well. There is the considerable matter of A12 bragging rights to be considered. Harry Ferrier and Romford boss cavalier Jack Chisholm are both from-the-hip straight shooters, unafraid to voice an opinion. John Coward and opposite number Jim Parrish are strident, gregarious advocates of the merits of their respective clubs and all they stand for.

At this stage though, City are matched by their near neighbours, and it's more of the same a week later when the teams slug out a 3-3 draw in the Southern League Cup, watched this time by 6,801. Back at Brooklands nine days later and the teams know all there is to know about each other, playing out a no-score draw in front of 6,139 fans.

Suddenly, an impressive 2-1 win at Hereford with Nicholas and Mason on target sparks what will be the most fruitful spell of the season – six league victories out of seven, a 2-1 score line at Romford among them, and, believe it or not, two more important clashes with the same opponents.

The 1962 'Dream Team'
Back Row Left to Right: Alec Moyse; Peter Gillott; Derek Tiffin; Alan Collier; Len Phillips; Mike Collins.
Front Row Left to Right: Tony Butcher; Denis Hatsell; Tony Nicholas; Bobby Mason; Ron Smillie

Now things are looking up and belief begins to surge as the newcomers start to gel with an old guard in which ever-present Peter Gillott is a rock. You always need the fellows at the coal face doing an often unsung job although as usual it's the star names who tend to catch the eye.

Nicholas is fast becoming a favourite with the fans – blond and highly visible; he's busy and enthusiastic, he's everywhere and establishing himself as the man most likely to pop the ball in the net. It's easy to imagine why Chelsea were so excited when he was promising to do just that as a kid alongside Greaves, and why later Brighton paid their club record fee to sign him. We can all stand more of this.

Don't imagine anybody tiring of the Romford saga, either. A 3-0 Essex Professional Cup victory at The Stadium (attended by 5,359) is a rehearsal for an even more significant New Writtle Street meeting in the fourth qualifying round of the FA Cup.

Although Arthur Turner's benchmark Oxford United had successive Southern League titles to their name, the biggest point of difference between the clubs at June's League AGM was all about making a flourish in the FA Cup. More than ever, then, the pressure is on to deliver a Cup run and results to catch the attention of the wider football world.

All's well that starts well this time, City racking up a 2-0 victory thanks to goals by Dennis Hatsell and Tony Butcher, who have hardly featured in the side up this point. A 7,034 turnout means six matches against Romford spread over the first two months of the season have attracted 36,862 customers – 26,223 in four games at Chelmsford.

That volume of support shouts to the world that New Writtle Street surely can sustain League football and what better way to demonstrate the rightness of those claims for recognition than to use the FA Cup as a platform.

And so to the day supporters of hundreds of little clubs fantasise about, the first round proper. Three times in the past four seasons, Chelmsford have blown their chance to win first-round ties at home whereas only last season, Oxford made it to the third round and enjoyed all the attendant rewards and publicity. Perfect timing, you might say, and the perfect example to try to emulate.

Bearing in mind their exploits, and those of other giant-killers before them, a decent show in the Cup is just what City need to put its name to the fore. Shrewsbury Town at home sounds like a good opportunity, they're Third Division, not what you normally would call giants but a scalp like theirs would do nicely.

The league tables suggest they don't travel especially well, that's what all City fans tell themselves, although their player-manager Arthur Rowley, notwithstanding a thickening waistline, is renowned for knocking in goals like there's no tomorrow.

And wouldn't you know it, there is no tomorrow.

An exuberant 8,752 crowd at The Stadium arrives with high hopes for something special, but whatever surprises City were hoping to spring remain disappointingly under wraps as Shrewsbury prevail 6-2.

It's a tough day at the office and especially so for stalwart centre-half Derek Tiffin, part of the furniture for years but exposed on this day as now half a yard short of his awe-inspiring best. Four months will elapse before his return to first-team duties.

***

I've been a regular observer of all of this, recording a few of the club's happenings in my still-fresh *Soccer Star* gig and in free-lance contributions to national newspapers. Out of the blue, my involvement becomes much more full-on.

Bernard Webber, sports editor of the *Essex Chronicle* (Fridays) and *Newsman-Herald* (Tuesdays), telephones to tell me J.C. Chaplin, for years the regular reporter on all things Chelmsford City, has been diagnosed with a terminal illness.

I don't know John Chaplin, but like thousands of followers of his commentary and coverage not just of Chelmsford but the non-league stage at large, it feels as if I do. Certainly I've read and devoured just about every word the man has penned in the local columns for the past few years, since I became aware of the club and its place in the scheme of things.

Bernard, who also edits the sports section of the *Colchester Express* with all the enthusiasm you would expect from someone who has supported the Us since he was in short trousers, wants to know if my commitments allow me to cover City matches and the Southern League scene for the newspapers which regularly feature at or near the top of my required reading list.

It takes me all of five seconds to bite his hand off. Before even raising the matter with my London bosses, I'm sure they won't mind (they don't) and it's a huge boost to my ego, not to mention a new source of free-lance income which won't go amiss given the cost of commuting from High Roding and a season ticket to and from Liverpool Street.

Not that reporting on sport is about money. It's always been and hopefully always will be about being close to the centre of the action, on an inside track with players and officials and enjoying the perks that come with actually being paid to attend games. And with every indication John Chaplin won't be back, this is a great opportunity for me.

I detect the hand of Len Menhinick here. I've known him since I was about eight years old; he has given me encouragement and sage advice at various stages and taken a keen interest in my career. It's obvious he has given me a glowing reference and now Bernard has just handed me the keys to the door behind which a whole new adventure is waiting.

I'm into my new role with relish and for a few weeks after Shrewsbury, the City's results and performances hint at a renewed ability to grind out results to keep them there or thereabouts in the title stakes.

It's a settling-in period for the new scribe, made easy by the access to the hierarchy. Harry Ferrier rarely holds back if there's a pithy summary, or more likely a detailed analysis to be made, John Coward is a non-stop human headline with his grandiose plans for the future, the players seem a pretty amenable bunch. As often as not I'll make my own way to away games, but the offer of a ride on the team coach is open and, from time to time, gratefully accepted.

The atmosphere is light, punctuated by the sort of banter which is much the same in sporting teams all over. Peter Gillott's laugh is a recurring feature on the sound track. Tony Nicholas is always noisy, Bobby Mason quiet and remarkably unassuming, Ron Smillie invariably earnest, and the manager's cigar-perfumed anecdotes and character references never fail to capture the attention of an appreciative audience.

On New Writtle Street match days, Howard Southall of the *Essex Weekly News* clearly is the eminence Gris of the press box. I had some of my first pieces – a series on Essex cricketers – published in his paper while I was still at school and when the time came to leave, it was his suggestion that I try my luck in London. We're rivals now but he's welcoming and entertaining.

The 'box' is a glass-fronted sanctuary at the back of the main stand, bang on the half-way line. It can house half a dozen, maybe seven at a push – and with a visitor or two, is usually a platform for lively and companionable debate. The sweet briar from Howard's pipe, though, possibly constitutes a health hazard in the longer term.

***

Any of us hoping Christmas and the New Year might signal a further upswing in City's fortunes obviously reckon without the intervention of the weather and one of the coldest winters on record.   From the end of December until late February, vast swathes of the country are ice and snow-bound, the fixture list takes a hammering and week after week the pools panel is called upon to pronounce on what results might have been.

Chelmsford are no different from anybody else. They go without a game from December 29, a cheerless 1-0 defeat at Wisbech, to the Monday night of February 27 without seeing any on-field action. I'm flat out churning out thousands of words through the best part of two months in which virtually nothing is happening. Not quite in the same class as cricket's *Test Match Special* experts on the radio, skillfully finding topics of worthwhile debate in rain breaks, but a lot of it is pretty good value, if I say so myself.

City's return after that little hiatus is memorable, almost entirely for the wrong reasons.

Depending upon your point of view, their performance in a Southern League Cup tie at home to Cambridge City is among the worst ever served up at New Writtle Street – or, I'd prefer to call it the most scintillating display by a visiting side anybody could witness.

The visitors skate lightly across the frosty surface with a sureness of touch and liberal dashes of improvised brilliance all of which adds up to a thumping 6-0 score line. Former Nottingham Forest FA Cup Final winner Tommy Wilson orchestrates the rout along with spike-haired ex-Blackpool half-back Sammy Salt; electric winger Mike Benning and quicksilver inside forwards Alan Banks and Albert Derrick are all but uncatchable.

It's a night to become seared in the memory bank – Cambridge are on the way to the Premier Division title as well, a tiny consolation footnote perhaps, and in the end all the shell-shocked Stadium faithful can do is applaud them from the ground.

This is a watershed for everyone at the club, an emphatic realisation that whatever heights City are straining to reach, that probably isn't going to happen with the current set-up.

A few days later Bobby Mason is on his way, transferred to Leyton Orient to aid their ultimately unsuccessful bid to preserve their First Division status. Orient manager Johnny Carey knows Bobby of old, has an up-to-the-minute reprise of his talents in an Essex Pro Cup semi-final which Orient win 6-3 after extra time, and makes a £4,500 bid which is promptly accepted.

Come the weekend Mason is making his return to the top flight in slating rain at Brisbane Road against an Aston Villa side who prove too smart, winning 2-0 thanks to goals by Phil Woosnam, their recent capture from nearby West Ham, and Ron Wylie.

City, meanwhile, prepare to welcome Bobby Grant, a one-time Glasgow Rangers reserve included as part exchange in the deal. Whereas Mason is deft and delicate, Grant is a blunt instrument, but a welcome acquisition for all that. He's a beefy, bustling attacker who enjoys making defenders aware of his presence and a talkative addition to the dressing room. In 15 appearances he collects seven goals, City simply don't lose when he gets on the score sheet, and he features in 4-0 wins over Cambridge United and Bexleyheath which statistically are the team's best in the 40-match League programme.

The Easter double over Cambridge United (City win the home match on Easter Monday 2-1) is a killer blow to Alan Moore's boys who finish on 53 points, three adrift of local rivals Cambridge City … and Chelmsford, everybody's pre-season tip for the top, manage just eighth place on 46.

***

Harry Ferrier pays the price for that, departing with uncharacteristic stealth before the season is out. His expensively assembled, much lauded 'Bank of England' squad has given glimpses but failed to deliver the ruthless consistency required to elevate them above the pack.

In the space of 10 months, the hopes and expectations of the Chelmsford City faithful have been to the moon and back, Marilyn Monroe died, President John F Kennedy stared down the Soviets over the Cuban missile crisis, there's an emerging phenomenon in the pop charts with the Beatles leading a new wave of British artists, in cinemas where Sean Connery as James Bond is making hearts flutter, and the Boston Strangler has claimed an eighth victim.

We won't forget this season, the giddy dreams it provoked, suggestive hints of a golden future flickering across our consciousness only for the clammy reality of ultimate disappointment to become the unavoidable memory etched in the record books.

It remains to be seen whether the newly-appointed Billy Frith, the one-time Coventry manager lured from his enforced sabbatical to take over from Harry Ferrier, can turn the tide, recapture the hearts and minds and deliver the conviction the class of 1962-63 has not managed to provide.

Experience has taught us to be sceptical, but there's not much fun in that. No doubt cockeyed optimism will be back in vogue before long.

6

THE DREAM BECOMES A NIGHTMARE

Len Menhinick has long been associated with football in the town. Firstly as a player for and then secretary of the Old Chelmsfordians, latterly becoming a referee and administrator for local leagues. Appointed by John Coward he transformed the administration of the Club to be a truly professionally set-up to rival any in the country. He still lives in Chelmsford and now recounts his view of the remarkable season of 1963/64 that ends in disaster.

I like Billy Frith; a thoughtful, measured and decent man. Not a Justice of the Peace by accident and diligent in all he does on and off the football field.

I have watched some of his training sessions during this summer of '63. They are well constructed and organised with Billy getting more out of the players than I've seen of late and the boys look sharper. He can take a joke too.

I knew the team were up to something when I saw them skulking around the dressing rooms and giggling. Billy had to leave training early to get to a meeting and left the boys on the pitch at New Writtle Street so he could shower and change into his suit, collar and tie.

I could not understand why the boys stopped exercising and waited – looking down the tunnel. They stood in one group, laughing. Still they waited; Billy emerges wearing his overcoat and a pair of shoes – his bare, hairy legs showing out of the bottom of the coat.

'*You b******s, I'll have you for this!*' He shouted as he opened his overcoat to reveal the stark truth of his credentials and went off laughing too, as the boys were literally rolling around on the pitch.

He had to go home to pick up new clothes hoping the Police didn't stop him on the way. If that had been done to Harry all hell would have been let loose.

***

Billy's mileage records tell me he's clocked over 2,000 miles on his scouting missions, but after last year's sensational signings those this summer appear decidedly low-key.

We know Owen Medlock, who had been at Chelsea and then Swindon as a youth, to be a good 'keeper at his most recent club, old foe Oxford United. I'm surprised he's been released but he did miss most of last season with a broken arm and Billy sees him as useful back up to Alan Collier.

Swarthy Bobby Smith, defender or half back, joins from Barnsley having had only a few League games – perhaps Peter Gillott, now having more of an influence at the City as club captain, knows him from old.

Right back Roy Jacobs comes from Peterborough and half back Trevor Harris from Colchester. Of these signings Harris is the oldest at 27. Billy tells me he is determined to develop a team – a team of young men prepared to give their all for City. He is set on bringing in players to win matches and not simply so-called stars to please the fans. He knows that success on the pitch is the first step towards the Football League and only then should we implement Chairman John Coward's vision. I'm not sure this is how John or the fans see it panning out but they only have to look at last season to see the glory, glory route of expensive 'stars' waltzing us into the big time is just a pure flight of fantasy.

For my part I'm continuing with the restructuring of the back office with Len King alongside – there was much to be done when I arrived and we continue to strive to improve.

Like most managers, Billy starts to bring in players he knows from old such as John Richmond, a wing half from Derby, and Colin Holder, an inside forward from Coventry. Billy managed Holder at Coventry and describes him as a mercurial talent, but apparently not strong on discipline, but Billy's confident he can turn him into a great player, so we shall have to wait and see, but let's hope so. Wesley Maughan, a utility forward, comes from Reading and is an interesting character. A devout Salvation Army man he is nevertheless a 'man about town' and I hear already has a string of female admirers around the town!

From one of his weekly meets with Martin Rogers of the Chronicle, Billy comments: '... *that most of the players are in their early 20s and have enough incentive to give of their best. We are not exactly over staffed and negotiations are ongoing for a centre forward but there is still room for additions.*'

Billy also sees the need for local youngsters to step forward and 28 are invited for trials.

One matter I have given priority to this summer is to pay the outstanding fees for Alan Collier, Tony Nicholas and Ron Smillie. The Board is determined to ensure that all players on our books are a 'City player' and not second party owned. With the Football League looking to ban clubs from applying for election whilst money is still owed, we want to be seen as whiter than white. But what concerns me is that we never did pay any fee for the likes of Bobby Mason and other players, who are no longer on our books and in Mason's case secured a transfer fee when he was sold on – what can Wolves have thought about that when they received nothing! We were entirely working within the Rules, but will that course of action come back to haunt us?

There are some concerns in the club that our overdraft is excessive for a club outside the Football League at over £9,000 and it is not something we would want to escalate. One player off the payroll and reducing some of our wage bill is Roy Isherwood, one of the 'dream forward line', who has returned north. We did make a trading profit last season of a little over £2,000 but were it not for the Supporters' Club raising £18,000 we would have struggled.

***

On an upbeat note Martin Rogers has watched these new young players blending in well with what remains of last year's squad and believes these players will be 100% grafters. He does worry about the reaction of the fans with no 'known signings' of any significance and a cutting back on the friendlies that have seen so many great players grace the New Writtle Street pitch. Might this create apathy in the supporters? Billy and the boys will certainly have to win them over.

It will not be from the want of trying. Billy's mantra is for superior fitness and hard work. Peter Harburn takes the fitness training and Bill Watson the strengthening – two men not to be taken lightly, by the way. Billy has a word with each player regularly about their technique and their attitude. I'm thrilled to see him working so well with Tony Butcher who has a spring in his step after hearing what Billy has in mind for him this season. Tony's already feeling his game has improved a notch or two in such a short space of time with the help of Billy's coaching. That says something when you think Tony has been with us for nearly ten years, but Tony needs this – to feel wanted with an arm round him. He will always get goals; it's in his nature but he has to fight against the unfortunate, and most often unjust, criticism he seems to attract from our fans.

27-year-old Peter Gillott, the new club captain, enhances the harmonious atmosphere. Ebullient, enthusiastic with abounding Yorkshire grit and determination (what an excellent choice by Billy); Peter is liked by the players too – a true leader. The ex Barnsley triumvirate of Gillott, Smillie and Smith have certainly made the dressing room and the training ground this pre-season an exciting (and amusing) place to be.

All at the Club are pleased the Reserves have moved to the Metropolitan League and away from the Eastern Counties. If we want to develop our youth and provide a higher standard for those senior players not currently in the First Team, the Metropolitan is the answer; playing the likes of the 'A' teams of Tottenham, Charlton, West Ham and Arsenal will provide quality opposition with better grounds and, most importantly, swell the home attendances to a level in excess of 1,500 – adding more to our coffers.

Billy is keen to monitor the health and well-being of the First Teamers and I arrange for all the players to have a medical. The Doctor reports back that he has never seen such a group of fit young men. (What would he have made of some players in the past – some crocked and on their way down the football ladder?). Perhaps this level of fitness will stop the fans moaning that the players are never properly trained and fit!

We have much to look forward to this season. I'm convinced Butch will remain our main goal threat and sparkle under Billy, having been pushed out by the star signings last season and on the transfer list. I expect only good things from him this year and I have a funny feeling that he might just hit it off with Bobby Grant as our attack spearhead. Uncompromising Scot Bobby (ex-Rangers and St Johnstone) made an impact last season. He is Arthur Adey like, yet less forthright, more skilful, and more studious in approach – a crowd favourite because of his attitude, but with more discipline than Arthur off the pitch. Grant has a lighter side and does an impressive take off of Harold Steptoe, so earning him the nickname 'Harold'.

19-year-old Colin Holder might be one of our more skilful players but he is not the most sylph-like young man and has been dubbed 'Chubby Checker' by his teammates. I do hope he doesn't become a wasted talent and would do well to take Derek Tiffin as a role model. Derek starts his 13th season with the Club, in this our 25th anniversary year. Whilst young Eades will probably take over his place in the First Team, Derek will remain an influential player especially with the youngsters in the Reserves.

With most of the 'stars' having left, I see crowd favourite, Tony Nicholas, as the team's talisman.

In the Reserves stalwarts like Mick Butcher and John Thurgood will persevere and answer the First Team call if required, but what of Robin Gladwin? I saw him play at left back in one match for the Reserves and he looked most comfortable there – whereas at inside forward or wing half he is rather ordinary. Although it is not my place to tell Billy his job I do mention it to him and he seemed to take it on board.

***

In the wider world what a summer 1963 has been with the newspapers full of the Profumo affair and the revelations of upper class decadence through the trial of Stephen Ward, but all this ends when Ward commits suicide. There is talk of Mr Macmillan resigning as Prime Minister, after Profumo, Minister of War, lied to the House of Commons.

Then on August 8th we have the largest robbery ever with millions of pounds stolen from an overnight mail train from Glasgow to London. The Police have started this huge hunt for the robbers who actually stopped the train before making off with the sacks of money.

Back at City there is much chatter about these goings-on, but the players are single-mindedly looking forward to the new season. Billy Frith looks like he has found a pearl in Bobby Smith – absolutely outstanding in a 1-1 draw with Millwall, incidentally a club I've supported since a boy, in a friendly with over 3,000 there to watch.

The opening league match against Guildford sees Roy Jacobs get the nod for right back and the rest of the team is as expected – Collier Jacobs Gillott; Harris Eades Smith; Smillie Grant Maughan Tony Butcher and Nicholas.

In his column this week Martin Rogers makes a very valid point that other clubs love to hate City and up their game when they play us. Perhaps they are jealous of our big name signings supported by the money from the Chairman and this plus the large home crowds also inspire visiting teams. I very much agree with Martin that we need to dominate teams more, especially away from home; silence their crowds and become a team to be feared on the pitch to bring the success we crave.

'Actions will speak louder than words' says Martin who asks if this could be, 'our season with a positive challenge for the title under Mr Frith'. Let's hope so.

***

The task of bringing the off field side of the club up to scratch is proving greater than I could ever have imagined, but I feel we are making progress which is more than I can say about what is happening on the field. Looking back at the end of the December and following the awful 4-2 reverse at Hastings on Boxing Day it has largely been a season thus far of huge disappointment.

We did have a good start and by the end of October had won eight league games, drawn one and lost three. One loss was to arch enemy Romford who are running away with the League. We did beat them in the FA Cup at The Stadium in front of 8,500 and then beat Cambridge United away in the next round before disappointingly losing at home to Bedford 1- 0 in December with a huge crowd of over 9,000. Bedford have a plum draw away at Newcastle to be played on January 4th. If only we could have won that match and had the same draw against a Division One club in the Third Round of the Cup. Making an impression on the football world in the Cup remains as distant as it has ever been.

The team from the 1963/64 season
Back Row: Left to Right: Roy Jacobs; Tommy Pettigrew; Bobby Smith;
Owen Medlock; Tony Lowe; Peter Gillott
Front Row: Left to Right: Ron Smillie; Bobby Grant; Tony Butcher;
Wes Maughan; Tony Nicholas

The City public is not satisfied with our performances and has written in numbers to the Chronicle complaining, in particular, of the harassment of the referees and the petulance on the pitch, not something City could be accused of over the years. There has actually been booing of our own players as a result.

Bernard Webber wrote an interesting piece in the Chronicle: *'The Southern League is rough, tough soccer demanding the strictest self-discipline for the players and stronger referees who are moving up their ladder to the Football League.'*

He is right about that and as a referee myself I find the attitude of some of our players unacceptable. There has always been toughness in football but as the 60s progress we are seeing different attitudes in players – they are more aggressive towards both opponents and referees, with an air of self-importance that was not there in the 40s and 50s. Perhaps this is as a result of the money earned by players these days and their new found status, even those at our level.

***

The Reserves start well with a good win over Tottenham 'A'. Against West Ham they lose 3 -1 with Holder and Pettigrew sent off in a violent match, as if to prove my feelings about the way the game is changing. I cannot recall City having many players sent off over the years and certainly not two in one match. I am told Tommy Pettigrew, an uncompromising player, was hard-done-by, but Holder showed his immaturity and ill-discipline – something that doesn't surprise me.

One interesting piece of gossip went round the Club that former Scottish International Stewart Imlach might be signing – he was previously at Nottingham Forest and played in the 1959 FA Cup Final. He was later under Billy at Coventry and Billy confirms to me that there is some truth in the rumour, but he cannot agree terms – however, he remains hopeful Imlach might sign in the future. Such a signing would certainly galvanise the fans and perhaps kick start the season.

Suddenly Billy bursts into my office in December to announce he has secured the services of Tommy Wilson, a Forest colleague of Imlach in the 1959 FA Cup Final where he scored the winning goal. This only goes to show it is not difficult to attract players to City with what we pay here. We remain an attractive proposition for a player dropping down the divisions with wages as high as anywhere outside the top two divisions: we can add to this our excellent facilities plus the ambition to match.

The fans remain unsure of what to make of Billy. He starts the season playing a 4-2-4 formation with two wingers and two spearhead attackers – this is five years after Brazil introduced it into the World Cup in Sweden and continued with their success in Chile in 1962. We, like many clubs throughout Britain, have been slow to copy this successful style of playing. Add to that the footballs are now much lighter and players becoming more skilful as a result, we should expect more free flowing football. However, there are not the goals around that we saw post war. Defenders are leaner and fitter and expected to have more skill than previously; as a result defenders shackle attackers more comfortably.

The Reserves have averaged more than 2,000 per home match for their opening games which sees them top of their league. The crowd numbers exceed even my expectations – but there was crowd trouble at a home match with Watford Reserves when stand seat cushions were thrown on the pitch towards a Watford player who had caused a serious injury to a City player. I have to deal with some serious issues arising from this, some with the FA.

Since Martin Rogers took over from John Chaplin as the 'City correspondent' on the Chronicle, he has been excellent in looking at the positives with some excellent reporting and comment. In October he writes that: 'in a few years' time City could have one of the finest sports facilities in East Anglia if John Coward's £1.25m plan linked with Chelmsford Cricket Club comes to fruition. This includes an international sized swimming pool on the Barn side of the ground backing onto the river.'

Martin praises the Chairman's enterprise and foresight, especially as leisure time is becoming more of an issue now the post war recovery sees people better off than ever before. Looking into his crystal ball Martin can see crowds flocking to the facility – including the football club.

What concerns me about the Chairman's proposals (and with my feet planted firmly on the ground) is how the whole thing might become a white elephant – and an expensive one at that. Last season the wage bill was over £28,000 and not sustainable, although many of the higher earners have now been moved on and been replaced by the current younger set of players on lower wages, but larger league crowds are needed. Currently we average fewer than 4,000 but need over 5,000 and what is galling is that we have twice that average attend FA Cup matches (even if against Southern League opposition) but we need a thousand or so of them to return every other Saturday. The money from the Supporters' Club is absolutely vital, but it is less than it was yet remains the main reason we do not slip into very serious debt.

To add credence to my views about ill-discipline, and to my dismay, Alan Collier, a quiet, easy going fellow, punches a Romford player to the ground in the Essex Professional Cup match at Romford in November for no apparent reason. We are lucky in that we hold on for a 2-2 draw with Bobby Grant performing heroics in goal after Alan is sent off.

To make matters worse we have to suspend Colin Holder for a breach of club discipline and Bobby Grant has a falling out with the management and is not even picked for the Reserves – a rumour circulates that he has left the club, but that is not true.

The First Team's poor run starts the day after President Kennedy's assassination on November 22nd when we lose at home to Yeovil. We are all shocked by the previous evening's news but clearly Yeovil were less so and this heralds the start of five straight league defeats for us and the loss to Bedford in the FA Cup. What alarms me as much as anything is that we have over 4,400 for the Yeovil game but the next two home games are barely over 2,000. Yes, it is the time for Christmas shopping and the weather was poor but …

On a lighter note, I have the chance to watch a training session. This is the first time I have seen Tommy Wilson in his kit. He looks overweight to me and this, allied with his short, stocky build, makes him look very little like a top professional footballer. However, my view changes when he is put up against Mick Butcher for some short sprints. Sleek Mick looks a clear favourite for the twenty-yard dash, but Tommy shows him a clean pair of heels not once but on every occasion they are set against one another.

***

That Boxing Day defeat at Hastings becomes our low point after a succession of league defeats and something of a watershed for us. That day I'm in my office at the Reserve match and have the radio tuned to listen for the football results. With Millwall being my 'other team' I have to wait some time before I hear their result (actually a heartening 3-0 win over Luton Town who we leapfrog in the table but remain in the bottom four), but Division One is always the one we all want to hear. I have to check the calendar when the results from the top division are read out to make sure it's not April 1st! The results run like this:

Blackpool 1 Chelsea 5
Burnley 6 Manchester United 1
Fulham 10 Ipswich Town 1
Leicester City 2 Everton 0
Liverpool 6 Stoke City 1
Nottingham Forest 3 Sheffield United 3
Sheffield Wednesday 3 Bolton Wanderers 0
West Bromwich Albion 4 Tottenham Hotspur 4
West Ham United 2 Blackburn Rovers 8
Wolverhampton Wanderers 3 Aston Villa 3

That's 66 goals or an average of 6.6 per game – the previous set of ten matches produced only 29 goals! My son Kevin despite his tender years is a Burnley fan and goes to bed a happy little chap with Burnley trouncing the illustrious United.

A few days later the reverse fixtures take place and City beat Hastings 4-2 to set us up nicely for the New Year. Little Kevin's joy is short-lived as his Burnley are thrashed 5-1 at Old Trafford. The trend of unusual reverse results is continued when Ipswich beat Fulham 4-2 and West Ham win 3-1 at Blackburn.

***

Looking back over 1963 as we now enter 1964, what a year it has been. Martin Rogers reflects many of our views in his piece in the Chronicle. It started with the 'big freeze' followed by a 6-0 home defeat in our first game back and then a season that promised so much meandering to a close.

Golden Boy Bobby Mason came and went along with most of the other star signings. Harry Ferrier resigns and trainer Jack Pritchard is sacked with NINE players given free transfers.

However, Billy remains cool and calm – efficiency personified – and he seems to be setting City on a different road; one I hope that leads to success. However, Billy is not popular with everyone around the club and has ruffled a few feathers with some upset that Len Phillips was allowed to leave when he should have been offered a player/coach role to tap into his experience to help with the younger players. Martin Rogers is critical of that decision and considers Bath City's gain is our loss. The problem for Billy, to be fair to him, is that with the club more mindful of expenditure, financing Len might have been at the expense of recruiting two young players for the future.

One bright spot has been Bobby Smith who Martin Rogers considers as a steal, both as an able replacement for Phillips and a loyal club man.

Bobby Mason left a memory of a great talent – you don't play for Wolves at the top of the English Football League for several seasons without a lot of skill – but perhaps he is more suited to the more refined play of top League football, as opposed to doing enough for City but not grafting and giving his absolute all in the hurly burly of the Southern League.

But what can we look forward to in 1964? Hope lives eternally of League status and there is still talk of a super league at the top of English football with regional lower divisions. This would make economic sense as the cost of travel and overnight stays are making it so expensive. These lower leagues would be increased with the expansion of numbers putting City in a good position. How many times though have I heard of such proposals? I'm certainly not holding my breath that something will happen in the very near future.

The removal of the maximum wage a little while back has coincided with the down turn in attendances at most levels of the game with the result that revenue is falling whilst costs are rising, something I've alluded to before. The post war years saw a surge in attendances mainly due to little else being affordable at a weekend. Now, though, with more people having cars and looking further afield for their entertainment there are many other things to attract them on Saturday afternoons.

Clubs outside the top division of the Football League have seen gates on average reduced by a third and, unless there is a local benefactor to prop up the club, many have become run down with poor facilities and pitches. City have something better with a superb ground but we need more people through the turnstiles and we do seem to be swimming against a very strong tide.

It is interesting to read comments in the Chronicle from both reporters and the club's supporters. At times, John Coward's grandiose ideas are mildly ridiculed with the fans choosing a more realistic view and wanting to see success on the field first, a thought echoed by our manager: certainly, winning the Southern League will set us on a pedestal and the Football League may not be able to ignore us.

I see one letter in the Chronicle from fan, Mr Matthams of Avon Road, who says: *'A football team cannot be run on sentiment never mind how long a player has been at one club. I am afraid Manager Frith has missed the bus for this season at least and before we start shouting about the wonderful stadium we are going to have in the future let us have a team worthy of the old stadium! I cannot see the signing of old players is going to be much help.'*

Is he referring to Tiffin (recently having a run back in the First Team) Butcher and Gillott? Perhaps he sees the signing of Tommy Wilson as that of an old man at 30!

I agree with Martin, though, that Billy Frith has done well especially having to start almost from scratch. What we need is a dominating centre half to build the team around and to play alongside Eades with a ball-playing inside forward to help provide more ammunition to the forward line of Butcher, Grant, Maughan and Nicholas who have shown they can score goals. Perhaps adapting the line up to play 3-4-3, like Colchester have done successfully, might help.

Possibly with change in mind, Billy decides to take drastic action to arrest our slump by dropping the whole of the half back line following the Boxing Day defeat at Hastings and for the re-match at home two days later. This win is our first for two months.

***

As 1964 arrives, the Chairman is downcast – this season is not fitting in with his grand plan. We are fifth in the league and out of both the Southern League Cup and FA Cup with just the replay of that Romford game in the Essex Professional Cup to look forward to. Perhaps Wilson will be the spark for Billy – he, too, is feeling the pressure of expectation and the fans are voting with their feet. Billy, I know, has two important irons in the fire and looking to sign two key defensive players. He is also hopeful Wilson will fire up Tony Butcher who is playing well but not netting his normal quota of goals. Billy tells me he wants to have Butch spearheading the attack with Tommy playing deeper behind him. This reminded me of the system the Hungarians used when they beat England 6-3 at Wembley in 1953 – it has only taken us ten years to catch up.

***

Now at the end of January we can look back with pride, with the First Team winning all four matches during the month scoring fourteen goals with six coming from Butcher. Bobby Grant's fit of pique with the Club did not get 1964 off to an auspicious start and Billy says it is up to Grant (recently left out of both teams because of his attitude) to fight his way into the Reserves and then the First Team, but with Wilson arriving to partner Butcher that seems some way off.

Grant's cause is not helped when in his first game back, annoyed or possibly frustrated, he lashes the muddied football towards the advertising hoardings around the edge of the pitch, but misses and the ball hits a young schoolboy full in the face. Grant made no apology at the time, but was later taken to task in the changing room and it now looks like he is destined to spend the rest of the season in the Reserves.

However, the Reserves are top of their League and have many players who can capably slot into the First Team. One of those will not be Colin Holder who has left the Club and is not yet fixed up with another. I am not surprised as I could see this happening right back at the beginning of the season, yet he could be a great talent but, like many before him, will end up too early on the scrap heap of wasted opportunity. His leaving follows that suspension for poor discipline off the field and his record on it was not much better.

Back to the First Team and I can see reasons for our change of fortune in terms of league points. Wilson, brought in to supply the ammunition for Butcher, has certainly fitted in beautifully with Butcher duly playing as the spearhead – exactly where he wants to be. Possibly more significant has been Billy's signing of Sammy Salt from Cambridge City to bolster the half back line. I remember Salt from that 6-0 defeat in the first game back after the freeze last year when he was outstanding – head and shoulders above the rest. He spent his early playing career at Blackpool watching the greats there like Mortensen, Matthews and, more recently, Jimmy Armfield. Sam is still only 25 and I can see him dominating the middle of the field like Len Phillips used to do, but how Sammy is not playing at top league level leaves me baffled.

***

February becomes 'Romford month' with two huge derby matches; one in the league and the other the much-delayed Professional Cup replay. So far this season we have seen over 20,000 watch the three matches against Romford.

Bobby Grant perhaps seeing the writing on the wall eats humble pie by returning as a wing half for the Reserves scoring the winner in his first game back.

The First Team remains unbeaten in the league through February with four wins and a draw and I overhear Billy Frith chatting with Martin Rogers after beating Merthyr Tydfil 5-1 away from home: 'We have been improving all the time and this was the best yet.'

Our home league match with Romford on February 1st sees over 7,500 through the turnstiles – that is over 5,000 more than for our last home game three weeks earlier. What an effect a good run has, especially thumping away wins and with this match a local derby to boot.

Romford, who have led the league table for most of the season to date, are fading. Butcher and Wilson put them to the sword in a 2-1 win to delight the home fans. John Coward is equally delighted and I turn a blind eye to the extra bonus he dishes out to the players as a result. His long-standing (fairly) friendly rivalry with Romford Chairman, Jim Parrish, knows no bounds!

I have long held the notion that a Floodlit League for teams in our region would be a money spinner comparable with the floodlit friendlies over the years since the lights were introduced, but a league would have more of a competitive edge. I have sounded out a long list of clubs including some in the Football League, such as Watford, Southend, Colchester and Orient; they all show interest. Now these plans for the Eastern Professional Floodlit League are moving along at pace. We have set up an initial organising committee of which John Coward is to be Chairman and I have taken on the Secretary, Treasurer and Referee's Appointment Secretary roles; The Stadium will be our headquarters. We definitely have four clubs – City, Romford, Cambridge City and Cambridge United and these will guarantee bumper gates, as they are always our top league matches every season in terms of crowd numbers. Each team has pledged it will field its strongest team and this will almost certainly be incorporated into the new League's rules.

Watford, Guildford City and Bedford are most interested and Bob Last, one of our directors, will provide a league winner's trophy.

***

Back to playing matters, it is clear during the run to the end of February (eight league wins and one draw) that, as well as Billy's changes mentioned already, moving former right winger Ron Smillie to inside forward and Wes Maughan to outside right has been a stroke of genius. With Salt linking successfully with Smillie as the central two, the team has symmetry as good as I have ever seen. Billy certainly can read a player.

The half back line of Salt, Eades and Bobby Smith is the best at City in all my years of watching. I will be surprised if Eades does not play League football at a high level and perhaps Sammy will return to his rightful place there. Bobby Smith, a gem and a talent well spotted by Billy in Barnsley Reserves, has settled in the town with his new wife and they are now living in one of our houses – what a bonus these properties are for our young players. Since Alan Collier's suspension after his stupid fight at Romford, Owen Medlock has been absolute class in goal.

By the end of February we are sixth in the league but thirteen points behind the fading Romford with two games in hand. Yeovil and Bath remain in contention and I am sure the League winners will be one of these four clubs.

The Reserves remain top of the Metropolitan League and Bobby Grant is back knocking in goals after his problems, scoring five in the 8-1 win away at Romford. Home gates for the Reserves average more than 1,500 and continue to help with the balancing of the books.

Interspersed in this fine run in the league comes that Romford replay. I have to say that this is one of those games that will remain in the memory forever. The Chronicle headlines read:

IS THIS THE GREATEST MATCH IN CITY'S HISTORY?

You judge – here is what happened.

Firstly, you will recall that in November we played away at Romford in an Essex Professional Cup tie and secured a 2-2 draw after Collier was sent off and Grant went in goal; Robin Gladwin and Butcher scoring the goals. This was at a time when Romford were leading the way in the Southern League and we were in the middle of one of our worst ever run of results. For various reasons the match was delayed into 1964 and played at the end of February, but 6,714 turn up for the floodlit replay. The City team reads:

Owen Medlock
Joe Ling   Peter Gillott
Sammy Salt   Terry Eades   Bobby Smith
Wes Maughan Tony Butcher Tommy Wilson Ron Smillie
Tony Nicholas

With seconds remaining City trail 2-1 having been two goals down at one time until Ron Smillie scored with about fifteen minutes left on the clock – some of the crowd start to leave as the minutes tick down to the ninety: the Romford fans are singing their hearts out in the packed cricket ground end.

We win a corner and it's our last chance, Owen wants to run the length of the field to add height and confusion in the Romford penalty area, but Billy waves him back. Tommy Wilson rushes over to take the corner but there is a hold up as some irresponsible City fans are throwing objects at Billy Dunbar in the Romford goal (I find out later these are pennies and three-penny bits). Tommy swings the ball in – it is caught on the wind and heads to the near post. It is above head height and a Romford player patrols that post. Dunbar sees the danger and runs towards his near post, but crashes into his defender, smacks his head on the metal goalpost and is knocked out whilst the ball sails into the net. Dunbar is comatose and needs urgent attention but the referee has blown for time. Dunbar is carried off on a stretcher and rushed to the hospital in London Road, where we later hear he is being kept in overnight with concussion.

The players wait in the centre circle whilst all this is happening; extra time will be necessary. A Romford defender dons the goalkeeper's jersey and this has shades of the first match when Grant took over; perhaps one day we will have substitutes allowed for injury.

The Romford supporters, ready to celebrate a famous win, are now quiet and being taunted by the younger City fans at the Wolseley Road end. Extra time starts. Tony Nicholas on the left wing turns on the style – not seen for a while – rampaging past his full back at will and sending over a stream of crosses. Maughan twice and Butcher get onto the end of these and it becomes 3-2, 4-2 and then 5-2 as the goals fly in. There is delirium in the City crowd whilst the 'Romford End' empties rather quickly as Nicholas slams in the sixth and for most of extra time we have had the unusual sight of the whole main stand on their feet – something I have never seen before and may not see again. The noise around the ground is greater than when we had over 16,000 at the Colchester game in 1949 yet this is only a Essex Professional Cup match but it's the nature of the win and how from being down and out against our nearest and keenest rivals, we snatched such a dramatic result.

As the game ends sections of the crowd flock onto the muddy pitch and I spot some on their hands and knees at the Wolseley Road end –

later I hear they were collecting the loose change they had thrown there earlier!

What a game and I'm not sure it gets much better than this. What a way to celebrate John Coward's birthday and he is delighted, of course, not least at getting one over on Jim Parrish!

Later in the week I hear from a friend that his great uncle left the game shortly before that last minute corner. Uncle is over seventy and wanted to miss the squeeze over the old iron bridge leading to Central Park – always a bottleneck when there is a large crowd. Being quite deaf – but, apparently, too stubborn to wear a hearing aid – he failed to hear the roar for Wilson's equaliser as he passed under the railway viaduct and headed for his bus. The next morning his Daily Express arrived and he thumbed through it before heading off to work. He casually glanced at the football scores expecting to see Chelmsford 1 Romford 2 but instead it had a 6 against Chelmsford, but he dismissed it as a misprint. When he got to the factory there was a surprising buzz – unusual for such an early hour and he did not take in what the men were talking about and went to his office. Later at tea break he discovered what he had missed the previous night and vowed never to leave a match early again: perhaps a lesson for us all.

***

As if that Romford match was not enough excitement, we are making an attempt to link into the current pop music craze. The clamour for The Beatles and other pop groups is changing our society – not that they are my cup of tea, just give me Frank Sinatra and Perry Como – but we are keen at the Club to offer more than just the football. Fans traditionally arrive just before kick off, but if we can attract them earlier we might sell more programmes, draw tickets, food from the various outlets and collect money over the bar in the Social Club before the match. A pop group might also encourage young and not so young women to attend matches if there is more than simply the football to watch. Look round the terraces at any match and there are not many women – yes, a few in the main stand but not many anywhere else on the ground.

So we are going all '*Mod and Rocker*' as the Chronicle calls it. The local pop group, 'The Alpines', will perform before the next home game against Wellington about 45 minutes before kick off. What some fans will make of it I'm not sure, but many have clamoured for some entertainment like we had in the early floodlit friendly matches, so instead of the Dagenham Girl Pipers we have a pop group … times change!

During the week before the Wellington game I read in the national newspapers that Bobby Mason has been transfer listed at Leyton Orient – it's a shame that he can't settle and I wonder if he regrets dropping down to play for us from Wolves: surely he should still be playing in the First Division?

I bumped into Derek Tiffin the day after. He's waiting for a hernia operation and is pretty sure this will bring his career to an end. Billy is making good use of him by having him do our scouting role and we all hope he continues with this even if he does call a halt to his playing career.

I have occasion to speak on the telephone with my counterpart at Clacton Town regarding the Floodlit League, and it is sad to learn they will be dropping out of the Southern League for financial reasons and joining our Reserves in the Metropolitan League. To think five years ago we saw them as an archrival before Romford became full time and took over that mantle.

Billy Frith gives another interview to Martin Rogers saying *'we did not expect to win the Southern League this season, but ironically we could; or at least finish in the top three and the lads think they can pull it off.'*

As we still have to play Yeovil and Bath away in April I accept there is still a glimmer of hope that we could take the league title with these two clubs becoming our main rivals if Romford continue in poor form. We are up to fourth and seven points behind Romford with still the two games in hand but Yeovil and Bath are ahead of us and have one more game in hand, so we face an uphill task and we have a poor past record at both Yeovil and Bath.

The Reserves remain one point ahead of Spurs 'A' and two ahead of Cambridge City and Arsenal 'A'.

'The Alpines' perform manfully at the Wellington game. It is most definitely not my sort of music and yet we did get an influx of fans – 1,500 up on the previous non-Romford home game – but the sound quality was poor, which was our fault and not the group's. It's unlikely we will repeat the exercise but might try other forms of entertainment. However, the music inspires the players, who probably like that music more than me, and we wallop Wellington 5-0 with Butcher getting a hat trick.

***

In the week following I have a meeting with John Coward and he is more excited than I've seen him for a while. He truly believes we are the best footballing team in our league and our final position will support that. We mull over where we are with the Floodlit League and talk more of his ideas to develop The Stadium with his £1 million plus plan. I do feel we might have problems with permission to develop that land behind The Barn, but we do agree to approach Chelmsford Cricket Club and the French family regarding the land directly behind the goal at one end. French's yard separates us from the Cricket Club and is less likely to be flooded than the land behind The Barn, which could cause a problem for any building put there. Mrs French might be amenable to sell especially as it was from her family that the site for The Stadium was purchased in the first place.

John had made it known to all who wished to listen last year that he was keen to move the pitch round ninety degrees, put in a new 1,000 seater stand, a swimming pool, a ten pin bowling alley and a directors' restaurant that overlooked the pitch. He wanted to make our ground the social centre of the town and open to the public seven days a week. I must say I admire his foresight but quite how this was to be funded he has never made clear, although a third party had heard John had suggested setting up a new and separate company. I'm sure all football clubs could offer more than just action on the pitch and I've started up some initiatives within the Social Club and can see how this could be extended under John's vision.

***

We continue to receive excellent coverage in the Essex Chronicle now celebrating its 200th year with over 40,000 readers. Martin Rogers, someone I have known since he wore short trousers and seemingly now barely out of school, has been a revelation under Sports Editor Bernard Webber, who I always thought has more of soft spot for Colchester, but even he is warming to the City. The coverage they give the club each Friday normally covers at least two full pages with sister paper, the 'Newsman Herald', providing match reports from the Saturday and Monday night matches in its Tuesday edition. We could not ask for any more publicity and I know the fans revel in the facts plus the comment, reflection and perception brought by Martin and Bernard. Howard Southall in the Weekly News also provides a very professional view of City matches and of what goes on off the pitch. The Chelmsford public is well-blessed with having such men doing whatever they can to support the club with their comments – that's not to say they will not be critical when they feel it necessary.

It is my belief, also shared by many old hands including these reporters, that we currently have one of the best footballing sides assembled in the club's history, but now without a host of costly 'star' names. Billy Frith's original strategy seems to be coming together.

One particular thing I have noticed at the Club this season is that everybody appears so positive and loves being involved – I can best describe it as a family atmosphere. We are the best-supported club in our league and the players enjoy the bigger crowds with the atmosphere that generates, especially under the excellent floodlights. We offer decent wages and the club houses are an excellent way of attracting the players the manager wants.

Whilst the gate for the Wellington game was up, I have calculated that 22,795 spectators have watched the three Romford games at The Stadium this season and yet, at the next home game against Nuneaton, the gate is back down to 3,500. I realise the crowd is swelled by a good few supporters down from Romford and the local rivalry, but what do we have to do to increase our regular support? Fifteen years ago we had over 16,000 for that league match against Colchester – is it too much to dream that we could draw half that number on a regular basis in the Football League? Chelmsford is designated to be a London overspill town and will cease to be the quiet county town its insular image has provided over many years. It will become a centre for industry and commerce with the population expected to rise from

50,000 to 80,000 – even more reason for the town to have a Football League team!

In early April news reaches me that Barrow in the Fourth Division are seriously in debt as are Stockport, Bradford Park Avenue and several other clubs with anyone one of them possibly going the way of Accrington Stanley at any time. Were this to happen we would be on the threshold of taking their place with the best ground and best gates outside of and even inside the lower divisions of the Football League – our position in the Southern League will help too.

On the playing side, Romford approach us about signing Bobby Grant. He has disappointed this season and simply seems content to bang in the goals for the Reserves having exploded onto the scene in the First Team last season, but has not played for the First Team since December following his falling out. I believe Billy will let him go.

I watch the Reserves play St Neots Town and in their ranks is none other than John McCorkindale who played for us a while back. I always thought of him as a great talent but like so many before him he seems to have wasted it and has drifted like a nomad around the lower reaches of non-league football. Still he's a cracking lad and it was good to see his friendly face once more.

Due to my secretarial duties I often watch the Reserve matches and continue to be impressed by Robin Gladwin. In March I saw him score a hat-trick and I really rate this lad, but he has had only a few First Team games this season and played in many different positions, but I see him as one of those late developers and am still of the opinion that he will make a good attacking left full back. However, out of the blue Billy tells me he is signing a left back, thus scuppering my idea of playing Gladwin there. Frank Austin, one of his old Coventry players but now at Torquay, is an experienced defender and comes to City to perhaps relieve Peter Gillott who has been playing when not fully fit and I know Billy wants to give him a rest. I still think he should try Gladwin at left back!

***

John Coward, being a local lad made good, has always been keen to promote youth football and a while back asked Ossie Willsher to put a team together to compete in the top local Mid Essex League. Through that team goalkeeper Peter Clarke, from my old club the Old Chelmsfordians', has already made a considerable mark when deputising for the suspended and then injured Alan Collier in the Reserves.

Ossie's boys bring us at least one trophy when they win the Mid Essex League Cup Final at The Stadium on Easter Monday with Terry Charrington, an excellent cricketer already on the MCC ground staff at Lord's, scoring the winning goal. John presents the trophy and is clearly delighted – seeing a rosy future for many of the players with one stand out player in young Johnny French ex of Trinity Road School. I know of him and worry about his temperament; without doubt he has all the natural skills but like McCorkindale and Holder before him it might need more than just the talent.

The Chairman is seriously thinking of buying a holiday property in Portugal, or at least that is what he tells me, when he spots in the Chronicle that Taylor & Co are offering foreign properties for the first time with bungalows in the south of Portugal, called The Algarve, on offer between £1,300 to £2,800 and I know he is tempted. It would be good for him to have somewhere to go off to and relax as he drives himself on so hard at times with the City and all is other business interests and I fear he will burn himself out before he reaches 60.

We secure three wins out of three over the four day Easter weekend including a 3-1 win over Bath at home in front of over 5,000 (that's more like it!). A week on from Easter we win at Kettering and so from the end of February we have played eight league games and won seven and drawn one. That win over Bath puts us in a better position to win the league title than them but Yeovil have been winning just like us and now we face a weekend away in the West Country with Yeovil on the Saturday and Bath on the Monday.

I stay back at The Stadium and the telephone is red hot at 4.45 with fans wanting to know the result down in Somerset. The 2-0 loss on the infamous Huish slope is our first since December and this is followed by a draw at Bath which is normally a most commendable result, but after this long weekend it is now almost certain we will finish behind Yeovil.

***

With April coming to an end so does our season. Looking back it has been one of the most successful on and off the field. In some years we would have walked away with the league title but Yeovil are fully deserving of their success, yet we pushed them hard. Our record since Boxing Day was played 23, won 18, drawn 4 and lost just the one to Yeovil. So, 40 points from a possible 46 – title winning stuff but we lost five and drew two of seven consecutive games in November and December. If only!

We are beginning to look forward to next season and beyond, with the comfort in the main stand a priority. There are no back supports on the seats so we are looking to fit tip up seats this summer with the stand itself extended above the social club and so increasing the capacity. The pitch still remains a worry and not helped by the number of matches played on it this spring. This includes local league cup finals plus the normal run of league matches, with over twenty games played on it in a little over four weeks. It now resembles a veritable dust bowl and my one concern for next season is the extra games the floodlit competition will bring only adding to its wear and tear.

It is sad to learn the great Derek Tiffin, at 34, is leaving the club. Club captain for eight years he has been the epitome of what Chelmsford City is about – stylish, passionate, single minded and honest. He has played 447 league games and 229 other senior games and all this while an amateur and then part-time professional: he has certainly never let us down. It will not be the same without him around the club.

Other players being released come as no great surprise. Roy Jacobs has been out of favour for a while as has Tony Lowe and, with the signings of Joe Ling and Frank Austin plus the presence of the ever reliable Gillott, we do have a surfeit of full backs.

Holesund, a Swedish league club with several internationals, visit as part of the Gillott/Tiffin testimonial matches. City win one-nil in a thoroughly enjoyable game with almost 4,000 present to help fill the coffers for our two stalwarts. Holesund's management team and directors are most impressed with our set up saying they would not be out of place in the Swedish First Division.

Sadly, the Reserves unbeaten run of 23 matches comes to an end against Hastings away in the first leg of the League Cup semi-final. In the second leg City are cruising to victory on aggregate at The Stadium when a tropical storm turns the pitch into an ankle-deep paddy field and the referee has to abandon the game. It is replayed the following night but this time we lose on aggregate.

In the League the Reserves, like the First Team, just come up short but what a season for both teams. To cap the season City pick up the Pearson Trophy from the Mayor of Chelmsford when they beat Colchester 3-0 in the one sided final of the Essex Professional Cup. There is another wonderful gate of 6,207 to see Tommy Wilson's finest match so far.

Billy Frith passionately believes that if City can get into the Football League for next season they will get promoted at the first attempt – this team, with strong Reserve support, is that good.

As Bob Dylan sang in his big hit earlier this year, 'The Times They are A-Changin'' and none more so than in the world of music. As if 'The Alpines' was not enough for those like me who prefer a quieter type of music, we now have 24-hour pop on our radios. Visiting the players in the dressing room before our last home game against Cambridge United, a transistor radio was on full blast. It can't be the BBC, surely, and I'm informed that this noise is coming from a boat moored off Harwich and calling itself Radio Caroline – apparently it's outside the jurisdiction of our broadcasting control and has been dubbed 'pirate radio' – it sounds dreadful and has awful advertisements but I cheer up when I hear most of the disc jockeys suffer from bad seasickness – give me the Light programme any day.

***

With the Football League AGM approaching I help draw up a most impressive brochure to be circulated to all League clubs. The Directors really do believe our pipedream can now become reality and as well as several interesting items, we set out ten reasons for us being in the League. They are not only good reasons but also sound reasons and they include details about the club:

- A weekly income in excess of £1,000
- Wages at around £600 per week
- £100,000 given by the Supporters' Club in recent times
- 14 houses owned and currently worth £60,000
- £40,000 spent on ground improvements in the past four years
- An average attendance of 5,100
- Further improvement plans including the leisure facilities to be enjoyed by the town – not least an Olympic size swimming pool

The club made a profit of almost £3,000 for the year and does not, therefore, have any spiralling debts like many League clubs.

Bernard Webber reports that *'all this smacks of vision and drive and the enthusiasm is clearly there. Good luck to the club with their great effort and may they soon be celebrating a place where they belong in the Football League'*. Praise indeed.

Perhaps as a sign of the times and following a few unsavoury incidents around our ground on some match days, early May sees disturbing scenes in the town when a fight breaks out in a group of gypsies on the land between The Stadium and the Market. One of their number dies from a stab wound and the town is shocked with the Chronicle confirming arrests have been made with three men charged with manslaughter.

On a lighter note the FA Cup Final arrives and there is great excitement in the town as former City star Charlie Hurst is off to watch son Geoffrey line up for West Ham against Preston. Geoffrey comes away with a winner's medal, scoring the second goal as West Ham win 3-2. What a journey for Geoffrey – a workmanlike wing half he has now become a rampaging goalscorer and is tipped to play for England, having already caught the eye of Alf Ramsey. And I remember Geoffrey as a kid with a runny nose kicking a ball around in the club's gym!

I arrive at the office one morning to learn the team's talisman and supporters' favourite, Tony Nicholas, has refused to sign for next season. Billy had to lower Tony's wages in the new offer, as it is now our policy to have all the senior players on the same basic wage following the unwise variations of terms used to attract the stars like Tony in 1962. We all feel the current offer made to Tony is realistic and commensurate with what he would get at a lower division League club. He told me he would dearly like to stay and start up a business in the town and says he is happier here than anywhere else he has been. He feels settled in one of our houses on the Moulsham Lodge Estate with his wife Darlene and young family and even helps out with some sports' training at Trinity Road School. It is a tense time but, in the end, Billy's charms work and Tony, much to everyone's relief, decides to stay.

***

Despair!! Our dream has been shattered, the rug pulled from under our feet, the walls have fallen in – call it what you like! There is sensational news from the Football League. We have been hauled over the coals for signing Bobby Mason from Wolves and Peter Corthine from Southend a couple of summers ago. As you know we were entitled to sign these players without paying a fee whilst we remained outside the Football League and they were both on what is termed the 'open to transfer list'. Wolves were most unhappy with the Mason saga – they lost the fee for the player – and have forced the issue. However, we acted entirely within any rules laid down by the Football League and the Football Association at the time, but we are now barred from applying for a place in the League for 5 years back dated to 1962.

To put it all another way we are found guilty of a 'crime' when in fact there was no 'crime' but the football world, it seems, has other ideas. Martin Rogers writes: *'Football League clubs have decided to retrospectively ban, from applying for admission, non-league clubs who have dared to take advantage of the rules loophole allowing them to sign transfer-listed players without paying a fee.*

If upheld, this decision of the club chairmen could be a body blow to City's burning ambitions. Natural justice suggests that such a nakedly unfair ruling can't stick, still less a five-year ban. The consequences are too ruinous to contemplate. Who knows what any of us will be doing or where we will be in 1967?

Hell hath no fury like a football club chairman scorned, it appears, but John Coward and his colleagues won't take this lying down, of that we all can be sure.'

Devastated we have to accept it and we are not the only club affected as others including Cheltenham, Cambridge City, Bath and Kettering have also been barred from applying should any League club wish to invoke this ruling. With renewed talk of the likelihood of 14 non-league clubs being admitted to a new Football Alliance of two regionalised fourth divisions, it is now almost certain we will miss out.

This is a sad end to a superb season for the club. The Board is determined to fight on and make sure our case is an even better one when the ban is lifted in three years' time. I can see first-hand how this has affected John Coward as he is devastated and I am sure his proposed ground re-development will now be put on hold and, perhaps, even ditched forever.

It is as if the Football League is a closed shop – 'an old boys club'. There are some clubs in the League with run down grounds, have crowds barely reaching what we get for a Reserve match and remain in a parlous financial position. Despite this they are re-elected each year, but perhaps one day the teams winning the Southern League and its equivalent in the north will be automatically promoted to the Football League; this would be a most logical and sensible step.

In the week following this momentous news Billy leaves for a well earned holiday in Sardinia but on his return I persuade him to play for the City team at the Old Chelmsfordians' five-a-side tournament, which City win; the final is against the hosts. Billy opts out of the final but with the side down by SEVEN goals Tony Butcher calls out for the boss to come back on the pitch but he declines! The team turns matters around with their superior skill and fitness to win 18-11. So, a trophy at last but, amusingly, it is a suitably engraved toilet seat! That just about sums up what we feel we have been dealt by the footballing authorities.

At the Southern League AGM we want to drive forward some improvements and propose that a player's maximum bonus per game is increased from £2 to £4 with an increase to the match officials' fees and a new rule that the referee should be at the ground at least two hours before a match. This would allow time for matches in doubt to be properly called off and not at the last minute or go ahead when they should not.

Not one of the 41 Southern League club was prepared to second the monetary proposals, although the early attendance by the referee was agreed. Martin Rogers, in his weekly column, criticises the Southern League and he sees the City as a progressive club, full of ideas but, much like the Football League, the elderly gentleman representing the clubs do not like change, even if it is for the better. Perhaps they have issues with us born out of jealousy.

I have discussed with the Board the level of season ticket prices for next season. I have agreed with them that supporters will be able to pay in instalments so there is not one large amount to find during the summer. The stand ticket will be £9 9s in full with the lowest terrace season ticket at £2 12s 6d. This will include, as before, all First Team and Reserve League matches. I also manage to persuade John to include the cost of the Floodlit League matches in this price – at least for this one season to see how it goes.

***

Now as the summer progresses the stand extension is almost complete and we arrange an opening of the newly extended Social Club when 450 revellers have a thoroughly good evening. This is a proud moment for me as one of my aims when taking the job was to improve this facility to help with funds and to have it on a proper professionally run footing in order to achieve this.

Young Vic Vale, only eighteen years old and his assistant, the even younger Rod Butler, are working hard on the pitch. If we have another wet winter and with the extra floodlit games, he will be under greater pressure to keep it up to standard. I have received details of artificial pitches and I am sure that at some time in the future these might be introduced. The freeze in early 1963 hit clubs hard with no money coming in yet with bills and wages to be paid and these artificial, all-weather pitches would have meant we could have carried on playing.

Before I leave for my holiday ahead of gearing up for next season, I'm surprised to see Tony Nicholas doing some running carpentry repairs around the ground – he was trained as a carpenter and joiner. It was not agreed with me that we would be paying him, so I assume he's doing this of his own volition. It does show what sort of club we have here with this player who only days ago was in dispute with the club over his contract now helping out in this way.

The last act I carry out is to arrange for Peter Harburn, our fitness trainer, to attend an FA coaching course at their Lilleshall facility. He has management qualities but not in the Frith mould, far more abrasive and not one to suffer fools gladly – it will be interesting to see how he fares on this new career.

7

THE CRACKS START TO APPEAR

David Selby is a City man through and through. Currently the Club's Historian he has fond memories of those halcyon days of City in the 1960s, when that cloud of football fever always hovered over the town throughout the months of each season. Expectations had always been high and the Chelmsford football public remained demanding, but in the summer of 1964 all of our dreams were in tatters. As the club picked up the pieces following its ban from applying for a place in the League, David tells his story from that defining season.

It's the summer of 1964 and my teenage years are fast approaching, now that's a sobering thought, but I already have four seasons of following City behind me. I have got a few sporting heroes; Babe Ruth, surely the most amazing sportsman ever, the man who was so good at what he did, and so much better than any of his peers, that he saved the sport of major league baseball almost single-handedly following the 1920's Chicago White Sox scandal; Colin Milburn, the Northamptonshire cricketer, whose debut test hundred followed his duck in the first innings, something I can vividly remember recording in my little cricket score book. None of them though rank as high as my number one, Tony Butcher, who scored twice in my first ever City game, a 3-3 FA Cup draw with Wisbech Town in October 1960. He is a Chelmsford lad playing for the City, and he has done so throughout one of the Club's golden eras, the early 1960's. He is my real sporting hero!

However, in the summer of 1964 I have that sense of anticipation as the new season is about to start. Runners-up the previous season, Billy Frith's first at the Club, and still there is talk of the Football League. I am still young enough to be able to dream, Oxford United got in two years ago, so why can't City follow suit? I know little of football finances and such like; I just turn up, watch the game and go home. To me the thought of City getting in the Football League is just about waiting for the inevitable. That's what the Board have been telling us through the local press, who am I to doubt their word? However, everyone connected with the club – players, directors and fans – have all been affected by that awful news that we will not be able to apply to be elected to the Football League until 1967 at the earliest assuming, as is likely, any League club objects to any application, which I am sure they will.

So when City make the long trip to face Yeovil Town, the previous season's champions, on the opening day of the season the side will show their championship credentials surely? I am now old enough to make the occasional away trip, two or three times a season, with the usual regime to go to a First Team game one week and then down to watch the Reserves the next week, but I am not at The Huish to watch the Yeovil game. Instead I am at New Writtle Street watching the Reserves. As my father and I leave the ground at the French's field end we hear someone say that the First Team have lost 5-1. Of course it would be helpful if the man on the tannoy gave us the score from Yeovil but we remain in suspended anticipation. It is a Saturday ritual for me to accompany my father to the Railway Station in Chelmsford in the evening and to wait by the little wooden hut at the bus stop for the arrival of the trains carrying the Saturday night edition of the Evening News, a better read than the Evening Standard I believe, and the Ipswich Football Star, colloquially known as 'The Green 'Un', to get our result and match report. It isn't unknown for us to walk up to the 'Golden Fish' opposite the bus station to get Saturday's evening meal as well.

There it is in print though. Yeovil Town 5 Chelmsford City 1, surely not! I read through the report, 3-0 down at half time, Tony Nicholas pulls one back early in the second half but then City concede two more, including a penalty. It can't be true though can it? Frith has resisted the temptation to sign any new faces, presumably feeling confident that the squad that finished just four points behind Yeovil the previous season can do the job this time around. But there it is, a 5-1 defeat to start the season.

Despite my tender years I am feeling so crestfallen with this opening. I have been clinging to the hope all summer that this season is going to be the one. City haven't won the Southern League championship for nearly twenty years (and it was more regionalised then with fewer teams); surely Billy Frith will lead the side into that treasured 'Promised Land'.

I live in Lewis Drive on the Moulsham Lodge estate and have done so since my family moved to Chelmsford in 1957. Number 4, Lewis Drive is a Club house occupied by new City full back Frank Austin and I'm a regular visitor to his house. Not because I want to talk to Frank about all things City, although the subject does crop up from time to time, but because his son has the most amazing collection of American comics that you can imagine, Superman, Batman et al, they are all there. We make our own entertainment, which mainly consists of kicking a ball about the streets or the garage areas behind the houses on Moulsham Lodge, or, especially during this summer, finding a piece of wood to use as a cricket bat and playing the summer sport. So to have a friend with a large collection of American comics is a bonus. The others in 'the gang' can't afford to buy them so here is our opportunity to while away the hours reading about the goings on in Metropolis and Gotham City rather than participating in some sporting activity.

On the same day as we were hammered at Yeovil there was a first on TV. The new station, BBC2, is showing the highlights of a top match on Saturday evenings but not many people can watch this yet as it can only be seen in the London area at present. The first game is Arsenal's visit to Liverpool where they lost 3-2 and I read in the papers that this coverage is to give training to all those technicians etc. who will be covering the 1966 World Cup in England. The programme is called 'Match of the Day' and on quite late but I hope to get to see it when we have BBC2.

Returning to our start of the season, it is, surely, just a hiccup. Tonbridge are at New Writtle Street on Monday evening, so things will be put right won't they? City having to open the season with a visit to the reigning champions is a tough start if ever there was one, but here is a chance to remedy things against the newly promoted side from Kent.

I love these Monday night games. New Writtle Street is an atmospheric stadium, especially with 3,825 people in it, as there is for this match. Floodlights are a relatively new innovation and I had just started watching City when they were installed just four years ago. I don't know about the Wednesday afternoon games that pre-dated the floodlights and were played in front of pitifully small crowds, they were before my time. All I know is that after a day at school I can't wait to get down to the ground and revel in the atmosphere of a game played under these bright lights that illuminate my heroes. The City ground may well be capable of holding up to 17,000 people but even with just 4,000 the Stadium manufactures a unique atmosphere.

I know I am someone to be avoided at school on a Tuesday morning if the City have played poorly the night before. I take a failure badly, and by failure I mean anything other than a win, and a convincing one at that. My father is a bit more laid back, telling me, not infrequently that it is only a game. Only a game? Not to an eleven years old schoolboy it isn't! So when City only draw 2-2 with the new-to-the-Premier-Division Tonbridge after twice being ahead I am like a bear with a sore head the morning after. This was going to be our season but here we are with just a single point from our opening two games, not what is expected. Wes Maughan and Tony Nicholas had given us hope each time they put City ahead but on both occasions we were pegged back. The playground the next day is a lively place to be as my group of friends discuss what went wrong as we kicked a ball around replaying the crucial moments from the game.

The season's start may be a disappointing one but this is still a great time to be a City supporter. The City, under Chairman John Coward, is known as a go-ahead club with ambitions to play in the Football League and there are many innovations as the Club moves forward. One brought in at the start of this season is the installation of heaters into the roof of the stand. As someone who stands with my father on the half way line just in front of the Barn, surely this heated area is the most impressive piece of covered seating in the whole of non-league football, but then Coward & Co Ltd is a heating engineering firm! I am not likely to have any experience of how successful this improvement to customer comfort will be but I do know, thanks to spending at least some time in the classroom, that hot air rises so, presumably, if you were sitting on the roof of the stand you would be nice and warm, but underneath the roof?

I manage to persuade my father to let me go to these Monday night games even though I have school the next day. With the matches finishing at 9.10 we are straight onto one of the Eastern National buses (their works are almost opposite The Stadium) outside the ground waiting to take fans to various points around Chelmsford and its outlying districts. So when that final whistle goes my father and I have merely to exit the stadium, cross the road and clamber aboard a 44A going to Moulsham Lodge and we are home in next to no time.

Of course, City being City, things are soon back on track, so much so that on the first Saturday in September City go to Cambridge United and win 6-2, with Nicholas getting a hat trick, my hero Tony Butcher getting a brace and City's newly appointed skipper Tommy Wilson getting the other.

Many of the players have been with us for some time and no one ever seems that keen to leave. So we must pay them quite well and with the facilities, the crowds and our status, players like Butcher, Peter Gillott and Bobby Smith have already racked up a huge number of games and will, no doubt, continue to do so.

A week after the trip to play Cambridge United, City make the same trip again, this time to visit United's rivals Cambridge City. This is one of my away trips and although my father cannot drive and does not have a car his brother can and does; so four of us make the trip to Milton Road – me, my father, my uncle and his brother-in-law. The game is something of a non-event but Tony Butcher scores twice as City win 2-1, but I must say the Milton Road ground is an imposing one. I have never been to a ground with so much room, not only in the immediate confines of the spectator facilities but around the ground as well. Cambridge City are the bigger of the two Cambridge clubs at present and over 4,500 saw this game against us. In fact both

Cambridge clubs are attracting bigger crowds than we are right now, over 4,000 were at the United game the week before. I'm sure the area around the ground will soon be built on – some factory units are already being put up and there was talk in their programme of greyhound racing being held within the ground – there is certainly plenty of room for it.

***

The FA Cup takes a little time to come around, after all City are regularly exempt until the Fourth Qualifying Round, so we have to wait until mid-October for the fun to start. This year though there is some more excitement before the Cup gets underway – a new competition, the Eastern Professional Floodlit League. Since City's floodlights had been installed in 1960 with the sole purpose of increasing income and replacing the poorly attended Wednesday afternoons (traditionally half day closing day in Chelmsford), those high profile friendlies were introduced but that novelty soon wore off. Yes there are a few league and cup games played during the week but City have now been instrumental in the formation of this Floodlit League, a competition that will add an additional six home games to the City calendar.

So to the FA Cup and City are drawn at home to amateurs Oxford City in their first game and such is the pull of the nation's favourite knock out competition that over 4,300, well above City's average league crowd for the season, see the game. City win easily with the forward line of Wes Maughan, Tony Butcher, Tommy Wilson, Ron Smillie and Tony Nicholas all getting on the score sheet, along with full back Peter Gillott. The prize in the competition proper is a trip to Fourth Division side Notts County who are a middle of the table side playing just one division higher than City. Could this be a major cup upset?

My father spends a lot of his working life abroad and he is away in California when this game is played. Thankfully my Uncle Stan's car comes to the rescue and a car load of us set off for Nottingham. This is a big occasion and it calls for special measures. My Aunt Margaret stepped up to the plate and I left Chelmsford adorned in the claret and white bobble hat, scarf and mittens that she has knitted me. I am especially proud of the mittens that have the letters C-I-T-Y on my four fingers of each hand. We arrive in Nottingham some time before kick-off and I feel proud walking through Nottingham town centre resplendent in my City 'uniform'!

I'd like to think that my Aunt's hard work has conjured up a lucky charm but City are to have yet another disappointment against a Football League side and lose 2-0, in front of nearly 10,000 fans. Ron Smillie's broken leg didn't help the cause though – it's such a shame no substitutes are allowed. So another F.A. Cup run is over, almost before it has started, time to concentrate on the league!

I'm still young enough to believe that 'the more the merrier', but the formation of this new League leads this season to the dilation of the attraction of the derbies with Romford. In fact City and Romford meet five times; they are also drawn together in the Southern League Cup, with 16,364 watching the games at an average of just over 3,100 per game. This is well down on what we saw just a couple of years ago when the six games between the two clubs attracted over 36,000 fans. To me, though, the rivalry is still just as intense, no matter what the competition is.

Romford's Brooklands is a lovely ground, being only a short journey from Chelmsford helps of course, with a magnificent stand that wouldn't look out of place at New Writtle Street. Its tip-up seats are far better than the wooden 'bench' type seats that City have. What is shortly to become the speedway track round the pitch doesn't seem to affect the atmosphere either. There is no covering behind the goals so effectively most, but not all, of the crowd either sit in the stand or stand in the covered side, known as the 'clock side', opposite.

I love the rivalry though; it's so intense. The matches against Romford bring a special atmosphere to both grounds, and the games are eagerly awaited. To a young schoolboy it is something special and a win for City makes it even better. We should be allowed to play these games at Christmas or Easter to maximise the crowds, but this season they are to be played on Saturdays in October and March. City lose the game at Brooklands, Sammy Salt getting City's goal in a 2-1 defeat, but I wasn't there. I remember the home game though, not because City win 3-2 but because centre forward Billy Brown gets two of City's goals. I like Billy not just because we have signed him from Romford (he was their top scorer in 1963-1964) but the Brooklands crowd got on his back and he asked for a transfer. Billy Frith has brought him to New Writtle Street and, as an eleven year old, getting one over your local rivals makes you feel good, especially pinching their top scorer. I have that feeling of smugness that not only do we beat the 'Boro but Billy rubs salt in their wounds by scoring a couple of goals.

When I started supporting City in 1960 the floodlights had already been installed, so to see City playing in white shirts with a single or double claret hoop or hoops was not unusual. It was introduced to make the players easier to pick out under lights and has now become the regular strip. That is not to say the side don't wear claret shirts with a white hoop or hoops from time to time. Traditionally we are the 'Clarets' and have always been so and never the 'Whites' – perhaps one day as the quality of lighting is improved we can revert back to the correct main colour. Like when the players run onto the pitch to the sound of 'The Waltzing Bugle Boy', some things should never be changed! You can't beat tradition.

To most of our supporters Cup matches are considered to be as important as league games and City play in the Essex Professional Cup, along with West Ham United. Leyton Orient, Colchester United, Southend United, Romford and Clacton Town. It is the chance to see some Football League players strutting their stuff at New Writtle Street, a chance for me to see some players who I previously have only seen in pictures in 'Soccer Star' or 'Charles Buchan's Football Monthly'. These two excellent publications are essential purchases, pocket money allowing, but, disappointingly, are about all there is around. I can't lie and say that I buy them every time they come out but when I have enough change in my pocket I'm straight over to the shops in Gloucester Avenue to snap up a copy. That's if the paper shop stocks them of course, but, if not, I have to wait for a trip into town and a visit to W.H. Smith.

Leyton Orient come to town for a semi-final game in the Essex Professional Cup (the shortage of clubs means that City came straight in at this stage in January) having already beaten City 2-0 at Brisbane Road in October in the final held over from the previous season. It is another Monday night thriller and, having rushed home from school in eager anticipation of the visit of the Football League stars, I take my place alongside my father on the half way line as City win 4-3. Perhaps Orient have not put out their strongest team, I just don't know, but it doesn't matter to me. City have won against their illustrious Essex neighbours. Roll on the final!

We lose the final 1-0 to Colchester United with nearly 4,000 turning up at New Writtle Street for what is the last competitive game of the season. By then though things have become confusing with what happened earlier in the month.

I am by now just a couple of months away from my twelfth birthday and I am still young enough to believe that what happens in life, and in football, only happens for the good. So when manager Billy Frith is suspended by the Club in April I'm neither surprised nor upset. It just happens. I have no real opinion about it. There will be no big exodus of players; the manager has been suspended, no big deal as far as I'm concerned. Things move on.

Trainer Peter Harburn is put in charge and he selects exactly the same side for his first game as Frith had done for his final game. The players are the same, the kit is the same and the ground is the same. City beat Folkestone 3-0. Life goes on.

Of course Frith is not likely to return. He has reportedly left the Club after falling out with the Club's Board of Directors over the composition of the retained list, although some supporters say there is a darker reason. For me it is no big deal though. There is little discussion about his successor and Harburn is appointed immediately; perhaps an interim measure. Mr Frith was a most successful manager for City, results wise. Runners-up in his first season the side has slipped a little, but his two seasons were hardly unsuccessful.

I am a member of the Junior section of the Supporters' Club; this season I have attended one of the functions laid on for the junior section and this has changed my perception of how football should be played. Although I am a regular at New Writtle Street, I do make the very occasional visit to Arsenal and to Ipswich Town as a guest of my friend Barry Broom and his uncle, who has a car and could drive us to Portman Road. So I have seen top flight players in the 'flesh' and watched top class football live. The Supporters' Club announcement that they would be showing a film of the 1959-1960 European Cup Final between Real Madrid and Eintracht Frankfurt wasn't to be missed though. So along with dozens of other youngsters I walked into the Social Club under the stand, somewhere I had never been before, and grabbed my bottle of pop and bag of crisps and sat down to watch the match. For those that don't know 127,621 fans crammed in to Hampden Park, Glasgow to watch an amazing game that Madrid won 7-3. The young City supporters as well as me were as amazed at what we saw as were the hordes who actually watched the game live in 1960.

So the 1964-1965 season ends with City in a disappointing fifth place; disappointing as after the runners up position had been achieved the previous season we all thought that more progress would be made but it is not to be. That 5-1 defeat at Yeovil in the opening game of the season must have knocked the players' confidence and they never really seemed to recover. That defeat must have been the lowlight of the season, coming as it did at a time when we all hoped that things would start off with a flourish. There were highlights though, even if the FA Cup proved to be another disappointment with that long awaited win over a Football League club seemingly as far away as ever. The side scored plenty of goals, although the total in league games of 86 was short of the previous season's 99, a total rarely likely to be matched.

As the season ends I'm glad it's over. Mr Frith has left, although that in itself is not a major problem to me as my youthful enthusiasm and optimism keeps telling me that an even better manager lies just around the corner. The real disappointment was the way the side fell away after Christmas. The 4-3 win over Rugby Town on Boxing Day meant that City reached the half-way point in league fixtures with just four defeats but the next twenty one games brought nine defeats, although to be fair we finished just six points behind champions Weymouth. It was a relatively disappointing spell given the optimism that prevailed as the season started.

I look back fondly at all the Floodlit League home games with crowds totalling over 14,000. I just loved the fact that all the games, by definition, were played under floodlights. Both Cambridge clubs, City's arch rivals Romford, Kettering Town, King's Lynn and Wimbledon were all involved.

To a young eleven years old schoolboy personalities abound in the

Southern League and especially at New Writtle Street. It is not unusual for players to finish their careers with a spell in non-league circles, in fact almost all the Clubs have at least one 'name' in their side. For me it was thrilling to know that both Stuart Imlach and Tommy Wilson are plying their trade in claret and white just five or six years after having played in the FA Cup final, the most important and eagerly anticipated game of the season. Imlach arrived during the season but Wilson has been here for the whole campaign and despite being 32 years of age he has scored 22 goals to finish second top scorer behind my idol Tony Butcher, who has notched 30.

Then there's our elegant wing half Sammy Salt, prised away from Southern League rivals Cambridge City and sporting a blondish crew cut haircut that makes him look every inch an American, although of course he isn't.

The Southern League may be the last stopping off place for many players but Frith's youth policy was beginning to pay off and 'Keeper Bryan King and defender Robin Gladwin have begun to make their mark and may well embark on Football League careers, as the Essex Chronicle always has stories of them being watched by scouts from top clubs. Tony Nicholas has had another successful season playing up front, but it looks likely this will be his last. Nicholas, with his rolled up shorts (the current fashion) and his perpetual tan is a fine player when 'on song' and a fitness fanatic something that will, no doubt, enable him to continue with a longer career than most. If he does go it is likely he will continue to live in Chelmsford as he now has his Do-It-Yourself shop in the town that is apparently very successful.

I have never taken too much interest in away players. To be honest it is only the City players that concern me. These others only play for the opposition because they aren't good enough to play for City – that is it, isn't it? One I do take an interest in is Yeovil Town goalkeeper David Jones. All goalkeepers wear a green jersey, apart from internationals where they wear yellow; Jones has a problem as Yeovil play in a green kit. His answer is to wear an all-white kit, which, bearing in mind the state that pitches get into these days, must leave who ever washes his kit with a headache or two! Still, if he's out to make an impression, it certainly works!

So the 1964-1965 season has ended and although it has been a disappointing one my youthful optimism will override this disappointment and I look forward eagerly to next season. I have now spent five seasons supporting City and they have continually finished near the top of the table. This is the way of the world, isn't it? A new season and City always finish near the top of the table; that's how life should be surely! Life goes on as it always has done. Next season will be no different as far as I am concerned.

Of course you can't have everything and Billy Brown is gone by the end of the season, sold to Bedford for £750. The fact that not long after and during the summer they sell him for £2,000 to Gillingham, thereby making a handy little profit, doesn't matter to me. I will forever remember the day he put one over our Essex rivals. That would do in my book!

Regrettably Austin is also released at the end of the season and moves out of the area taking with him his son and that collection of comics. Still it was fun whilst it lasted.

8

MANAGER PROBLEMS, BOARD DISPUTES
BUILDING A NEW TEAM

Now into my late teens and playing in local football, my Saturday afternoons are more often than not spent ploughing through the mud of Melbourne Park for Westlea United in the Mid Essex League than watching my heroes at New Writtle Street. Still, there are plenty of Monday night games (plus Wednesdays for the Youth team) and early and late season matches to watch. The end of this coming season will see the World Cup held in England, something to look forward to but let's hope the City can whet our appetite and win the Southern League. There is much to look forward to in the 1965/66 season but no doubt much will stay the same – Steve Little.

With the end of the 1964-65 season the excellent Wes Maughan joins Frank Austin on the transfer list, Billy Brown has gone and long-time favourites Tommy Wilson (now player manager at Brentwood), Tony Nicholas and Ron Smillie have been released. What great servants these latter three have been to the club and perhaps we may not see the likes of them again.

The supporters love this time of year despite no football to watch.

Having pored over the retained list, or more likely who is leaving, the expectation rises as we await the new signings with no little excitement. Director Fred Langton tells the Weekly News that we are looking to sign eight or nine players. Young star goalkeeper Bryan King is on semi-professional terms but it looks like Sammy Salt might not accept the terms offered and return to play for Wellington Town – we hear his family cannot settle. The most pressing need is for goalscoring forwards, with only Tony Butcher remaining from last season when he was again top scorer.

We still have no manager as such with Don Walker and Peter Harburn looking after the First Team and Mr Langton helping away from the pitch – we are apparently keeping our options open regarding a new manager; hardly a satisfactory position for Harburn and not something that will sit comfortably with the players. Is the Board waiting for the right man to become available? Are they waiting for someone they have in their sights to get the sack from his current club? It's difficult to understand why for the first time in our history we have gone so long without a manager. Perhaps it's a financial matter and a way of keeping our costs down.

In the wider field of football, tickets for next year's World Cup can be applied for and Club Secretary, Len Menhinick, has advised supporters that these can be purchased through him. He also explains about the new substitutes' rule introduced by the Football League on a trial basis this season – the one substitute allowed ONLY applies to Football League games and does not even extend to the FA Cup. At long last a step forward and I'm sure this will be adopted for the future and the absurd situation of teams having to play with ten men or a 'passenger' hobbling up and down the wing will be a thing of the past.

Through my connection with the Old Chelmsfordians I hear of an amusing incident (well, it could have been serious but we laughed about it later!) that occurred last Saturday when Len Menhinick (also an OCs' stalwart) and his wife Vera had an early night. Len was suddenly 'on fire' – literally not metaphorically – as there was a sudden shortening within his electric blanket, which set fire to the bedclothes. Vera quickly doused the flames and there was, thankfully, no damage to Len.

During the week after Fred Langton's announcement, we sign 27 year old Roy Summersby, yet another recruit from Portsmouth, and the Chronicle reports that John Docherty, surprisingly released by Colchester, will probably join us. Thankfully, and in an about turn, Ron Smillie is offered new terms and stays.

News from the Southern League – Barnet, a top amateur club, have followed Wimbledon's example and joined the professional ranks of the Southern League; referees will receive four guineas per match and the linesmen two; all clubs must now have qualified medical staff on duty at all matches. All this hints at a more professional approach to modern day football – a welcome development. One significant fact has also emerged in that City were one of the clubs instrumental in having a new rule adopted in the non-league allowing us to sign 'apprentices' to add to our professional staff; these, like their counterparts at Football League clubs, cannot be poached by other league clubs without the payment of a fee. There's an irony in this when in the past we've pinched professional players from League clubs without paying any transfer fee!

The supporters are excited to hear of the signing of former Peterborough United defender and captain, Ollie Hopkins. A player well-known enough to feature in my bubble-gum card collection! Six feet two inches, thirteen and a half stone and aged 28 Ollie turned down Bradford City and Halifax to come to City. He teams up with our former Barnsley contingent – Ollie having played there with Peter Gillott. He has played professional league cricket in Yorkshire and has a golf handicap in single figures – we also learn it's not advisable to wager on a frame of snooker with him as he'll wipe the floor with you!

John Docherty duly arrives and I've seen him play before – gritty, no nonsense, a little slow but a one hundred-per-center, that's for sure. At last a centre forward of note is signed to play alongside Butch and it is none other than Bud Houghton – ex of Birmingham City, Southend and Oxford but he comes to us from Lincoln City. He is signed the same day as flying Scots winger George Duncan, who comes down from Chesterfield having originally been at Glasgow Rangers. These are all players the supporters have heard of and have a good pedigree and, hopefully, this will rekindle the crowds to flock back to those levels of a few years back. Clearly Mr Coward's vision lives on but not perhaps with the same enthusiasm as five years ago. In fact, on this point, there is disquiet around the club. It is the talk of the Social Club and rumours emanating from 'people in the know' that certain directors on the Board are determined to undermine Mr Coward and say his 'vision' is no more than a 'pipe-dream' and that the club is struggling financially.

I am delighted for Tommy Wilson to secure the post of player manager at Brentwood and the players he has there is like a City old boys' reunion with Frank Austin, Joe Ling, Jimmy Elvin, Keith Abbiss, Mick Butcher and Tony Lowe – we wish him well, of course, and it was so nice to hear him say: *'Chelmsford have given me all the help possible as regards advice about administrative problems, players' concerns and all other things which crop up in the daily life of a soccer manager – I can't say how grateful I am.'*

What a compliment to our Club; one we feel proud to be part of and it is interesting that we rarely receive any criticism from ex-players, even those released and we have a marvellous back room led by the two Lens – Menhinick and King.

With the players returning for pre-season training in early July, I get a chance to watch them train at Lawford Lane but there is no Sammy Salt who has indeed returned to Wellington (his wife's home town) and Tony Nicholas has gone back to his old club, Leyton Orient. Whilst we had probably seen the best of Tony, Sammy still had much to offer and will be sorely missed – he is a player who could still cut it at the top level if he chose to do so and I have the impression he thrives as the proverbial, 'big fish in a small pond' but it's clear his move to Wellington is for very good reasons.

We all hope the new players gel quickly. Two constants are Gillott and Butcher – Butcher will miss Wilson who brought the best out of him, but Gillott will be able to claim back his left back spot having switched to right back to accommodate Austin.

I have helped Len Menhinick with organising some trials for boys aged fifteen and a half to eighteen with a view to developing a youth structure tapping into the now extensive local football scene. Unfortunately, I preclude myself from these trials having been told that there are two reasons I will not make a professional footballer, skill and ability! City needs to build a base of quality local players to form the nucleus of our Reserve team, which will be supplemented by the pros not getting the First Team call. Years ago we had the 'A' team playing in the Border League and that served us well but we want to improve our Youth team to compete in the Mercia League and have these players come through at least as far as the Reserves.

Len also has the idea of trials for some over 18s who might have been missed when they were younger and would be a useful addition to our Reserves. These trials will take place at the tail end of the summer.

All the trials at the Old Chelmsfordians' ground will be overseen by Peter Harburn, Ossie Willsher and Don Walker. Let's hope the news from there is all very positive.

The City fans have a laugh this week at the expense of top Chronicle reporter Martin Rogers as he is severely cautioned by the local Sunday League and fined £1 for his behaviour on the touchline at a St Margaret's match – he is manager/secretary of this fine club. He didn't mention his misdemeanour in his weekly Chronicle column, but a colleague clearly did!

To show how the club and the town like to support former players, hundreds attend the Hoffmans' cricket ground for the testimonial match for our former player, Gordon Barker, now the Essex opening batsman. It was wonderful to see legends like Denis Compton, Richie Benaud, Bert Sutcliffe and Sir Learie Constantine support Gordon's day.

I was at school with Malcolm Pannell and now play the occasional Sunday match with him at the Old Chelmsfordians. As a young amateur he has been with City on and off for some time and will play this coming season for City when he is home from Durham University, but whilst up there will turn out for crack amateur side, Crook Town. He will be most welcome back at New Writtle Street.

Len Menhinick agrees with the Board that we will offer season tickets to local football clubs at a discounted rate (five guineas for a seat and £3 10s on the terraces) so they can pass them around their members who wish to attend games. This seems an excellent idea.

Out of the blue City are approached to take Lou Costello from Southend and that will be an excellent signing as he is highly rated – apparently he is in a contract dispute with United and wants out. We turn down approaches from two former top stars in Mel Charles (ex-Arsenal and Wales – and brother of legend John) and Fulham's Tosh

Chamberlain. I hear we consider them a little too old, costly and injury prone.

After a 2-1 defeat by Watford in a friendly we win our first league game against Yeovil 2-1 with Butcher netting the 87th minute clincher.

The team at the start of the 1965/66 season
Back Row: Left to Right: Peter Gillott; Lou Costello; Owen Medlock; John Docherty; Terry Eades: Bobby Smith
Front Row: Left to Right: George Rosling; Tony Butcher; Bud Houghton; Roy Summersby; Stewart Imlach

Ollie Hopkins, now well settled into the town with wife Eunice and their three children, believes this is a really strong, well balanced team with bags of experience at all levels in the game. Howard Southall in the Essex Weekly News is as excited with this team as with that of the Mason, Hatsell era in 1962 from which only Gillott, Butcher and Smillie remain.

The opening day crowd is a disappointing 3,496, so again the fans don't seem to share our excitement but then it is August and holiday time. A loss to Cambridge City, a win at Rugby and a tedious 0-0 at home to Wimbledon followed by a draw away is not spectacular stuff but we'll accept this steady start.

Vice-Chairman Mr Fred Langton writes the *'Boardroom Comments'* piece in the match day programme for the Wimbledon game saying: *'One can feel reasonably satisfied with the season's commencement, after all with a degree of fairness in the result at Cambridge last week, at the time of writing we should have been unbeaten and at the top of the league. Taking into account our smaller staff than last season, I am still confident that given the breaks with not too many injuries, we shall once again be vitally interested in the championship race.*

*Now let us hope that the crowds roll up to see what our teams are like, only crowds can get clubs into the Football League, **NOT RESULTS**, but crowds and results will make our chance even better.'*

Very positive words but I can't help thinking this smacks of delusion. Does Mr Langton really believe our League aspirations hang on the thread of crowd support? Surely consistently being the top non-league club in the country so we cannot be ignored is the answer? This means winning the Southern League regularly and beating superior opposition in meaningful competitive matches not end of season friendlies. Most fans recognise this but have the Board been brainwashed by Mr Coward? His dreams are looking less and less likely to ever be realised as the years pass and I'm pretty sure I'm not alone in thinking that the golden era of the club is on the wane. Finances are not what they were, we are cutting back on the playing staff, support is dwindling and we seem no closer to being Champions than ever before. I really hope I'm wrong.

***

Looking back at the season so far from the end of October, I have to say we are all disappointed, especially as so much was expected from this team. Four won, four drawn and three defeats in the league sees us in 8th place but we are in touch as it's tight at the top with no one running away with things. To not reach the First Round Proper of the FA Cup for the first time in eight years is bad enough but losing to Romford makes this a bitter pill to swallow.

But we can take some positives. Houghton has been excellent but has missed October through injury. He is yet to link well with Butcher who looks like he misses Tommy Wilson who played in the role just behind Tony, but now Tony appears to be playing that role to the more direct Houghton.

There have been a few unsavoury incidents around the club none more so than when trouble broke out in the crowd in the home game against Wimbledon. The constabulary had to step in to pull rival supporters apart but there were no arrests. The trouble is symptomatic of a worrying trend of an undercurrent of violence surrounding football generally and this needs swift action from the authorities.

Not before time the club has an improved PA system and with it comes a new feature when a music request was played for a fan at our last home match; dedications and further requests are now welcomed and the club has bought in some pop records to replace the military marching music of old. Add to that various details of forthcoming matches; some half time Football League scores all read out by an announcer with some professional training and it is all rather exciting! This innovation was the brainchild of Jimmy Hill, Chairman at Coventry City, and has caught on across the country.

Back in 1962 someone at the Club composed a Chelmsford City song which was played and sung before an end of season friendly against Luton Town and this was to be what "Glory, Glory Hallelujah" has become for Tottenham. 'Our song' was set to the tune of "Knees Up Mother Brown". Suffice to say it was not a success and did not catch on but now we've adopted 'Glad All Over' by the Dave Clark Five as our celebration song; it was first played recently at the final whistle at the end of a game we'd won. Those of us in the Barn ran to the corrugated back of the stand and hammered out the beat to '… *And I'm feeling* … **'BANG BANG'** … *Glad All Over'* – I'm not sure what the more senior citizens thought of it but there was a good deal of muttering and shaking of heads.

***

In November, the Chronicle carries news of the club's accounts showing a loss to 31st May 1965 of £2,993 (£2,361 the previous year) – salaries rose from £32,000 to £36,000 but donations were down from about £29,000 to £22,000. Our saving grace is that we have fixed assets of almost £85,000 (mainly the houses) to shore us up with John Coward's inevitable support too. The problem highlighted by Bernard Webber is two-fold – what if we lose the support of John Coward and, also, if we have to start selling off the fixed assets of the houses? The fragility of lower league and non-league clubs is highlighted by reports in the National Press that Bradford City at the bottom of Division Four have an overdraft in excess of £15,000 AND are losing £300 a week. We look in great shape compared with that (although there is an unsubstantiated counter-claim that our overdraft has suddenly risen to over £17,000) and they are also competing with Bradford Park Avenue in the same city, probably an unsustainable situation. It is their places in the League we would ultimately like to fill.

We have one valuable potential source of funds for the future. The initiative of the summer trials has unearthed some excellent local talent and, with Peter Collins and Russell Rosling the stand out performers in the Youth team, we potentially have assets available later to sell on to league clubs. We already have Bryan King being watched by many league clubs and he is another we can cash in on.

I know Len Menhinick is proud to have 'unearthed' Peter through the trials. I played against Peter at primary school level and it was plain then for all to see what a talent he could become. Len tells me Peter will become the club's first 'apprentice' under the new FA guidance and is sure Collins will make it to the top bringing City its substantial cash windfall.

***

Whilst our home attendances started off averaging over 3,000 they have fallen away as winter arrives. The crowds have been getting on the players' backs, serving no purpose, and disgruntled fans have been writing to the local papers in droves with all sorts of criticism. Only 1,500 or so attended one recent Monday night league game against Tonbridge as if confirming the disappointment and frustration.

With Houghton injured and Butcher out of form we are desperate to find a centre forward. George Duncan has been disappointing on the wing and Roy Summersby something of a failure although he had an excellent game against Colchester in our Essex Professional Cup game at Layer Road at the end of October when we lost 2-1 after extra time. This game did at least show glimpses of what our team could achieve and even Bernard Webber, a Colchester man, praised us highly saying we went down 'with all flags flying' with our Barnsley trio of Smith, Smillie and Gillott outstanding.

As I thought he would be John Docherty is a no-nonsense hard tackling leader on the pitch, sometimes over-zealous but never one to shirk a challenge.

Suddenly there is a wave of interest in the town as it is reported that centre forward Bobby Smith, the former Spurs and England international, who two years ago starred for England in the FA centenary match against the Rest of the World, may be coming to City. He is now at Brighton and wants a move – they want £3,000 and apparently we are prepared to meet this fee. However, we disappointingly lose out to Hastings United who opt, as we had done with Mason et al, not to pay the fee and are, as a result, able to offer Smith very generous wages. There's no doubt that players are becoming more mercenary than in the past and this hints at a worrying trend, although as Smith edges towards retirement you can understand why he would want to cash in before it's too late. City fans are upset and write in to the Chronicle to express their views, largely that the club has no ambition and making the point that increased crowd numbers would have covered the extra outlay. I'm not so sure; we have ploughed that particular furrow before with Mason and it was a financial failure.

Bernard Webber writes at length in the Chronicle about the standard of football in the Southern League believing it to be falling whilst that in the Third and Fourth Divisions is on the rise. Martin Rogers on the other hand is in more positive mood suggesting no one should write off the City; yes City are not yet setting the League alight but once Houghton returns he believes we can expect greater things from this team – I really do hope Martin's right.

In his weekly column Martin has been critical of the fans who continue to voice their opinions in his paper or verbally at the players, management and directors at home matches. When we played Wimbledon in the Floodlit League on November 1st there was a mass supporter walk out near the end of the game – or that at least was how some saw it – despite City winning 3-1. The comments made vary from … what a load of rubbish it was, to why were so many reserves drafted in to play and that is not what we pay full price for, to … everyone had to leave to catch their buses as the services now provided by Eastern National are abysmal after nine in the evening! Some say a thousand left early but Roy Gisby on his hospital radio commentary called it only a 'small minority'.

With that win City top the floodlit league, so all is not as bad as some make out. In fact, in mid-November we have an astonishing 7-1 win over Kings Lynn in the Southern League Cup with Bud Houghton scoring FIVE, to equal a club record, and in the next round in early December we beat Margate 6-0 with a Butcher hat-trick.

The Reserves are faring well but their gates are falling. On a brighter note, the five home Mercia Youth team matches have been watched by close on 200 at each game. When the boys play Ipswich Town, Brian 'Tich' Honeywood is in their team yet he is still registered with us and John Coward has to come to an agreement with his Ipswich counterpart, instead of reporting them to the League. We are not told what this arrangement might have been but I suspect it might involve handing over of some cash.

Bernard Webber suddenly changes his tune and writes that 'City are beginning to look a goodish bet for Southern League honours' – but perhaps he would have had second thoughts if he'd watched the away defeat at Hereford at the end of November when we went down 5-2 to John Charles's team where the game ended in a near riot! When we met for a drink recently Len Menhinick passed on Ollie Hopkins' version of events:

'Bud Houghton was caught in the face with a nasty swinging arm from Hereford centre half, Ray Daniel, the former Sunderland and Wales player. He and I had a few words and I threatened to get even. Unseen by the referee there was, let's say, a little confrontation between us; Daniel ended up on the ground. He got up and swung a punch and was seen by the referee who sent him off. The crowd had seen my involvement and were incensed with the referee, Mr Mason. At the end of the game their fans swarmed onto the pitch gunning for Mr Mason and me. Lou Costello stood firm beside me as I was threatened. The worse offender was a Hereford fan – a middle aged gentleman wearing a long mac and carrying a stick – he came towards me through the throng of their fans. Lou took the law into his hands and, how can

I say, stopped the man in his tracks! There was a police inquest after the game but it was decided Lou was only defending both of us. It turns out the Hereford man was an off duty Police Inspector. We got away from the ground safely – eventually.'

In mid-December we play a Friday night game against old rivals Guildford City. In the past playing games on a Friday was seriously considered so we could attract those working or playing (like me) on Saturday afternoons. In one aspect the switch works in that we win 8-0! However, the gate, a disappointing 2,066, is only a little higher than the last home Saturday game. It's a shame this latest idea is not as attractive to the fans as the club might have hoped, but a few more 8-0s might help!

George Duncan and Stewart Imlach are now in top form on the wings and Summersby has *'eased into top gear at a time when he was widely written off as a flop'* – Robin Gladwin has been playing at left back since the beginning of October and despite not securing a regular first team place in the past is being coveted by several clubs, most particularly Norwich City.

As we arrive at the end of 1965 we are 10th in the League with seventeen points from sixteen games with Wimbledon top with twenty-one points but from seventeen games, so it's quite close.

CHELMSFORD CITY BOARD OF DIRECTORS

Chelmsford & Essex Weekly News Picture

Standing: H. A. Phillp, Esq., F. R. Kearsley, Esq., G. S. Last, Esq., H. D. Benge, Esq., L. G. Menhinick (*Secretary*).
Seated: S. W. Harrington, Esq., J. W. Coward, Esq., (*Chairman*), F. J. Langton, Esq., (*Vice-Chairman*).

The Directors pictured in the programme for the match against Wimbledon in September 1965. They all look happy enough but splits and divisions were already beginning to pull the club apart

The club is shaken to its roots on the very last day of the year when it's announced that Messrs Benge, Kearsley and Last have been asked to resign from the Board. Clearly the rumours of unrest and disagreement circulating for the past month or so are true.

John Coward says, '*It is in the best interests and the smooth running of the club*', but Mr Kearsley retaliates by questioning the club's financial state and Mr Coward has responded with '*this is never better*'. These are worrying times for the club and clearly all is not right. Kearsley might have a point as we know expenditure is exceeding income and perhaps it's only those club houses that are shoring up the club, achieved perhaps with the houses being used as collateral for bank loans, something many Football League clubs use to add to their funds or cover the shortfall in their Income and Expenditure account. Could John Coward with all his positivity and bluster be leading us down the path to possible ruin? Will he be bringing in his own men to the Board allowing him to maintain his apparent dictatorial style? Does this dramatic sacking of these directors hint at desperation? Len Menhinick who knows John Coward better than anyone sees a man under great stress whose health is not what it should be. These are worrying times.

***

This news follows defeat at Nuneaton over Christmas on a pitch so dangerous from frost that Medlock ends up in hospital with cuts and bruises, Imlach damages ligaments, Eades breaks a bone in his wrist and Duncan has a thigh injury. City management are upset with the referee in allowing the game to go ahead and are to take up the matter with the League.

As we slip into the New Year with the World Cup in England only months away, we secure a draw at Margate then beat Cambridge United away in the Floodlit League. This signals Robin Gladwin's last game as he is transferred to Norwich for £3,500 with another £1,000 due after twelve first team appearances. Perhaps it was with the knowledge of this money coming that John Coward could confidently say our financial situation was '*never better*'! I find the Gladwin situation baffling. He has been with us some time but has never really made it in the First Team and no City manager appeared to rate him. I know Len Menhinick has always considered him a special talent, but at left back – more of an overlapping full back, a role that Alf Ramsey talks of requiring from his full backs, normally Cohen and Wilson. In Gladwin's case perhaps the presence and excellence of Peter Gillott prevented managers from opting for Gladwin at number three. One thing it does go to show is how fine the margin currently is between playing in the Southern League and at the top level.

In our next match Bobby Mason returns to The Stadium with Poole Town adding a few hundred to the crowd and he takes us apart, showing us just what he can do and what we might have been missing. This is typical Mason – on his day he can show the real quality of a top player but, as ever with Bobby, he is great when he raises his game and really wants it, but, too often when with us he seemed to be going through the motions.

With Houghton back scoring goals along with Butcher and Summersby, we secure a great win at Yeovil at the end of January having had a three-week break due to the weather. In early February we beat Barnet over two legs for a place in the League Cup Semi Final where we are due to play Guildford – the team we recently blitzed 8-0.

The next bombshell, although some saw it coming, is that Crystal Palace want Stewart Imlach as player coach and at 34 I cannot see us preventing him from missing out on this chance.

Indeed he leaves but what service he has given us. He had doubters at first but won them over and he is quite a character off the field too. So much is happening in and around the club it is difficult to keep up! The latest is that Doug Rollings, Chelmsford lad made good in the building trade and aged only 27, has joined the Board. His younger brother Martin has been playing for the Youth team and looks a promising centre forward. Doug hopefully will bring some young mindedness to a Board traditionally made up of old men! He joins newish appointee, Claude Seymour, another local man who farms at Little Waltham. Claude is married to my father's cousin and the two couples were close friends before children came along. Claude was a massive Pools winner a few years back which helped set him up financially.

As if all this change was not enough Peter Harburn is officially given the Manager's job after ten months acting in a caretaker role, having won the confidence of the professional staff some of whom were apparently sceptical at first. Mr Coward is quoted in the Chronicle: *'We felt Peter had been doing a good job over the last few months. He's got the club and the players at heart … we have complete faith in his integrity, honesty and ability to tackle the job'*. A ringing endorsement indeed!

As Harburn is promoted Len Menhinick leaves. This was expected as Len had always said his other business interests would eventually need his full attention, but he will become a Director and maintain his connection with the club. John Coward is effusive with his praise for Len on how he has truly placed the club on a professional footing in all areas and also schooled Len King to take over.

John Coward pronounces in the Chronicle that *'Everyone wants to set City alight as of years gone; we have the team to win the League and we can look forward to the rest of the season with the utmost confidence'*. He also scotched rumours that the Reserves would be dispensed with next season, but confirmed the club intend to play more Friday night matches next season following the Guildford experiment: a change that suits me and, no doubt, many others.

This is a good time to look at Mr Coward's position. He clearly remains extremely positive about our chances of making the Football League. The ban set us back but even before that the votes were negligible and it seems we have little support from the league clubs, as do most other non-league clubs. The taking of 'dead man's shoes' would seem the only chance the non-leaguers will get, as Oxford did as Southern League champions when Accrington Stanley folded. United have maintained an admirable consistency in the league having been promoted from Division Four at the end of last season and were the first Fourth Division club to reach the sixth round of the FA Cup in the season before that.

With the removal of the maximum wage smaller league clubs have struggled to maintain full time football and many are on the brink of collapse, as with the two Bradford teams. The Southern League is very competitive and difficult to win, but a club must do so to stand any chance of Football League status. Southern League champions just have to hope that their success coincides with a League club folding.

Mr Coward's 'vision' is clearly on hold following our ban but this will soon end and winning our league will again take on greater significance.

My father has heard that the land between The Stadium and the Chelmsford cricket ground is to be sold for building development, probably housing. Developers are likely to offer inflated prices due to the returns they can make from the burgeoning demand for houses and the French family, who still own the land, will surely take the best offer. A few years back the club might have been able to compete when funds were plentiful, but now that time has passed and with it Mr Coward's vision of a sports centre, hotel and the extended major stadium.

I fear for my club. Diminishing crowds, less funds coming from the Supporters' Club and now an uncertainty over how much financial support Mr Coward can continue to provide leaving the club perilously placed for the future. Even if League status is achieved there would not be a significant improvement to our income and this will filter in as seasons pass, but we would have to pay higher wages, much greater travel costs and so on from day one. The Chronicle suggests we need liquid assets of about £30,000 to £40,000 to deal with this greater expenditure in the first season or so in this higher division, funds we do not have unless we sell off fixed assets such as a half of our club houses. Yet these houses have been used to attract top players with Ollie Hopkins and Peter Harburn, to name but two, preferring us to League clubs because of the availability of a house into which they can settle their young families.

Much of this remains speculation so let's win our league and see where it takes us – knocking at the League door long enough will see it open eventually. But for whom? At the end of February Halifax Town are reported to be in dire financial straits and may not last the season, so a case of 'dead man's shoes' might rear its head again. However, it would only need one League club to object to our application for us to fail – at least until the five year period comes to an end next year.

***

What a three months we have had up to the end of March! Since Bobby Mason's Poole Town thrashed us on January 6th we have played twelve league games and won seven and drawn five with our only defeats during this period coming in the Floodlit League where we have fielded weaker teams. The Houghton/Butcher striking partnership has at last clicked. Terry Eades has been a tower of strength at centre half with Ollie Hopkins switching to right back in place of Costello. The only blot in this terrific run was an unfathomable loss away to Guildford in the League Cup semi-final by 3-0 – Guildford, the same team we beat 8-0 two months or so earlier. I don't think I'll ever understand the game of football!

One great moment for the town is when former City player Charlie Hurst proudly watches son, Geoff, brought up in Chelmsford and an old boy of Kings Road and then Rainsford School, make his debut for England at Wembley in February in the 1-0 win over West Germany. I have followed Geoff's career with interest both as a cricketer for Chelmsford and Essex as well as a professional footballer. He has been transformed by Ron Greenwood at West Ham into a free scoring centre forward from an average midfield player and is vying for a place in the England World Cup squad, but is up against Roger Hunt, Joe Baker and Jimmy Greaves amongst others for the honour – let's hope he makes it.

We can look forward to another local derby next season when Brentwood, with their newly installed lights, will join the Floodlit League. This should boost the crowd numbers especially as Brentwood have a sprinkling of ex-City players.

To temper all this good news there is always something to bring us back to reality. At a recent game a section of the crowd in the main stand, where you would think they should know better, directed unfair, abusive criticism towards Tony Butcher. We all know poor old Tony has had to put up with this through most of his time at the club, but on this occasion he snapped and ended up trading 'pleasantries' with a small number there. It was an extremely unedifying incident and does beg the question why some of these fans simply attend matches to moan instead of getting behind their team and cheering them on.

As if to illustrate this point and despite us having been on a largely unbeaten run, a 'supporter' writes to the Chronicle complaining about:

'… suffering yet another 90 minutes of unadulterated rubbish served up by the current team …. the City set-up has taken a giant step – BACKWARDS!'

Yes it's true. Some of the draws have been rather boring against moderate opposition but that's the way football is at times. After the 3-0 debacle at Guildford Harburn, apparently, lashed into the team after the game and there was a lengthy, closed door post-mortem with plenty of frank talking with no punches pulled. Good for them because the players know they must raise their game once more.

Martin Rogers is concerned Harburn is driving himself towards a nervous breakdown in his quest to replace the departed Imlach and Gladwin, especially now he has lost Bobby Smith for the season to a cartilage problem. We have signed McQuade from Millwall and 18 year old Billy Stack from Palace to fill Imlach's considerable boots and both look talented.

It seems youth is the policy when Peter Leggett (22) and David Kydd (20) arrive as a package from Brighton with Leggett a winger and Kydd, a centre forward. Kydd says: *'The City set up is as good as any in the Football League … and the only club with ambition outside of it'.* Quite something for a 20 year old to say and both players look promising. He and Leggett share a bachelor flat and I have already seen them out on the town enjoying themselves, let's hope their typical 60s lifestyle does not let them down. Kydd shows aggression on the pitch which might get him into trouble with the referees whereas Leggett skips past full backs like a modern day Stanley Matthews and looks capable of taking on the mantle of that former crowd pleaser and favourite, Tony Nicholas.

As we enter the final lap of the season and despite some adverse comments, the team is still handily placed only one point behind the leaders with 3 points covering seven clubs. After the Guildford debacle we beat them away in the League and go on a good run including a 1-0 win at old foe Romford with Kydd endearing himself to the fans with the only goal. Despite a heavy defeat at Dartford we remain second in the league. A 0-0 draw with title aspirants Worcester City is quite the worst game I have ever seen at the City and some of the crowd in the main stand threw their cushions onto the pitch at the end of the match. Good job we're not in the relegation zone! One good thing about this league is that we get to see some older, great players now in the last phase of their careers. Worcester paraded Peter McParland, the former Aston Villa player and Irish international. He was well shackled in this game by the impressive Terry Eades but supporters will recall nine years ago when McParland scored both Villa goals in their 2-1 win in the FA Cup final against the pre-Munich Manchester United. McParland was both hero and villain on the day having clattered into United keeper Wood and breaking Wood's cheekbone. He was reminded of that fact several times by our crowd.

A few days later I take the opportunity of attending the first 'Meet the Officials meeting' – an odd title – but it is most successful. Outgoing Secretary Len Menhinick hosts the meeting in the Social Club and is joined by Mr Coward and Peter Harburn. The audience, as is often the case with such things, is quite hostile to begin with, but by the end of the evening the honesty and forthrightness of the three hosts wins everyone over.

Mr Coward is asked about his stadium dream and what is holding up the development. He explains that the delay is due to legal hold ups, but work on the new road and car park area should begin shortly.

Harburn, on the other hand, vigorously denies there is any Board influence in selecting the team; whilst he might seek opinions, he absolutely makes all selections.

It is planned to have another such meeting later in the year. To involve supporters like this does help with providing a more detailed knowledge of what is happening at their club direct from the horse's mouth, as it were, and not via rumour or newspaper speculation.

Back on the pitch we secure five points out of six over Easter, with over 6,000 in the ground to see the draw against Romford thanks to a late Lou Costello penalty. The title is still anyone's but we do not help our cause by losing at close rivals Cambridge United but then beat league leaders, Hereford, 1-0 with a typical Tony Butcher goal. Even better is a 1-0 win at Weymouth who are favourites for the title due to the fact they still have so many games to play, most of them at home. The league positions are as follows before the last game for us on 30th April:

City 52 points from 41 games
Hereford 50 from 38
Weymouth 47 from 36

The retained list is produced with old stalwarts Peter Gillott and Ron Smillie released along with Roy Summersby, Dave Pye and George Rosling. John Docherty is to become player-coach next season but the more surprising news is the possible return of Bobby Mason on a match by match, part-time contract basis, as he has a good job down in Dorset.

Now don't get me wrong Bobby was, still is even, a terrific footballer and he must love City because to want to come all that way to play for us without a permanent deal seems to say so. He is very popular with the fans but to me he is all froth and no substance. I agree he is a delight to watch at times and seems to turn it on much more in home games but perhaps does not dig in and give his all on a cold winter's night in deepest Dartford! Amusingly, one player is said to have remarked recently that Bobby always has the cleanest shorts of any player on the pitch in any game!

With the excitement of this year's World Cup building and a good chance our local boy, Geoff Hurst, will be in the England squad, we all flock to New Writtle Street to see him play for City in the Peter Harburn testimonial match against Cambridge United. Over 3,500 come along, probably the largest testimonial crowd we have ever had. Geoff scores in a 4-3 win but what about this team in City colours?

Owen Medlock;
Lou Costello; Ollie Hopkins; Derek Tiffin; Bobby Moore (West Ham and England captain!);
Ronnie Boyce (West Ham); Peter Brabrook (West Ham and England);
Stuart Imlach; Geoff Hurst (West Ham and England); Jimmy Leadbetter (ex-Ipswich); Peter Harburn.

It was marvellous entertainment and indicative of how high a regard Harburn is held in football circles, especially with the two current England men released by Mr Ramsey to play for him. As well as some extra cash from this testimonial Harburn is rewarded with a new contract.

For the second time in three years we finish runners up – not at all bad but still fans have moaned all season. To be fair we have not played vibrant attacking football and it has been worse than dour to watch some of the narrow victories, mostly 1-0 with some awfully boring 0-0s too.

There is a controversial end to the season with Weymouth pipping us for the title. They had so many home games postponed over the winter that after we'd finished our games they had FIVE home games to play against teams who already know their fate with nothing to play for and often with players not retained for next season. Not a satisfactory state of affairs.

More controversy in the Floodlit League play off final in May with City winning 2-1 but, having been 3-1 down after the first leg, we lose 4-3 on aggregate. There was a fight between players in the tunnel as they came off the pitch with other club officials allegedly also involved. A Cambridge City player was knocked out cold by David Kydd (confirming my view about him). Cambridge are so upset they refuse to receive the trophy or stay for the eats and drinks and, instead, go to the Bird in Hand pub across from the ground to celebrate. It remains to be seen if action will be taken against Kydd by the authorities.

So what of the 1965/66 season? Second in this league is no mean achievement after a sketchy start with our Achilles' heel of not winning enough away from home haunting us once again. There was no FA Cup run having lost to Romford with this shortly followed by the disappointment at Guildford in the Southern League Cup. There has been none of the promised development of the 'Coward Empire'; whether this really is due to legal red tape remains to be seen. There are rumours circulating that Mr Coward is unwell and that none of his 'vision' will ever come to fruition.

On the playing side Bud Houghton is the league's leading goalscorer with 22 and Butcher his closest rival with 19. John Docherty has been Mr Consistency playing in 68 of our 69 games, quite something.

For me, it is the style of play that has been disappointing and the dwindling mid-season crowds voted with their feet to show their disappointment and disapproval. With no actual manager for a good part of the season it was difficult for Peter Harburn to operate effectively as simply the coach, knowing that someone might be appointed above him at any time. There are some strong, forthright characters in the City dressing room with the likes of Gillott, Hopkins and Docherty and this would have made Harburn's coach-only role really difficult. Harburn has publicly stated that he wants us to play adventurously next season and we certainly did play much better football once he was officially made manager, thus ensuring a positive end to the season. Harburn has also said that too many of our players have been shackled by teams playing defensively at New Writtle Street with their sole aim to secure a point but he is looking for a more expansive, attacking game using wingers next season.

***

There has been a disturbing trend in football this season with discipline on and off the field leaving much to be desired. We have had our own problems with the Kydd incident and the barracking of Butcher from the 'posh seats' and perhaps this is all down to the way society is changing so rapidly: time will tell.

From a financial standpoint we shall have to wait until the autumn to find out how the season has gone but Robin Gladwin's money from Norwich might balance the books and there are still the valuable fixed assets of the club houses.

At the Football League AGM some League clubs do invoke the ruling to veto our application to the Football League. However, the good news is we will be free from this restriction next season when the five year ruling is removed. However, with Rochdale receiving 36 votes (the lowest of those current League teams applying for re-election) and the highest number of votes for a non-league team being Cambridge United and Wigan Athletic with a mere 5 votes, it does not look like there is any chance of a non-league team getting promoted under the current set up, described by Bernard Webber 'as an old boys' club voting for their own'. Peter Gillott has been quoted as saying that many clubs vote for the status quo because next season it might be them in the bottom four and they will want to count on the votes of the fellow League members they voted for previously!

What of our other valuable assets at the club? Peter Collins is most certainly a star in the making and with goalkeeper Bryan King given a few Floodlit League games at the end of the season also looking as though he is destined for greater things, our future looks rosy and both could be big money sales. Ultimately, it comes down to managing expenditure but most importantly having the team and the characters to ignite the fans plus adding to that a good FA Cup run.

What saddens me is that in my ten years of supporting this great club, we have been promised much; we have expected much; yet, we have not achieved very much at all. I fear that dream we had when the new decade started of John Coward leading us to the Promised Land, is slowly fading along with local interest in the fortunes of City. There has been a surge in the numbers of teams competing in local amateur football with the Essex Olympian League, Mid-Essex League and the Chelmsford Combination full to capacity with hundreds of potential fans lost to park football. Social change has had its effect too as the 1960s seem to be changing the world as we once knew it. It was as if the great freeze in early 1963 switched off the old Britain and when, two months later, it started up again everything was so different. Perhaps our golden era is on the wane but for me and most other die-hard fans, we will continue to live our claret dream.

There we have it … another 'what might have been season' – no FA Cup run (again!); a poor start but good finish; tantrums in the boardroom but stability on the pitch and a promising looking team which augurs well for next season – I can't wait but, for now, 'bring on the World Cup' – the fever is building – good luck Geoff, we hope you make the team.

9

THE COWARD EMPIRE STARTS TO CRUMBLE

Imagine our Director viewing things a few years on from when he wrote of the hope and the excitement at the beginning of the Coward era – he did warn us of some pitfalls ahead but even he could not have envisaged how little of John Coward's 'Claret Dream' would actually be realised. The crowds have gone, the star players have by and large been a disappointment and there seems very little to look forward to now, but you never know – football is a funny old game! Here our director reviews the 1966/67 season:

From the Directors' viewpoint in this World Cup summer, I can see a season ahead of consolidation. Peter Harburn is a safe pair of hands in charge of the team. Lovely fellow but I do wonder if he has everything the job here requires. He's no Ferrier or Frith that is for sure, but he's done his coaching courses and, but for injury, could still be playing despite being in his mid-thirties. The players seem to like him and his pre-season training is well thought out and well received.

During the close season we enjoyed an uproarious evening out at the Civic Centre when John Coward pushed the boat out with a dinner for players, directors, the Press and local dignitaries plus their wives and girlfriends. In his speech he says, *'City should win everything hands down after coming so close last year'*. Ever the optimist and generous man I fear for John. I can see a change in him – he looks strained and has aged considerably in the past five years, yet is still shy of sixty. What he has done for this club is little short of remarkable. He has kept us afloat and given the public such excitement, but their interest has waned and John is disappointed. The plans for the stadium were only sustainable if we could get League football and with our ban that pipedream has gone – at least for now.

There was a lovely quote from Len Menhinick at the dinner when we presented him with a gold watch to mark his time as Club Secretary: *'For once, I am lost for words'* – he has been John's right hand man and, along with Len King, has made us the most professionally run club outside of the top two divisions in English football.

This time of year always gives us time for reflection. Looking closely at the club we now have Ken Orrin, Claude Seymour and Doug Rollings on the Board – all men from the town willing to help move the club forward, but we still need success on the field to rekindle our Football League ambitions when our ban comes to an end. Since John took over it has always been thus and we all say the same thing every year – the title and a good cup run. However, I just wonder if the fans do actually feel the same. Are they that worried about us getting into the League? Yes, they want success and to win the Southern League but is acceptance at the high table of English football that important to them? Have they long thought John's ambition is simply a flight of fancy? Perhaps the fans are the ones with their feet firmly planted on the ground and, after all, is it that important to have matches against Carlisle, Darlington and such like, teams from the other end of the country, when we can have a host of local derbies in the Southern League? I do just wonder if John and the Board are the deluded ones!

Still I'm sure every fan would like to see us in the Fourth Division, but it might just not remain the be all and end all for them. Anyway, I have to say that our finances are a problem. Len Menhinick, now our Financial Director, sees a falling away of our income stream from the Supporters' Club. They have been magnificent over many years and have kept us out of the red for such a long time, but they could never sustain this forever. Len's development of the Social Club has been a help plus the Football Pool continues to raise funds. However, declining revenue through the turnstiles and escalating costs make small clubs extremely vulnerable and we have not become an exception.

***

Training is underway and the start of the season is eagerly awaited now that August is here. This summer of OUR World Cup has almost come and gone but what a time it has been. The pulsating match last Saturday at Wembley brought to an end a July full of excitement and euphoria which slowly spread across the country, as almost everyone became caught up in the tension of the last week as England's dream crept towards reality.

An indifferent start to the tournament for England left us stuttering into the knockout phase of the competition to face Argentina, a team of sulking menace whose ill-disciplined performance culminating in Rattin's sending off was to prove the catalyst for England as our own Geoff Hurst stepped up to the plate. His decisive, incisive header was the only goal of this quarter final. For a while that afternoon it looked like little North Korea might be our unlikely semi-final opponents until Eusebio almost single handedly turned round a 3-0 deficit into a 5-3 victory and so Portugal it was in the way of our first World Cup final. What a match this was with our Geoff becoming provider for Charlton's goals to send us into the final to play old adversaries West Germany.

That match will become the stuff of legend. Unbearable tension around the country, empty shops, all sport cancelled for the day, new TV sets flying off the shelves and one hundred thousand at the match itself. We're behind, we're ahead, we've won it surely – only seconds left – that was never a foul ref! Free kick; the ball hits a hand, no it doesn't they've scored – there's a collective slump into armchairs as England restart the game only to hear the final whistle. Extra time. Nerves are on edge, we've won it once lets win it again was what Alf told the players as they sat distraught on the pitch at the thought they'd given it away. We're on top – Alan Ball skips down the wing, what energy, he crosses, Geoff brings it down and turns, shoots, underside of the bar and in. Roger Hunt turns away when he could have put it in – he knew it was over the line. No! No! The ref says 'No' – wait a second he's going to the Russian linesman – he's shaking his head at the German players – does that mean no it was in or no it wasn't. The Russian nods his mane of grey hair and points to the centre spot, the referee concurs but the Germans are beside themselves – *'you shouldn't even be in extra time'* I shout at the TV, at the same time jumping up and hitting my head on the lampshade hanging from the ceiling.

Our Geoff scoring the winner that's dream time but, wait, there's still the whole of the second half of extra time to go. The Germans look a spent force as Bobby Moore, serene as ever, calmly chests the ball down inside his own penalty area. We're in stoppage time – *'kick it in the stands'* I shout, but Moore doesn't play football that way and lifts the ball down the inside left channel to our Geoff, socks rolled down, he sets off, the ball bobbles on the turf cut up due to the earlier rain. There's some chap from the crowd on the other side of the pitch who thought the ref had blown from time – he's running towards Alan Ball. Geoff shoots high into the net. Millions of people jump two feet in the air with a collective *'Goalll!'* Someone next to me says, *'I have never seen such a great goal as that!'* And he was right. A hat trick for Geoff and it's over, we've done it and it's all down to our own local son, Geoff Hurst (well, almost!). How proud we are of him and to think I was keen to bring him to New Writtle Street a few years back when it looked likely he might not make it at West Ham! I'm pleased for his father, Charlie, who is now very much a Chelmsford man and, of course, an ex-City player. Well done, Geoff, let's hope the town recognises what you have done and that this great victory for English football will inspire the current generation and the next to lift this country's football to a new level and pull players and fans into the sport. It leaves us all desperate for OUR season to start in a couple of weeks' time when we expect fans to flock to games buoyed by this euphoria.

***

To say I'm disappointed with Harburn's new signings is something of an understatement. Of course, apart from John, we on the Board have little input into such things and we do have to accept that Harburn doesn't have the contacts of a Ferrier or a Frith. The new players are young apart from the returning Bobby Mason travelling up from his home in Dorset. He will remain living down there and train with Poole and Bournemouth. It does say something about our club when he is prepared to do all that travelling and might not even get a place in the first team. Winger John Dryden is a prospect but released by West Ham; only eighteen he is well thought of by Ron Greenwood (but not well enough to keep him!) and like the equally young Billy Hinton, a full back, will provide young legs in the team.

None of these three enthuse me at all but I do like the look of Peter Shreeves, a Wales under 23 international. He met Harburn on an FA coaching course in 1964 and joined from Reading last season but was soon injured. Harburn intends to drop him back a little to play a deeper midfield role – a wing half as against an inside forward.

We have attractive friendlies against Cardiff City where we get hammered 5-2 and then are unlucky to lose 4-3 to Doncaster Rovers in an exciting game. However, we do beat Southend and Colchester in behind closed-door practice matches. Dryden and Hinton look good but I hear that young Malcolm Pannell is putting his studies before a football career and returning as an amateur at Crittall Athletic. How disappointing this is for the football world, as this lad could have gone all the way in the game.

Harburn has been employing a 4-2-4 system with player-coach, John Docherty, acting as sweeper; a continental approach but not dissimilar to Bobby Moore playing a little off Jack Charlton for England. However, Peter then informs me he has told the players 'to go out and entertain and play like we always used to' and by that he means 2-3-5 but, and a big but, the five forwards have to defend when the occasion demands.

Across the country attendances fail to show that the World Cup win has created a wave of new fans, or returning old ones, and this has to be disappointing. I join John Coward at a Fan's Forum in the Social Club. He surprises many supporters there when he announces that: 'If our gates do not improve Chelmsford City cannot carry on as a full time club with 23 players'. Following this bombshell there is embarrassment all round when a member of the audience asks John to confirm the club is £30,000 in the red and presumably this is why the club wants 40,000 shares sold to raise £10,000? John denies it but it is pointed out that Len Menhinick issued this information recently to the local press. Cue embarrassment all round but John blusters his way through and the fans let him off the hook (All I can say is that the finances are not where we would like them to be). John is asked about the falling gates and believes this is due to, '… *a changing world where some wives have something to say, with cars and television and other attractions playing their part*'.

John is not his usual self when we chat back in the office after this fan's meeting. For the first time I see him losing his grip. That edge to him has gone and he looks pale and drawn, even ill. I decide not to tackle him on the delicate matter of his health but it looks to me that it is getting too much for him. He has some doubts about Harburn and is concerned he made the wrong choice. He's lost his right hand man in Len Menhinick and, although John would never admit it, I believe he can see his vision of where he wants this club to be as something perhaps even beyond his reach. For the first time in his life Chelmsford City FC could represent his one failure after all that success with his other businesses.

***

Once the season starts we are mediocre. There seems no spark. We draw too many games and the fans show their disappointment by booing off the team at one home match. John Coward is edgy and Harburn is feeling the strain. The new recruits don't secure a regular first team spot, including Mason. The Reserves look strong with Houghton and Shreeves having run outs after their injuries and supported by Hopkins, Dryden, Hinton, Gillott, Thurgood and so on: an excellent blend with some local youngsters in Martin Rollings and Peter Collins showing admirable promise.

The directors and most of the supporters are appalled by the actions of the players during a Floodlit League game with Romford. There was fighting on the pitch and retribution being taken by both sets of players throughout the game – a game the referee had so much difficulty in controlling. Harburn apologised on behalf of the team to John Coward afterwards in the bar.

John is not happy with the way things are going on and off the pitch and has called a board meeting at the Club for next Sunday morning.

After much discussion and deliberation, we decide to let Harburn go. John considers Peter is not the right man – perhaps too inexperienced for a club of this size. John wishes the parting of the ways to be by the traditional *'mutual consent'*. It seems likely we will re-appoint Harry Ferrier who has been helping out for the club in a non-official capacity with some fund-raising. I suspect Harry is still in debt to John from his gambling and perhaps this is why John has been so forceful in persuading us Harry is the man for a second time. One thing I am sure about is that, if he does return, it will be a fillip to the fans and the club as a whole.

John meets with Harburn alone. John, we find out days later, believes it has been agreed with Peter that he departs. But Peter contradicts this by saying that as he had to leave the meeting for a family commitment, he told John he would let him know the next day if he was agreeable to depart with a payoff.

The local press are immediately told Harburn has left but on the following Friday the Essex Chronicle publishes the following from Peter.

I think in fairness to the public of Chelmsford and myself that I would like to make it clear that I did not resign as manager of Chelmsford City FC. Unknown to me a board meeting was arranged for the Sunday morning, September 17th. On my arrival at the ground to see the injured players I was informed my presence was required in the boardroom. It didn't need a 'fortune teller' to guess what they wanted of me. I said if it would help save their faces I would consider resigning. I was told if I did resign I could stay on as trainer-coach if I wanted to as the Board felt I was such a good club man.

I told the chairman that I had some family business to attend to and that I would have to rush off and see to it, but I would let the chairman know of my decision whether or not to resign as manager and also my decision regarding the position of trainer-coach if I gave up the managership.

Mr Coward said that the board thought that perhaps an older man would be more suited to my job as manager and said the man they had in mind was Mr Ferrier. I made no reply, but left the meeting to attend my family business.

In the morning I told the Chairman my decision was to stay on as manager. I was then informed I had already resigned and that Mr Ferrier was the new manager apparently appointed some ten minutes after I had left the board meeting on the Sunday. There is so much more I could tell, but it would take far too long.

The matter is now being dealt with by my solicitor, so I will leave it in his capable hands. I will leave the public of Chelmsford to draw their own conclusions. I have worked tremendously hard for the club as indeed many of you have. I have always been a fighter that is why I am going to fight for my rights. All I want is what I am rightfully due. No more, no less.

PETER HARBURN

Peter Harburn, left with unique sideburns, Peter Gillott centre with Terry Eades, right, enjoy an after match drink in the Social Club

How unfortunate this all is. I was convinced from the board meeting that John had agreed with Peter that he was no longer manager based on the results and that we need an older man. Perhaps Peter feels upset that Harry was literally waiting in the wings. This is down to John, as is his right as Chairman, and he did clear it with us. However, only he and Peter discussed these finer points so it will be one word against another and Peter may well seek compensation. The note in the newspaper has the hand of his solicitor in it, so perhaps we are in for a protracted court battle.

***

At the club's AGM only about thirty supporters attend and is a further indication that interest in the club, so great in the early 60s, is now waning at an alarming rate. We made an £11,000 loss last year. The donations from the Supporters' Club are down and it was their contribution that has prevented losses in previous years. Thankfully our fixed assets of almost £80,000, namely the club houses, still give us a solid base to work from but I can see these having to be sold off if we continue to post losses each year.

Perhaps Ferrier's new broom and style of play will bring back the fans. He hopes to get the gates back to above four thousand but I have to say this is wishful thinking. John Coward remains bullish but I can see he is worried and perhaps my fears are correct in that the wonderful 'empire' he created is showing signs of crumbling.

Ferrier's first act is to transfer list Hinton, David Kydd, Dryden, Day and Lovell. Quite a clear out given that some of these were only signed in the summer. There is no immediate interest in any of them from other clubs.

The Reserves have a strong team out against Spurs 'A' but are hammered 8-1 and I hear that some of the players did not appear that interested and were not giving their all. Ferrier is annoyed when he hears and promises action if it continues.

Suddenly an event happens that is so shattering it defies belief. Some years back the Munich air disaster shook not only football but the world as a whole when so many young footballers from Manchester and a good number of journalists and club officials perished. However, the 21st of October 1966 will live with us forever when all those schoolchildren, some of their teachers and fellow villagers from Aberfan in Wales are wiped out at a stroke when a mine's slag heap, wet from all the recent rain, suddenly rushes down the hillside and smashes into the school. Reports so far suggest 120 or more deaths, mostly children. I have not seen such a sombre place as the changing rooms, the Social Club and within the ground itself the following day. No one had much heart to play but we had to. There was none of the usual banter from the lads as they prepared for the game against Worcester – not much celebrating of the win either – life has just been put into perspective.

A few days later and in the middle of the excellent run since Harry has returned we have a friendly floodlit match against Ipswich as part of the Terry Eades/Tony Butcher testimonial year. A fine match sees a 4-4 draw and, with over 3,300 attending, plenty of cash into the kitty for these fine club servants.

On another lighter note our younger supporters have now formed their own mini-Kop at the Wolseley Road end under the small covered stand and their chanting resonates with help from the acoustic effect of the cover. Their latest song is rather repetitive but using the refrain from the Beatles' 'Yellow Submarine' it says:

'We all live at the back of City end
The back of City end
The back of City end
We all live at the back of City end
The back of City end'

It's hardly Lennon and McCartney and they do need to work on a second verse!

***

Now Christmas has arrived we can look back on this great run under Ferrier with only three defeats in twenty one games, although there have been some lows: the Peter Harburn saga has left a nasty taste in the mouth and we hear he is proceeding with his court case for wrongful dismissal. The performance of the Reserves and in particular the senior players within their team remains a concern. We all hoped Bobby Mason would have an 'Indian summer' to his career but that has not materialised.

On the plus side Shreeves looks a magnificent signing by Harburn and is a younger version of Len Phillips. Peter Leggett with his Beatle-style haircut and bewitching wing play has been a talisman like Tony Nicholas in the past. Out of the blue, though, we hear that Leggett, nicknamed 'Ringo' by some, is being sought by Reading but in a long interview with Martin Rogers in the Essex Chronicle he confirms he has no intention of leaving.

In November we lose in the FA Cup first round having beaten Hornchuch in the previous round. This time it's away to Brentford and by 1-0 – no disgrace, but oh for a great cup run; it remains one significant missing link to success in recent years, but at least the income from a sizeable gate at Griffin Park provides us with a good payday.

At a Board meeting in December we hear that Ferrier has put Mason up for sale. Illness and injury has held him back but Bobby says he has lost his appetite for the game, which has seen him dropped from the Reserves.

More significantly at that meeting we make the quite momentous decision to drop the Reserve team from next season. John Coward says it will save us £5,000. We will run a Youth team in the Mercia League and have seventeen professionals in the Southern League. John says: *'If we were getting any sort of support for reserve football things might be different. But it's false economy to continue.'*

I fear there will be a backlash from this, but purely from a financial perspective it is the correct decision. Personally I would like the Reserves to stay and fill it with young local talent and a few potential first teamers.

One highlight in the run up to Christmas was the 7-2 thrashing of Romford in the Southern League Cup. They have fallen away as a club along with Bath City and a few others and, if we are not careful, we could follow, but to win by such a margin against our local rivals is quite, quite satisfying!

So, much has happened in the past six months as we enter 1967.

The Ferrier effect has pushed us up the league and if it were not for three defeats over the Christmas period we would be in touch with Wimbledon and Hereford at the top of the league.

In early January, Ferrier adds Russ Rosling and Billy Stack to the ever growing transfer list but there is still little interest for any of them – a sign of the times with all professional or semi-professional clubs cutting back on player numbers to save money. John Thurgood, a stalwart of the club and in particular the Reserves, is also available for transfer. He has been a loyal servant and it will be sad to see him go; he has never let the side down. There's a shock in store in mid-January when Ted Phillips signs. He made his name at Ipswich in their golden year of 1962 when they won the Football League. Since then he has moved on to Orient, Luton and Colchester. This is typical Ferrier a big name to stir interest in the press and on the terraces.

What Ted will offer I'm not sure and perhaps is seen only as a temporary replacement for the injured Tony Butcher. With Bud Houghton scoring regularly up until Christmas there is no worry on the goal-scoring front.

The problem within the Reserves has come to a head. Mason, Dryden, Hinton and Day are all suspended by the club for breach of contract and in particular the section that says: '(the player) hereby agrees to play in an efficient manner and to the best of their ability for the Club' – what a sad indictment of modern day attitudes and this is unprecedented to my knowledge during all my time in football. At the Board meeting when this was discussed, and the decision made, we all agreed it was a sad day for the club.

By the time February comes to an end we have won only one of nine matches in the league since Christmas Eve with patchy form in the Floodlit League. To my mind, Phillips is over the hill and has not added much (and at some financial cost); he is certainly no substitute for Butcher. Ferrier has previously said February was our key month but having failed to win a game we have slipped to mid-table.

Now we are allowed once more to apply for a place in the Football League, we set about a bigger than ever campaign for a place. Firstly, two of us on the Board clear the £16,000 debt. The Supporters' Club are looking to raise the £40,000 we shall need to sustain the first season in the Fourth Division. Our assets now stand at £73,000 with £85,000 already spent on the Club's infrastructure in recent years. Perhaps the public might provide financial support by buying shares, but we know their interest in the club is waning. Many of these facts will be put into our campaign literature, but I fear the same old problems will persist in that we will not be Southern League champions, have not had an FA Cup run to get national coverage for any giant killing and queered our pitch when we signed the likes of Mason and Hatsell.

With young goalkeeper Bryan King and centre half Peter Collins expected to attract wealthy League clubs we can expect sizeable income from their transfers. We don't want them to go but no one would want to stand in their way. King came in for Medlock in February and Collins made his debut in the home game against Hereford which was drawn 1-1, with Phillips missing a penalty. What a great thrill for Peter who played in a midfield role and came up against John Charles – the greatest ever Wales international and also a star at Leeds before becoming an icon in Italy playing for Juventus. Peter told me afterwards that Charles took the time to shake his hand at the end of the match and compliment him on his performance, which saw Peter mark the great man out of the game. If Peter is half as good as Charles, he will go far in the game, but I do wonder how long we can keep hold of this lad.

This Hereford game also saw the opening of our club shop run by the Supporters' Club. Set up in the committee room behind the main stand, we have programmes going back to before the war, some old football annuals and other memorabilia and I was able to obtain a News Chronicle annual for 1948-49 edited by Charles Buchan. I religiously buy Buchan's football monthly as it is a cracking publication and the Annual is its equal. What attracts me to the 48-49 annual is the coverage given to Portsmouth who win the Division One championship helped by none other than Harry Ferrier and Len Phillips whose photographs appear in its pages.

***

Our recent board meeting saw the bombshell of John Coward's resignation as Chairman. Although only 59 John has been advised by his doctors to slow down. I knew he had been ill for a while; it was there for all to see but it was still a shock. I am not sure what life will be like around the club without him. A great man – bluff and hearty he has given his soul to the Club and more time and money than anyone could possibly imagine.

John tells Martin Rogers: *'Although I am resigning from the board, the cash arrangements made in the past and more recently will not be affected. The club has a good future and just because I'm going there is no reason why the various plans for the future should not be carried out. We have been planning ahead for years'*.

I am one of John's most ardent fans but these comments suggest to me that they are for the ears of the press and the fans alone and the reality of the situation is not as rosy as John makes out.

There is a battle in the boardroom. Vice-chairman Fred Langton should take over as Chairman and certainly John would not want the likes of Bob Last, the local car dealer, to take over after John removed him from the board for a while in 1965. I'm not sure Fred wants it and it is too early for the rest of us plus Len Menhinick certainly would not be able to give the time.

Amid the boardroom shenanigans, Fred has categorically said he will not stand so it leaves the door open for an outsider. Bob Last has indicated he would like to take it on but does not have much support yet he has the financial clout we need.

The boardroom debacle continues. I can't say too much but Bob is keen to bring back Harry Benge who left with him in 1965. Suffice to say this is not seen as progress by some and certainly not by the ailing John Coward. Even the Essex Chronicle picks up the vibes claiming this is *'cloak and dagger stuff'* and their reporters do not like what they hear.

On the field the fans are buoyed by a 3-1 win over Colchester United in the Essex Professional Cup Semi Final. Lou Costello, through injury and loss of form and having lost his right back berth to Ollie Hopkins, surprisingly plays up front against Colchester with Bud Houghton, who scores two goals with Lou netting the other. The gate for this home match is over 4,000 but our league gates hover around the 2,000 mark and are falling all the time.

With Easter in late March we have a plethora of games leading up to the three over Easter – seven league games on top of the Colchester game. Of those seven we win three, draw two and lose the other two.

However, April is something of a disaster and only 1,500 turn up for a Saturday match against Corby. Of eight league games in April we only win one and lose four, so it is not surprising the gates continue to drop.

The club is in crisis with acrimony at Board level, disenchantment amongst the supporters, disquiet from the local press, poor performances on the pitch and an alarming dip in our finances. I have a chance meeting with John Coward. He is feeling poorly and is depressed about his health and the turmoil at the club. He does not say but I suspect he has cancer – the stress he has endured with the club over recent years may perhaps be a contributory factor.

John believes the playing side leaves a lot to be desired. There is some missing ingredient as we have some outstanding players with Medlock, Costello, Shreeves, Eades and Docherty forming a resolute defence supported in the last year by Gladwin, Gillott, Hopkins and Jones with King in goal and Collins stepping up when required. I ask if he really considers Harry to be past his best and lacking the necessary drive to motivate the team. He believes not and points to how we have missed the prolific Tony Butcher who has been in and out of the team through one reason or another for most of the past twelve months. Winning just four games between Christmas and Easter has not helped and has seen us drop down the table.

Peter Collins gets another run out on the famous Huish slope at Yeovil. For once, I travel down with the team on the coach and we are in the middle of a poor run that has extended into mid-April. I was there to see another defeat but also one of the weirdest incidents imaginable. A Yeovil forward blasted the ball over the goal and out of the ground but minutes later another forward had a clear run on the City goal when the first ball was thrown back onto the pitch into his path. The two balls were side by side. The forward shot the 'wrong' ball into our goal. Pandemonium! Players crowded round the referee. Surely it's not a goal, say the City payers: Yeovil want it to count but, of course, they knew it would not and the referee correctly awarded a dropped ball. We mused afterwards what would have been the situation if the 'right' ball had been kicked into the net? Resident Director/Referee, Len Menhinick, told us the ref would have to make the same decision as the game must be stopped as soon as there are two balls on the pitch – so there you are!

As if we don't have enough end-of-season games – seven competitive matches in May – we also have some friendlies. On the night before the FA Cup Final we entertain Newcastle United who are down to watch the match at Wembley. They have just avoided relegation from Division One but boast a team of star names. At left back they have Frank Clark, a local lad who has played regularly this season. Well, he would not have endured such a torrid time as he did against Peter Leggett who ran him ragged, somewhat embarrassingly. If any talent scout was watching this match they would have snapped up 'El Beatle' without any doubt! Disappointingly only a few over 2,000 came along to see a top division side – a far cry from the days of Third Lanark!

At an end of season Board Meeting an interesting item is introduced under Any Other Business and it concerns what responsibility the club should hold for players that leave us and retire from the game, especially through injury. Should we compensate a player if he receives a career ending injury when playing for us? Should there be some sort of pension payable to those that have been with us for many years like Derek Tiffin and now Tony Butcher? Should this be written into a contract?

It was observed that the Professional Footballer's Association are looking into these matters and anything introduced will apply at all levels of the professional game. We decided we would wait and see but in the meantime treat any individual cases on their own merits.

The Board was taken to task for weeks in the local papers by the fans for the dropping of the Reserves and we come to a conclusion that we should vote on the matter once and for all. By the narrowest of margins I am pleased to say the Reserves will continue in the Metropolitan League next season.

10

THE RESERVES AND
THEIR DOUBLE DREAM

Ingatestone lad, Brian Terry, joined City Youth in 1965 and went on to play countless games for the Youth and Reserve teams with just one call up to the First Team. After the Reserve team was eventually disbanded Brian chose a successful career in the City of London but played top level amateur football at Enfield and Grays, after trials at Chelsea. He later played for Old Chelmsfordians, before managing teams there and becoming Chairman of the Football Club and President of the Old Chelmsfordians' Association. Here he tells of his experiences from three years at the City, also reflecting on the 1967/68 season. He starts his story in the summer of 1967.

I was playing for Rainsford Youth Centre when Ossie Willsher approached me to join the City Youth team ahead of a Youth tournament in Southend in 1965.

Rainsford YC was an excellent platform for young players. Tony Butcher was spotted there by Leyton Orient but turned them down and settled on a successful career at City: Derek Foreman and John Dinan were Tony's team mates and both played for City teams in the early 50s before enjoying their best years in football whilst they completed their National Service.

In 1965 City were keen to encourage local under 18s to form the nucleus of the Mercia Youth League team with perhaps one or more of us going on to play for the Reserves and even the First Team.

With the Reserves now competing in the stronger Metropolitan League the team was seen as an excellent source to blood the youngsters, but also to give a game to the pros returning from injury or suffering a loss of form; after all, there's little point them sitting around doing nothing – except getting paid. By 1967 Bryan King and Peter Collins had already progressed from the Youth team to play for the First Team and a few others like Ian Johnston and Martin Rollings could follow.

Looking back over the couple of years I have been at the club there are some aspects that surprised me. One in particular was that in both the Youth team and the Reserves there is very little technical coaching (with a scarcity in the First Team training too – from what I hear) and with no real tactics discussed before a game. It's clear to me that the club's finances don't stretch to provide expert coaching. Apparently the club did finance an FA coaching course for Peter Harburn before he became First Team Manager but money has been tight to have a full time coach as well as a manager for the First Team with what's available being spent on First Team wages, the pitch and maintenance of the ground. So, with falling crowd numbers and rising costs even my basic economics learnt at the Tech tell me that cannot continue! Before I joined I was under the misapprehension that the club was wealthy – it's quite clear I was wrong!

In training sessions there are never enough footballs to use and training seems all about running; round the cinder track at the Stadium, up and down the terracing and all over Central Park, during the lighter evenings. After these jaunts in the Park we normally return to The Stadium by crossing the bridge over the river behind The Barn. Most times we have a competition to see if we can chip the football over the river, across the marshy area each side and onto the dry land immediately behind The Barn stand. Too often the balls have to be retrieved from the river downstream behind the cricket ground or by us wading knee deep into ground underwater. Forfeits are demanded for the miscreants!

Bill Watson helps with our power training but most of the youth players are naturally fit, but it has 'beefed' us up a little. I'm not sure the first team are extensively coached but the management seems to rely on finding round pegs to fit round holes in a sort of 4-2-4 formation but following England's use of a 4-3-3 to win the World Cup we have seen a move towards this by many clubs but City have kept the wide wing men not favoured by England. The system works for City so who am I to criticise and why should the team complicate what is, after all, a simple game.

When I first joined the City some players went out of their way to help and I have benefited by learning from the older pros – Ron Smillie was particularly helpful when he was here, along with Peter Gillott, whose left back position I coveted. Gil was away at Margate last season but is now back, so we have been told, to captain and lead the Reserves. Worried I might lose my left back position I sought Gil out to chat about it. He laughed in that hearty Yorkshire way of his and told me not to worry as he saw himself playing in midfield where he would have more freedom and could direct his troops better. He also told me to expect a season with a regular berth at left back; good old Gil, top man!

The youth, amateur players and even some of the part time pros train in the evenings and separately from the First Team, who normally train during the day.

The facilities to help with injuries are pretty sparse with Benny Welham our physio, sponge man and masseur. He has been with the club since it became professional and presumably had some training in physiotherapy, but in my experience he gains perverse pleasure out of inflicting pain as he treats your painful twists and bruising. He has his trusty heat lamp to help your recuperation but a more serious injury would be referred to the club doctor (Dr Quinnell) or the hospital if it was extreme. You can forget about treatment for a simple knock, you are told to get on with things in no uncertain terms! I was informed early on by one senior player: *'not to go into Benny's room unless I was really dying!'*

I can't wait for the 67/68 season to start and one good thing about the Metropolitan League is we have Arsenal 'A', Spurs 'A', West Ham 'A' etc. as opponents – we never play them at their big grounds, but usually the training grounds – nevertheless their set ups are impressive and I expect to come up against a few rising stars plus the occasional international.

As an amateur I'm paid expenses and that's it. All I really want to do is to play football and since 1965 I've often turned out for the school team on a Saturday morning, the City in the afternoon and Redstones the following day in the Chelmsford Sunday League. Next season I'll be playing for Saracens in the Sunday League along with Wicker Smith, Lance Gooch and Ian Johnston, also likely Reserve team players. The City management seems to have no problem with this. I'm a little surprised but perhaps as we are merely amateurs it is our right to do what we like. Is it a case of the club not seeing us as likely long term first team prospects? If they did surely they would protect us more – and as a result this isn't exactly inspiring for any of us.

In fact, in my time here to date I've never really been encouraged or coached to attain First Team status although I feel I could make it, perhaps along with a few others. It appears the club has set its stall out to have the Reserves filled mainly with local amateurs supplemented by a few first teamers and to concentrate on operating the First Team as an elite squad of fourteen or so with some of them, like Micky Block who also works as a London cabby, not on full pro terms. I understand this would make sense from a cost point of view as there is no point having two teams of expensive pros. But this does mean there is little money left to develop much else.

I shall have to see how the coming season pans out before I decide on my future. The scrapping of the Reserves decision was recently reversed but the writing is on the wall and perhaps we have another season before the inevitable happens. With rumours rife that the whole club might go back to part time as we were a few years ago, these are worrying times both on and off the pitch. All we can hope for is success on the field and see where that takes us.

11

THE CLARET DREAM NEARS ITS END ... BUT WHAT AN END!

Throughout the 'glory years' of Chelmsford City there was one defining constant – Tony Butcher; Chelmsford born and bred, a great talent who only very late in his career went to another club, truly a 'Man for All Seasons'. Despite being rarely shy of 20-plus goals EVERY season he still had the crowd on his back at times – perhaps it was because he was a local lad, who personally knew many of his sternest critics, but he never once stopped trying. If he missed two chances he would never shirk being in the right place to net the third. Tony still lives in the Chelmsford area and rarely misses a City game. Player of the Year for the 1967/68 season he reflects on that glorious time with the help of others who were also there.

We've done it and I can't quite believe we have – champions at last! What a night last night. I had tears in my eyes, seeing the thousands lining the route from New Writtle Street, along London Road and all the way through to the Civic Centre.

The great Tony Butcher – 560 Southern League and FA Cup games with 286 goals

As we stood upstairs there having been greeted by Mayor Landers, I could hear the crowd chanting *'We want the Champs; we want the Champs'*, and begging for us to appear with the trophy. Some were even shouting my name. It made me feel so proud as a local lad even if some of those voices might have given me stick over the years, making me their whipping boy, unable to do anything right. But I don't mind, if it had upset me that much I would have left years ago and I've generally managed to confound them every season! For now at least we're all friends and all that criticism is forgotten. *'Go on'* said Harry, *'you and Billy take the trophy out onto the balcony.'* Billy Cassidy gave me a sideways look and smiled: *'Come on,'* he said, *'let's give 'em what they want!'*

We each grabbed one side of the trophy and walked out onto the balcony above the crowd. The road below was packed and the roar that went up when we appeared almost shook the building. People were hanging out of windows above the shops opposite and some were clinging to lamp posts to get a better view; others were hanging from the trees now covered with May blossom.

Billy, tough Scot he might be, had tears running down his cheeks. His goals, over fifty in total, and nearly thirty in the league had got us there – and I chipped in with my share too. But we both knew this evening was our swansong – Billy is off to Detroit Cougars and there might be one last chance for me at 31 to play at a higher level with some League clubs showing interest. Terry Eades, too, might well be on the move and he deserves it – smashing lad and talented with it.

Peter Gillott joins Billy and me on the balcony; he's holding the Metropolitan League trophy and their League Cup – what a triple! He's followed by the players from both teams thronging behind us to wave to the crowd. All the club officials, wives and girlfriends remain in Centre having travelled with us on the open top bus. It was some party atmosphere. With the First Team runners up in the Floodlit League and the Essex Professional Cup, it has been quite a season!

The cheers and chants from the crowd continue for more than ten minutes before we file back indoors to hear Mr Landers congratulate both teams: *'You have won this through teamwork, through blood, toil and sweat. The whole town is proud of you – you are good teams well worthy of the honour.'* He added that whilst he did not want to single out individuals he felt the half back line of Shreeves, Eades and Docherty was undoubtedly the best in the Southern League – and he is absolutely right.

Mr Landers then tried to persuade the very Scottish John Docherty to sing *'Road to the Isle'* but with no success then warned us all that if he saw any players without a drink he would warn them, the second time he would book them and the third time would send them home! We didn't need telling twice and tucked into the buffet washed down by plenty of wine or beer.

Once the reception came to an end we adjourned back to the Social Club at The Stadium to continue the celebrations and when we arrived there we were again mobbed by the fans as we got off the bus. We carried on well into the night and I've more than a slight hangover this morning with the Alka-Seltzer already put to good use!

***

So what of this team? Over the years City has certainly had better players in the First Team with all those star names – Mason, Isherwood, Phillips, Hatsell, Smillie, Taylor and so on. On paper at least we might have had much better looking sides but for this past season we have been a 'team' and that to me has been the difference. Yes, Billy and I scored the majority of the goals – most successful teams have a high scoring duo – but we have achieved this success using a very small number of players and perhaps that is the key to forging a successful team. Equally important is how those not regularly playing step up to the plate when called upon. Take Micky Block; he came in for the injured Gordon Pulley and scored in our crucial win at Wimbledon. Roy Walsh scored the winner away at Cambridge United which virtually clinched the title for us. Watling came in to play in goal for the injured Medlock after Alan Collier initially took Owen's place for a few games. And Gillott, of course, managing the Reserves, but filling in at the back for the First Team none more so than in that 1-0 win at Cambridge. Only sixteen players used in the League and to think we could have had young Bryan King in goal, now a fixture at Millwall, and the even younger Peter Collins at centre half who is now pushing for a first team place at Spurs!

This season has, without doubt, been the greatest ever for the club and for me personally. To win the league from where we were in February after everyone had written us off, and with me and Billy dropped from the team, was nothing short of miraculous.

I have played with some super players at the City over my twelve or so years at the club but this bunch of lads have made me so proud. Having lived in the town all my life I know what this means to the people here, but I feel this is tinged with sadness in that it did not come when John Coward was running the club. He was there last night but now only a peripheral figure yet I still see him as the guv'nor, we owe him so much. Now struck down with illness and merely a director in name only, his day has gone and his little empire built at the club, I fear, is no more.

This triumphant winning of the league title may well signal the end of an era with a season the like of which the club hasn't seen before and may not see again. An immediate break up of this team will follow but let's hope we shortly see the dawn of a new era for the club.

Finance, I understand, is a major problem. Mr Coward's money is not there and new Chairman, Mr Last, wants the books to balance WITHOUT the Directors propping up the club with their own money.

The vitriol in the town has been significant following the

announcement to ditch the Reserve team next year with only an under 18s youth team to back up the First Team squad. With this coming at the end of the double winning season it seems hard to understand, but Mr Last says the club is losing hundreds of pounds a week running the Reserves – a team of a few professionals supplemented by a large number of local amateurs including youngsters like Brian Terry and Ian Johnston.

With overall finances stretched we presumably won't be able to pay the level of wages to attract players from the higher leagues like we have in the past, but then paying over inflated wages is possibly one of the reasons we have these problems. If you have more money being paid out than you have coming in even I know you'll eventually come to grief. Back in 1962 the gates would cover the extra cost of wages but, with gates now half what they were then, we can all understand how the club may well be finding it difficult to make ends meet.

***

Amongst all these celebrations, laced with a touch of reality about the future, my thoughts go back to last summer, 1967. After all the upheaval at the club the previous season off the pitch, the players nevertheless ended up a united group and we all looked forward to a new campaign but I'm pretty sure none imagined how successful we would be.

The close season ahead of 1967/68 is far from dull. One of my old mates Peter Gillott is returning from Margate to mainly play for and manage the Reserves, but Ollie Hopkins has left to join Brentwood and also released are Bobby Mason, Ted Phillips, George Duncan and John Thurgood, among a few others. The biggest shock to me is Bud Houghton jumping ship to join Cambridge United having been unhappy with the terms offered. At first I found it hard to form a striking partnership with him early last season but, once we had, we were prolific. Many of the supporters I've spoken to are up in arms that City wouldn't meet his demands. Lou Costello is at present unable to accept the terms being offered but I'm pretty sure he can be talked round and will stay. I have to say that signing Bobby M and Ted was over-ambitious and probably costly to the club. Their pedigree would've demanded higher wages that might have been better spent elsewhere and perhaps used to retain Bud. That's the way of football goes, I suppose.

It soon becomes plain the Board have decided wages will be aligned to a set pay scale and not to have one-off deals for individual players. This is fine for me but not everyone. Surely it means we lose some top players yet have to buy in new ones and this seems something of a false economy to my simple way of thinking.

Terry Eades is staying having been coveted by several clubs. He and I enjoyed our testimonials last season and perhaps granting Terry one so early into his City career was the reason he's still here. I'm convinced he'll eventually move on to better things but pleased he's here for this season at least.

At the ground in June I bump into young Derek Ablett collecting his belongings as he's leaving to join Great Baddow. I really did see a future for him and much of myself in him, but he was just that little bit short of what was needed at pro level. Whilst there, I took the opportunity of meeting our new groundsman, Jim Smith, who as with his predecessors has his work cut out turning a dusty sandpit into a pristine green, grassy surface by August.

Two weeks further on Lou agrees new terms and the boss has told the Chronicle he has a budget that will allow him to sign players in a number of positions – particularly two full backs, two wingers, an inside and centre forward – to me that seems almost like a whole new team!

'Keeper Bryan King is sold to Millwall for £4,000 – a lot of money for a club like us when you think this would buy a three bedroomed detached house in the town, but he's a fine player and will do very well. We have a good evening to see him on his way and all the talk is how the transfer money might be spent on new quality players but many fear it might be used to reduce our reported overdraft – time will tell.

***

Brentwood Town have been elected to the Southern League so we'll be doing battle against a considerable number of ex-City players this coming season – something to look forward to. Disappointingly the players learn from Len King that at the weekend's Football League AGM we only poll ONE vote – this our first try since our ban was lifted and followed an intense campaign with League clubs for their support.

Out of the blue Len Menhinick telephones me to say he's leaving the Board due to pressure of work, but I've a sneaking feeling he doesn't get on with Mr Last. With this decision Len severs a link going back several years but what a job he's done and it's a sad day for the club that he'll no longer be around.

On a brighter note and as pre-season training starts, new players roll in. Alec Wilson, a cultured left back and full Scottish international who was in their 1954 World Cup squad, is signed from Portsmouth together with inside forward Johnny Gordon, ex Birmingham City and Portsmouth (yet another signing from there!) who a few years back played in the Nou Camp against Barcelona in the Inter Cities Fairs Cup Final. Gordon Pulley arrives and is announced as: 'a diminutive, crowd-pleasing winger from Peterborough'. I find my new striking partner is Bill Cassidy; released from Brighton on a 'free' he has played for the Glasgow Rangers first team and is still only 26. He has big boots to fill in replacing Bud but let's hope he does well. Forwards Michael Block from Watford and Gary Townsend from Hillingdon arrive (perhaps the boss met them when touring round London as both are qualified black cab drivers!) – Gary starred against us last season which probably explains his signing.

My least favourite part of any season has arrived – pre-season training, which in the past has meant quite a lot of running, more running and yet more running. The boss tells us he's introducing training regimes based on those at Spurs and Southend, but they still seem to mainly involve running. Our first public pre-season match is against Peterborough United. Wow! Have we unearthed a gem? Bill Cassidy hits FOUR and we win 6-0. On a sadder note dear Benny Welham is being relieved of his duties now we've a doctor at matches and access to facilities at the hospital including physiotherapy etc. So Benny with his lamp to radiate its healing into our injured bodies is a thing of the past, but he'll continue to look after the many players from the local leagues who visit him at his home for treatment.

Disappointingly, I am not selected for the opening two games with Townend picked ahead of me. In Saturday night's 'Green 'Un' Harry

Ferrier says his choice for the first game: '... *is what I consider to be my best team after what I have seen in training and trial games'* – so that's me told – perhaps my dislike of pre-season training has finally cost me with training regimes now taking on a greater significance! A draw in the opening game at Yeovil is followed by a narrow 1-0 win at home to King's Lynn, but I return for the home defeat by Guildford when John Docherty is sent off for throwing a punch. Immediately the crowd is on my back, so nothing changes.

The Chronicle carries a story that the club are trailing Ben Hannigan of Dundalk FC (goodness knows how the boss hears about these players), but the League of Ireland need to give their permission. Ignoring this Ben is signed and lines up in a friendly hastily arranged against Arsenal Reserves when we have a free Saturday in September. Ben scores and Arsenal only equalise in stoppage time and their team includes first team squad players in Bob Wilson, Pat Rice, David Court and Sammy Nelson. Disappointingly less than 1,000 are at The Stadium to see it.

The Reserves look very strong; a mix of youth and experience with Peter Collins continuing to put in excellent performances and he has been watched in recent games by Nottingham Forest and Manchester United.

***

Now in October, we're all satisfied with only two defeats in twelve games but both were at home in the League, disappointing the fans. We seem nervous in front of them and seem to play with greater freedom away from home, but Billy and me are really hitting it off and scoring freely; he is big and strong taking the brunt of the attack with me playing off him. 'El Beatle' Leggett has thrilled the crowd, flying down the right wing yet still consolidating in the midfield with Johnny Gordon when necessary. Peter Shreeves is a real thoroughbred playing alongside Johnny. The fickle fans were slow to accept these two classy players much in the same way as they did with Len Phillips in the past. We have the making of a good season with all the new signings fitting in brilliantly. Disappointingly the crowds hover around the 2,000 mark and those that do come along to watch are often sceptical and harsh with their criticism at times. Gary Townend has been something of a flop and is heading back to Hillingdon.

One aspect of life away from football has changed this week with the introduction of the breathalyser. I'm told the Police have already been out on the roads pulling drivers over and there'll be a few leaving our Social Club who'll need to be careful – and this includes some of the players!

Over my years at City I've seen them all come and go. Local amateurs, young pros, old pros, expensive pros, disappointing pros but I have to say this is a club like no other. Yes, at all clubs up and down the country you have the same characters, be they players, directors or administrators. The dressing room is, by and large, the home of the working class: footballers aren't normally the most intelligent of men, with only a few exceptions and there are players who like a drink: then there's the know-it-all, the moaner, the shirker (often me, in training!), a joker and a ladies' man. All different but someone has to mould them into a team pulling in the same direction. Some players need a kick up the rear but others a friendly arm round the shoulders from the Manager.

I have to say that all my Managers at City have been great, but all different. Mr Grice was the arch typical manager of that time, Harry Ferrier was and remains a dynamic and forceful 'character' who has seen it all in his playing football career at the very top. Peter Harburn was a very good coach and perhaps he could've worked with a more experienced man to handle the day to day management of the club. Billy Frith, not everyone's favourite, turned my game around when I was at low ebb with some excellent one-to-one coaching and I owe him a lot.

Add these managers to what happened behind the scenes where Len Menhinick and now Len King have transformed the administration set up and you'll find a club boasting a level of professionalism bettered by very few.

The Directors have been led by John Coward – an inspirational bloke. Yes, he's put a few noses out of joint and that's probably what caused all the recent upheaval, but we still have local men on the Board – football men who care about the future of the club. I'm not one who subscribes to ex England international Len Shackleton's view of football club directors. I saw in his recent book he had one chapter called, 'The

Average Director's Knowledge of Football' – the page was blank! When I was first starting out, Shackleton was my hero and someone I'd like to imitate; he was an inside forward like me and he often scored penalties with a back-heel, played one-twos with a corner flag to waste time or would sit on the ball to torment defenders and, when he went round the goalkeeper with the ball, would stand on the goal-line with his foot on the ball but when the goalie or defender desperately tried to dispossess him would calmly back-heel the ball into the net! Unfortunately, I had neither the nerve nor ability to emulate him and there is another interesting story about Shackleton when he announced his retirement to assembled journalists. He showed what they'd be missing by tossing a penny into the air, catching it on his instep and then flicking it into the top pocket of his jacket!

Shackleton had to retire early due to a serious ankle injury and we full time players do worry about our futures, especially if like me you're the wrong side of thirty. Even at a young age a career might suddenly end because of a serious injury – look at Brian Clough, one of the great goalscorers but his career was over in his early twenties.

Most of us had little career training before we did our National Service ahead of turning pro. At City for a while we could have a trade and remain part-time but as for my future I have plans. Peter Gillott has his cobbling business and I know is interested in other business opportunities when he eventually calls his playing days at an end. But sadly, I've seen some players on a slippery slope once they choose to or are forced to retire, but I'm determined that won't happen to me when the time comes.

I spoke with Bobby Mason last week and he's turning out for a team called Parley Sports in the Dorset League; he says it's just a run out to keep fit. I'm not sure when my days as a pro come to an end that I'll want to drop too far down the football ladder. What can it feel like for Bobby to play at this level when a few years back he was scoring in the European Cup for Wolves against Barcelona and playing in an FA Cup semi-final?

One aspect of being a long term pro at one club is a testimonial year. This is a wonderful gesture to a loyal player and I've benefited not once but twice. In the 1962-63 season I shared one with the late Bill Parry (former player, trainer etc.) and last season with Terry Eades. Apart from the off-field events I've had testimonial games against an All Star XI, Gillingham, Ipswich and Crystal Palace. These two testimonial years have created a nice little nest egg which I hope to put towards setting up a little business, maybe a shop, when I finally retire.

This season it's the turn of Bobby Smith and Owen Medlock who, deservedly, have their testimonials and in October, as part of their year, the club has arranged a match against Detroit Cougars from the fledgling North American Soccer League. They're playing a series of matches in the UK, perhaps on the look-out for players and, you never know, next season I might be playing alongside the shores of Lake Michigan and visiting the Tamla Motown studios!

It was strange to hear American voices in the corridors under the main stand mixing with the more earthy Yorkshire tones of Gillott and Smith. A crowd higher than our recent average come along which is good news for Owen and Bobby and we win 2-0. This doesn't say much for the standard of the NASL, but perhaps shows our quality and Billy C scores both goals thus impressing the watching Cougars' management. I wouldn't be surprised if it's him and not me lighting up their League in their 1968 season which starts next summer.

Interestingly, we have signed our first African player; well, on loan at least. Eddie Dilsworth from Sierra Leone, who played for Enfield at Wembley in last year's Amateur Cup Final, is having a try out for us. He's just 20 and a goalscoring inside forward like me. We were told he was involved in the Amateur Cup tie last season when a Highgate player was struck by lightning and killed. I spoke with Eddie about it and he's still having difficulty coming to terms with what happened. The game was abandoned of course and replayed at Villa Park in front of 31,000; there to pay their respects to the lad who died.

Eddie scores in his first outing for the First Team in a Floodlit League game against Cambridge United and, if I were the Boss and Mr Last, I'd sign him immediately on full terms.

***

At the end of October Bryan King makes his long awaited debut for Millwall against Blackpool in Division Two and the Boss watches him play well, by all accounts, in a 1-1 draw.

Reading a report of this in the Chronicle my attention is drawn to a brief mention that the Club's deficit has risen to £15,400 for season 1966-67 – up from £10,800 – mainly due to wages exceeding gate money and donations. That to my untrained eye doesn't look very healthy and is picked up by the usually supportive Chronicle reporters who are more than mildly critical of the situation. Let's hope this financial position can improve this season as we've started like a train! Fans are returning with a decent gate in the FA Cup match against Banbury which we win with my two goals and now a plum home tie awaits us against old rivals Oxford United – that promises to be fun!

***

Having reached the end of November our success thus far has largely been based upon a settled team with very few changes but in the same Floodlit league game where Dilsworth made his debut, Owen Medlock fractures a cheekbone. This leaves us with a problem as we enter the busy Christmas month AND the Oxford game. Reserve keeper, Dave Pye, is fine at that level but has always found the step-up a little daunting. At least he's better than stand-in Lou Costello who gave a passable impression of a cat on a hot tin roof when he took over from Owen for the rest of the game, having the crowd in hysterics. To prove my point about Dave he's in goal when we're thrashed at Barnet 5-2; that's not to say he was at fault but the defence seemed to be lacking in confidence and disjointed in front of him.

This crisis, if that's what it is, is temporarily resolved when old mate, Alan Collier, returns on an emergency three week loan from Bedford which will see us through the Oxford game. Also arrived is Roy Walsh from Ipswich and, like Billy C before him, nets four in one of his early games. Roy's was in an 8-0 thrashing of City Old Boys aka Brentwood Town in the Floodlit League, sweet enough but Roy was playing in my place as I've missed a few games in November. However, I did play in the 2-0 away win at Corby scoring both goals but it was 'Ringo' Leggett who took all the plaudits. He had been out injured but what a comeback! The headline in the Chronicle said, 'Brilliant Beatle sparks City win' and was spot on. What I also found interesting was Martin Rogers talking about the awfulness of the Corby ground with its muddy, bumpy pitch and poor floodlights, awful changing rooms and showers with all this set in a run-down area of a steel town. Martin asked me what it was like to play in front of the reasonable crowds at City and then come to play in front of a few hundred at Corby's down at heel place. All I could say was that I know where I'd rather play!

It's reported in the Chronicle that Chelmsford Council have approved a new £8,000 athletics stadium to be built in the top corner of Melbourne Park: that should provide a welcome boost to the town and, with the Mexico Olympics less than a year away, there'll be increased interest in athletics and hopefully the town will eventually have a team to rival the Birchfield Harriers of this world!

The most important thing for the football club, the players and supporters right now is the upcoming FA Cup game against Oxford United. Will this bring us the success we crave and put our name in lights so the whole nation takes notice? Oxford have moved on since we last played them and look set to reach the second tier of English football if they maintain their current form. It'll be a good test for us and I do have the feeling that this team of ours is gelling into something better than any of our teams over the past ten years, so 'Bring on Oxford' and the FA Cup!

12

THE MAGIC OF THE FA CUP

David Billings was born in the 1940s and lived for many years in Arnhem Road – just round the corner from City's current home. His step-brother is current Chairman, Mansell Wallace, and together with Mansell's twin brother, James, their love for the Clarets grew in the heady days of the 1960s; a love that lasts to this day. The following is David's first-hand account, written as at that time, of the glorious cup run in 1967/68 centred round the titanic trio of matches against Oxford United; a side that secured promotion from Division Three of the Football League in 1968 and a perfect example of where the City might have been, or where they still might be, had the footballing gods not conspired against us!

Up until England's triumphant 1966 World Cup campaign I had little or no interest in football, it brought back too many unpleasant memories of being kicked about on the cold, wet, muddy playing fields of Rainsford School. I much preferred the alternative option of reading a book in the comfort of a nice warm classroom!

But this changed dramatically during that summer of 1966 when it seemed the entire nation was preoccupied with the World Cup competition and whole families gathered round their television sets eagerly watching England's progress through the league stage and subsequent knock-out phase to reach and win the final.

With live football on TV a rare occurrence, the comprehensive coverage of the tournament was a real novelty for us. My twin step-brothers, Mansell and James, as well as my step-father, George, would take up their seats in our living room for each match. This being our only TV set in the house I had no alternative than to join them or face social exclusion. I did so reluctantly at first and then with a degree of resignation, but by the later stages with equal fervour, even my mother was showing mild interest by now.

And so, with my new interest in "the beautiful game" firmly instilled, it wasn't long before Mansell and James persuaded me to accompany them to a Chelmsford City home game. The three of us and some other friends were soon regularly attending home and away games in fair weather or foul.

Like most youngsters I kept a diary for a short while a few years ago and now in my early 20s I have decided to restart such a record detailing our FA Cup run because something tells me this could be 'our year'!

Saturday October 28th 1967

The 1967/68 season has started with the perennial call for 'a good cup run'; always a necessity (but usually a failure) to obtain some national attention to help our cause towards league status especially now our 'ban' has come to an end. We gain a "bye" until the fourth qualifying round by virtue of having reached the first round proper the previous year. Banbury United of the Southern League Division One are our opponents. It is a cold, wet and windy autumn day on which City emerge the victors in an unconvincing 2-0 win watched by 3,475 spectators.

City stalwart Tony Butcher scores both goals in the 42nd and 88th minutes respectively but both teams hit the woodwork and miss several good chances, so the release of tension was enormous when that second goal was scored. The Essex Chronicle in their report quote City manager Harry Ferrier's post-match comment – *"We weren't good and the tension that builds up for these cup games is so different from anything in the ordinary league programme. It should not be so but it is a fact of football that the cup generates great anxiety when success is so vital."*

Anyway, we are up and running – could it be our year?

Monday October 30th 1967

And so, having successfully overcome that difficult Banbury encounter, we eagerly await the draw for the first round proper which takes place today and now includes teams from the Football League Divisions Three and Four. Rumour passes round Marconi's this afternoon that it is Oxford United at home, but I have to wait for it to be confirmed in the 'Stop Press' of the Evening News. I am more than pleased it is indeed a home draw with Division Three high-flyers Oxford United with the tie due to take place on Saturday December 9th. Earlier in the 60s, so Mansell tells me, we regularly played Oxford (previously known as Headington) United in the Southern League before they were elected to the Football League when Accrington Stanley went bust. He and brother James are looking forward to us renewing acquaintances with old foes Ron and Graham Atkinson – career long veterans still plying their trade with United.

Sunday December 3rd 1967

I have just returned from watching a Sunday League game between Park Avenue and Saracens at Melbourne Park – feisty stuff and a large crowd, where the talk on the touchline was of the forthcoming Oxford match, especially as three City Reserve players, Wicker Smith, Brian Terry and Lance Gooch were playing for Saracens. There is also an increasing air of excitement and anticipation among the City followers in the town with the Oxford game less than a week away. Harry Ferrier is upbeat and confident about the team's chances. We are not on a bad run with a thumping Floodlit League win 8-0 against a woeful Brentwood and yesterday we beat Dover 1-0 away with a Peter Leggett goal. 'Keeper Owen Medlock broke his jaw against Cambridge United in mid-November and Dave Pye (from the Woodhall Estate and the Tech!) had two contrasting games as his deputy with the 8-0 then a 5-2 reverse away at Barnet. Former 'keeper Alan Collier (he left us in 1965) has returned on a month's loan, played yesterday at Dover and is set for the Oxford game. We are lucky to get him – nothing against Pye but Collier has the experience.

Saturday December 9th

Ferrier is able to field an unchanged side from that at Dover, namely: – Alan Collier, Lou Costello, Alec Wilson, Peter Shreeves, Terry Eades, John Docherty, Peter Leggett, Tony Butcher, Bill Cassidy, Johnny Gordon and Gordon Pulley. Bobby Smith is named as the substitute.

In an interview with the Essex Chronicle's football correspondent Martin Rogers, Ferrier says:

"We have had a worthwhile week in training, nothing fancy but our efforts have been concentrated on sharpening up for what is sure to be a really interesting match."

A local bookmaker is giving odds of 7-4 against for a City win, with Oxford the favourites at 6-4 on and 7-2 for a draw. Oxford have one or two regular first-teamers out with injuries and were knocked out of the FA Cup by non-league Bedford Town last season, so they might be nervous ahead of the game later today.

I have to queue (some time since that last happened!) across the old footbridge from Central Park to take up my usual position on the terracing in "The Barn". Not sure about Oxford being nervous, I certainly am as the two teams run onto the pitch. I feel rather uneasy and apprehensive about our chances as Oxford's players appear very large, fit and sturdy; they make ours look rather lightweight by comparison!

The Oxford line-up is, according to the programme:

1 Brian Sherratt –goalkeeper and back after a month's injury absence.
2 Cyril Beavon – 400 games – regular in their Southern League days.
3 Tony Jones – one of Oxford's "old guard" wing-half/inside forward.
4 Ron Atkinson – another stalwart of the club, a wing-half. He has the most muscular physique and huge thighs – I wouldn't want to be tackled by him and he makes Tony Butcher look like a waif!
5 Rodney Smithson – once of Arsenal, drafted in because of injuries.
6 Colin Clarke – defender, another former Arsenal player.
7 Ken Skeen – signed the previous season from Swindon.
8 Graham Atkinson – the younger brother of Ron.
9 Mike Bullock – £10,000 summer star signing from Birmingham City.
10 John Shuker – a "play anywhere" man but usually at full-back.
11 John Evanson – senior team debut and can play on either wing.

The weather is very cold and overcast with a light wind – the pitch rock-hard. A whisper goes round the ground that Oxford's manager, Arthur Turner, tried to persuade the ref, Mr. R. Johnson of Lowestoft, to call the game off but the ref thought otherwise and the game duly commences. The ground is pretty full on the terracing with the corners quite crowded – always a good sign that there is six or seven thousand in. The atmosphere is fantastic with a good number up from Oxford behind one goal.

It quickly becomes evident that City are by no means overawed or intimidated by their illustrious opponents, indeed are coping better with the slippery conditions and causing the Oxford defenders plenty of problems. There is little to choose between the two teams, hard to believe Oxford are two leagues higher than City. In fact the programme tells me Oxford have not won any of their last 17 away games notwithstanding their third place in Division Three.

To my mind City's two most effective players are Tony Butcher and Terry Eades who are the only ones in the team not to have played League football. Butcher is a constant threat to the Oxford defenders and Eades a veritable rock in central defence keeping £10,000 Mike Bullock constantly shackled.

City are firmer in the tackle, quicker in distribution of the ball and altogether keener to play in the appalling conditions. It comes as little surprise when City take the lead after 13 minutes, Bill Cassidy heads the ball across to Peter Leggett (looking more like City's answer to George Best every time I watch him!) whose strong drive skims in front of Brian Sherratt and runs to Gordon Pulley who without hesitation slams it into the back of the net. **1-0 TO CITY**

The first Oxford equaliser comes on 34 minutes and is an unsatisfactory affair for City. Eades and Bullock contest a ball, which is chipped to the near post from a free kick by Edmondson, they both miss it completely. Collier has the ball covered and appears to call for Wilson to leave it; Wilson pulls back but the ball strikes him, bounces against a post and to our horror rolls into the net. **CITY 1 OXFORD 1**

Our spirits are lifted again on 42 minutes when the ebullient Cassidy heads the ball on and Butcher speeds past the despairing sweeper, Ron Atkinson, and then past Sherratt to make it – **CITY 2 OXFORD 1** – and now it's half time.

Queuing for our tea and hot-dog with City so deservedly in the lead, the buzz of elation is very evident. The second half kicks off in a snowstorm, lasting all of 20 minutes and it almost obliterates the pitch markings. With eleven minutes of the second half played in these dreadful conditions our hearts sink again when Oxford equalise once more after Beavon sends a 20-yard free kick over City's defensive wall. The ball strikes the bar and rebounds to Shuker who shoots home after stealing in unnoticed. **CITY 2 OXFORD 2**

But City take the lead for the third time when Butcher scores a sensational goal on 69 minutes. Docherty drives a long ball out of defence that Butcher latches on to, challenging and beating two defenders before striking home from the edge of the penalty area. **CITY 3 OXFORD 2**

Cloud nine again but we know the last 20 minutes or so will seem like an eternity; however as things stand it seems all the might-have-beens will not matter and the tantalisingly close Butcher header which glanced past a post in the first half and the Shuker "goal" in the second half ruled out for a minor infringement will count for nought.

With the clock ticking at an agonisingly slow pace and with just eleven minutes of ordinary time remaining, Oxford strike yet again when indecision in the City rearguard allows Clarke a clear shot at goal, which he eagerly accepts. **CITY 3 OXFORD 3**

Mr Johnson adds a minute or so and we are relieved to at least get the draw but we were that close. As we slope off across the footbridge the consensus is that our chance has gone. Oxford will be stronger in the replay with home advantage. Still, we are in the draw for Monday.

Monday 11th December 1967

I can't believe it! Colchester United or Torquay United at home if we get through – the players will need no more incentive than that to pull off a shock on Wednesday! The Colchester game was postponed on Saturday and is due to be played tomorrow. There were a few surprises from Saturday (although a huge number of games were also postponed) and none more so than Runcorn beating Notts County 1-0.

Wednesday 13th December 1967

Colchester draw at Torquay and so we are none the wiser as to who we play if we get through. The Marconi Sports and Social Club has hastily organised for several coaches to transport interested employees to the replay with its 7.30pm kick off tonight. The coach picks us up from the Company car park in New Street in late afternoon with time off being generously allowed. We set off in good time but the driver has decided on an AA route to the north of London to avoid the rush hour and the infamous North Circular. With it being dark and the windows steamed up, I cannot make out much of where we are, except that it is mainly countryside.

I have a good supply of sandwiches and a flask filled from the coffee machine in the factory; the only good thing about it being that it is hot. The driver tells us he has no plans to stop and we are all bursting for a wee when we eventually arrive at the Manor Ground in Headington on the outskirts of Oxford. The ground is similar to New Writtle Street and we opt to stand on the terrace. We have mixed emotions as City had matched Oxford in overall performance in the previous game but could we repeat such a feat again, especially away from home? To be realistic we will, in all probability, bow out but hopefully not without a fight. We are well aware that this match will test City to their limits and that the superior fitness levels of the Oxford players will be a factor. However, there is a significant incentive for City; the prospect of a possible home tie with Third Division Colchester United and all that entails! The crowd builds impressively ahead of kick off. We estimate perhaps 1,500 from Chelmsford – brilliant for a midweek game.

City field an unchanged side again but Oxford make two changes from the Saturday match with Ken Hale and Barry Thornley coming into the starting line-up at the expense of Tony Jones and John Evanson. Hale is an inside forward who has played for Newcastle and Coventry, whilst Thornley is a teenager who Oxford have obtained on a free transfer from Brentford, who paid Gravesend £2,500 for him when just 17 years old.

Oxford start the match in a very positive way creating gaps in the City rearguard which looks rather indecisive and hesitant. Hale, Graham Atkinson and Clarke are mounting increasing pressure on the

City defence forcing Collier to make a string of excellent saves with Eades and Costello doing their best to stem the tide of attacks. Butcher is, not surprisingly after Saturday, being heavily marked but despite enduring a real battering is not being completely subdued. City's two wingers Leggett and Pulley are proving effective in the rare attacking forays City are able to muster.

Seeing them in action someone nearby in the crowd shouts: *"Look at that, they've got George Best on one wing and Charlie Drake on the other!"* This causes considerable mirth among the Oxford fans within earshot and it is true to say that Leggett, with his flowing locks, slight build and delicacy of touch bears more than a passing resemblance to the Manchester United star. Conversely, Gordon Pulley is short and stocky with a round face and mop of blonde hair but he is no comedian so far this evening and it is he who looks the most likely to score in the early stages of the game. There is no hint of slapstick as he speeds down the left wing causing consternation in the United ranks!

City fall behind on 24 minutes when United take a deserved lead when Collier parries a Clarke shot but the ball goes straight to **Skeen** who makes no mistake. City rebound and Leggett forces three corners in quick succession but the finishing touches are missing. At this stage United look really menacing as Collier tips over a fierce Graham Atkinson drive and seconds later scurries to halt Skeen who is through on his own. Butcher has a snap shot saved at the other end but on 40 minutes United go 2-0 up. Thornley squares the ball to Hale who beats three City defenders before passing back to Thornley who finds **Bullock** in the goalmouth to turn the ball in. I expect the worst at this point fearing a heavy defeat is now more than likely.

City aren't finished however and with just over a minute of the first half remaining **Butcher** heads a fine goal from a Pulley corner to make it 2-1. We feel a bit more optimistic or, at least, less pessimistic at half time because with a one-goal deficit City are still well in contention.

United begin the second half robustly with City mounting sporadic raids but midway through proceedings **Graham Atkinson** beats City's ineffectual offside trap to put United 3-1 up and seemingly out of reach. City have an enormous task ahead of them and the prospects look pretty bleak to say the least, but they continue to mount attacks from the wings and a life-saving opportunity to reduce the arrears comes on

65 minutes; Leggett crosses to Butcher who is hacked down in the penalty area by Ron Atkinson as he approaches the goal. The referee points straight to the spot and we hardly dare to look as **Peter Shreeves** steps up to take the penalty kick. He hasn't been experiencing the best of games but he strikes the ball firmly into the far corner of the net to give us hope again at 3-2.

United continue to press but Leggett still looks dangerous on the now increasingly rare occasions City are able to break free from the relentless pressure they are forced to endure. The ever-dependent Collier continues to make fine saves and Eades remains a tower of strength and inspiration in central defence. With minutes left it looks all over and some of the Oxford fans are beginning to file out of the ground. I overhear one say as he walks past: *"They aren't a bad little team but class always tells in the end."*

But City have other ideas and are still mounting raids on the United goal which results in an astonishing 89th minute equaliser. Docherty passes to Cassidy who lobs the ball to **Pulley** at the far post. There is not a custard pie or banana skin to be seen as the Charlie Drake look-a-like slots the ball home. We have to rub our eyes and pinch ourselves to make sure we aren't dreaming we've come back from almost certain defeat and scored three goals against a top Third Division team on their own patch!

In extra time City are well in contention to gain an incredible victory with Collier a spectator for most of the time. Both sides come close to sneaking another goal but we are well pleased with the way City have battled, their heads have never once dropped and a draw is the least they deserve.

Tired and hoarse we leave with the prospects of a second replay at a neutral ground and we speculate where that might be. We all feel we'd like to go to the pub but our coach driver had earlier made it very plain that he would leave at 10pm sharp if there was extra time.

Exhausted I settle down in my seat, what a day. Although there is a supply of food and drink on the coach, I still have the remainder of my sandwiches and the rather tepid 'coffee'. I wait for the celebratory singsong but everyone is too knackered after the almost full working day, the journey and the tension of the game itself. We all agree our boys have done us proud and we have scored six goals in the two

209

games without leading scorer Billy Cassidy getting one! Perhaps he'll save one for the next match.

Suddenly I wake up and wipe the window to look out to see the 'Leaden Roding' sign. We are on the A414 with not far to go. I suggest to John Butcher, Tony's youngest brother, that perhaps we could persuade the driver to detour up Chignal Road and along Melbourne Avenue so we could get off at the Park, saving us a trip from New Street. The driver kindly agrees and nearing 1 o'clock my bed is most welcome.

Thursday 14th December 1967

Next morning the talk at Marconi's is dominated by City's exploits, it seems the whole factory is in the grip of acute cup-fever which even exceeds the excitement generated by the World Cup last year. The second replay is to be staged at Brentford's Griffin Park ground next Monday.

Monday 18th December 1967

With Shreeves scoring the winner on Saturday against an always competitive Yeovil to keep up our good form in the league and our title challenge on track, I decide to drive to Brentford for the evening game. Nobby Harris navigates using a large fold-up map of London with very small writing which he has trouble reading in the dark. Not leaving enough time to get there and getting stuck on the North and then the South Circular roads, we find Nobby's map does not show the ground. We know we are in the Brentford area and are about to ask for directions when Nobby spots the floodlights. Now we have to find somewhere to park and the streets are full of cars. We find space two or three streets away from the lights. As we get out of the car there's a cheer. Possibly a goal – is it City or United? We're worried we won't be let into the ground as we're late but we are soon on the terraces and hear King Billy has scored. We're not the only late arrivals – all missing the goal, of course. My watch tells me we have missed the first ten minutes.

City have an unchanged starting eleven from the first replay with

Bobby Smith again named as substitute. Oxford bring in debutant Alan Farsdon at left back and move Maurice Kyle back to the centre half position; their substitute is Tony Jones.

We learn Cassidy's goal came after only 50 seconds when he headed in from under the bar from a Leggett corner. However, we are in time to see Graham Atkinson miss two half chances in rapid succession shooting wide on both occasions. As the first half unfolds the play is becoming a very scrappy affair peppered with numerous free kicks and stoppages for minor injuries. The conditions are not conducive to good football with the pitch a combination of mud and frost with light rain falling for most of the ninety minutes.

Neither side is able to stamp their authority on the game. Both goalkeepers are tested but Sherratt is the busier of the two. Butcher beats him on 27 minutes but the "goal" is ruled offside. Half time arrives and as we queue for our tea and burgers the Beatles' "Hello Goodbye" is played over the public address system, it is the current number one single.

The second half continues in much the same fashion as the first with neither team gaining an advantage and although Sherratt looks nervy at times Collier appears much more confident. The game is drawing to a close and our nerves are really on edge when Jones, who has come on as substitute for Skeen, is put clear but the advancing Collier is able to push the ball aside. The crowd is announced as 4,350 but more than half are City, all by now willing the seconds away, with a crescendo of whistling and cheering. When the shrill blast of the final whistle comes the roar is deafening, as though we had won the FA Cup final itself!

They play 'Hello Goodbye' again as we file out of the ground – I feel that song will always remind me of this fabulous game and result.

As we have no coach to rush to, we have time for a pint in a pub near the Brentford ground. We are talking excitedly about the result and are overheard by some locals. They are unaware a game has taken place only a short distance away. When we tell them more of the circumstances surrounding the match, they become even more interested. However, they have no idea where Chelmsford is and assume we are an amateur club. They are impressed, though, that we have beaten a team they consider much better than Brentford, who are in the Fourth Division.

The drive home takes about an hour and a half and feels much less fraught than the outward journey. Our only regret on the night is missing King Billy's goal!

Friday 20th December 1967

Two days now and I have still not come down off cloud nine! Colchester beat Torquay in their replay as we were winning at Brentford and so it is United in early January. The Chronicle is full of the Wednesday match and reports that a rather subdued Arthur Turner, the Oxford manager who watched on forlornly as his Division Three side bowed out to Southern League opposition for a second successive year said afterwards:

"Our defence stood off when Cassidy scored the goal. I had to give them a rucking at half time. Unfortunately we didn't get any better in the second half but I still feel we had chances enough to have won well."

A jubilant Harry Ferrier didn't allow the euphoria to sway his judgement.

"Perhaps we were a little fortunate. The Oxford forwards' finishing was often wild, even so our lads fought all the way and their application made me a very proud man."

And who can argue with that? The first Football League club City have beaten in 29 years and now we can prepare for a titanic clash with Colchester! Win that and we are in the Third Round with the big boys – surely then the League clubs will take note and vote us into the Fourth Division?

Sunday 7th January 1968

What a disappointing day yesterday! Football fever had hit the town for more than three weeks over Christmas when we won one, drew one and lost one of our league games in the festive period. We certainly lived the Cup dream but it is shattered by a very polished and professional Colchester United performance.

The police imposed a crowd limit of 17,000 for the all-ticket game, prices were: – Ground 6/-, Enclosure 7/- and Stand 8/-. The official attendance given out last night in the 'Green 'Un' was 16,403, not far short of City's record attendance, 16,807 for a Southern League match also against Colchester back in September 1949.

The build-up to the match was phenomenal with the Chronicle devoting pages to it. Martin Rogers expected a City victory with Butcher and Cassidy playing so well this season and the team possessing a greater degree of understanding and co-ordination than Colchester. City were 5/4, Colchester 2/1 and the draw 3/1, making us the favourites!

Queues for tickets to the main stand stretched the length of New Writtle Street and local league games were postponed to allow players to go to the match. Although Colchester might return some tickets to be sold on the day most of the terrace tickets had been sold already. It was announced beforehand that the City players would receive an extra 2s 6d for every 100 attending over 3,500, so with over 16,000 there it was, at least, a rewarding pay day with an extra £16.

Once again City are able to field an unchanged side from the last Oxford United game with the exception of goalkeeper Alan Collier whose loan period has expired. Owen Medlock is still out injured so Barry Watling is taken on loan from Bristol City for a two-month spell. Peter Collins is named as substitute.

Colchester's line-up as:

Ernie Adams

Denis Mochan; Duncan Forbes; Bobby Blackwood; Brian Hall

Terry Price; Derek Trevis; Tommy McKechnie; John Martin;

John Mansfield; Reg Stratton;

Substitute: Bob Walker

Hopes of a City victory were very high. Johnny Gordon expressed the mood in the dressing room by telling the Chronicle: *'There is a spirit here, a lot of guts and ability in this side. Overall, we have probably played better away from home – but we have yet to see the best of this team.'*

With Martin Rogers tipping City to win most of us thought a draw the least we could expect. After all Oxford had failed to get the better of us in three attempts and Colchester were much lower down in Division Three than Oxford. That's how the reasoning went, how wrong we all were!

A huge cheer greeted the teams as they ran onto the pitch to the strains of 'The Waltzing Bugle Boy' over the (as usual) defective and crackly P.A. system. To accommodate more fans some were allowed beyond the white walls and onto the cinder track, adding to the atmosphere. The game commenced and although City started with plenty of spirit they lacked any penetration, even Butcher and Cassidy, the goalscoring 'dynamic duo', were constantly thwarted and Leggett was ineffectual for most of the game. City's most impressive player in the early stages was Johnny Gordon who looked dangerous coming forward on numerous raids.

In the 17th minute City were struck a severe blow when Butcher was caught offside and Forbes thumped the resultant free kick downfield. Eades, under pressure from Stratton attempted to head clear but the ball glanced away towards McKechnie who struck it past the diving Watling.

Colchester's wingers, Price and Martin, were causing City problems with their speed and pace; both missed good chances to increase the lead before half time. Other than that the game was fairly even but Watling in the City goal looked rather jittery at times when put to the test.

Early in the second half City had their claims for a penalty brushed aside when a Butcher effort hit the hand of Forbes. There followed a period of intense City pressure which, although promising much, came to nothing.

Brian Hall was stretchered off on 65 minutes having been concussed after a clash of heads and Bob Walker substituted. This did not affect Colchester's composure and they stood firm as City continued to press. Costello almost snatched an equaliser late in the game when he headed inches over the crossbar and Pulley was unlucky with a shot that went just wide of a post.

Any hopes of a City equaliser evaporated in the dying seconds of normal time when they were again caught offside. Adams took the free kick, which Mochan collected and passed on to Stratton. He found Martin unmarked on the left and then ran into the penalty area just in time to meet the winger's cross and to head it past the despairing Watling.

⚽ 214 ⚽

Anglia TV captures the scene from their gantry above the main stand as Eades and Wilson defend a Colchester attack – a crowd of 16,403 packs into New Writtle Street with some seated beyond the perimeter wall

And so ends City's F.A. Cup aspirations for another year – no dream tie at White Hart Lane or Old Trafford, but we can look forward to the rest of the season – we are just above halfway up the league table but within touching distance of the front runners. From a financial standpoint it is reported we have made over £4,000 from the Cup run: so at least Mr Last will be pleased.

Disappointingly the national press coverage of the Oxford games was sketchy and the most high profile comment was from TV celebrity, Clement Freud, sitting in our main stand in the first Oxford game and writing for one of the national Sunday newspapers. He commented that the viaducts of the nearby London to Norwich railway could hardly be discerned through the driving snow and reminded him of the Trans-Siberian Railway!

13

BRING IT ON!

Elation soon turned to deflation as the team succumbed meekly to Colchester after the Oxford heroics, but with more than half the season still to play the League title was far from being out of the question and the Floodlit League too. Tony Butcher still had 35 games to play from January through to May. Glory waited at the end of this but, for now, Tony picks up the story after the Colchester game on 6th January.

We're all bitterly disappointed with our performance against Colchester. Such a huge, noisy crowd made for a terrific atmosphere at the old ground. I've never experienced anything like it. Johnny Gordon said he felt more nervous here than when he ran out at the Nou Camp to play Barcelona in front of 80,000 and perhaps it was our nerves that got to us. The City that beat Oxford just did not turn up yet we felt we'd given everything but were beaten by a better, more professional outfit. Disappointingly we find that Colchester have now drawn West Bromwich Albion in the next round: what a great experience that would have been with a game at the Hawthorns.

***

There is still much to play for. We're tenth in the league with 22 points from 18 games with Wimbledon top on 26 from 20, so if we win those two games in hand the four points will bring us level.

In the aftermath of the disappointment of Colchester, the players are upset with the comments made by Martin Rogers who writes: *'Buy or it will be Bye-Bye to our title hopes'* and *'Tony Butcher is out of touch and could do with a rest'* – something of a contradiction to what he said in the build up for the Colchester game! I take this up with Martin when I see him and he apologises claiming he felt I looked tired but in this week's column does mention that: *'Butcher never hides and whilst he might miss two chances will always be in place to score the third and his goalscoring record is phenomenal'*.

Disgruntled fans write in to the Chronicle and one says: *'one or two players suggest by their performances that they are disenchanted with Chelmsford City'* and another writes: *'There is a breakdown in liaison and sympathy between players and management'*.

The boys talk about this at training and are, quite frankly, astounded as well as being upset as nothing could be further from the truth. After all, we've beaten a team two divisions higher than us but lost to another – no disgrace in that – and we've a good chance of winning the league with so much of our season left. We've a great spirit largely brought on by having this very settled team, only changed so far through injury, and, with the Reserves doing so well in their league, everything at the club remains very rosy indeed. It's just a pity that some of the fans fail to see it that way.

***

To prove my high expectations for the rest of the season are well wide of the mark, I can't recall as bad a month as February in my time at City with one win in six league games and three draws; we play badly too. I get dropped and miss the Floodlit League game on February 19th and the Southern League game on the 24th but Billy Cassidy is also not spared and is due to sit out today's game at Nuneaton. Sitting on the long coach journey I have plenty of time to try and understand what's wrong. Billy is certainly having his head turned by Detroit Cougars who have, apparently, made overtures with their summer season not far away.

Perhaps Martin Rogers was right and I'm tired and could do with a break, but I feel fine. Owen Medlock is back in goal having not played since mid-November. Barry Watling has done quite well as his stand in but he's no Owen. Many in our home crowd have been on our backs and what amazes me is that we had over 16,000 for the Colchester match but at our next home league game it is less than 2,000. I can never quite fathom out where they all go and why a few more don't come along regularly. With our 4-1 win last Monday against Burton Albion perhaps we can embark on a run; we're still in contact with the front runners and not out of it.

Peter Collins duly left for Tottenham in January for a whopping £5,500! Good luck to him; he's a talent and we've not yet seen the best of him as he's had only a few senior outings. What irony though in that his first game for Spurs 'A' is against City at The Stadium playing alongside the great Mike England, captain of Wales, returning from injury.

The poor old Reserves! Riding high in their league they're told there won't be a team next season. We heard this last year but the decision was reversed; however, they're apparently losing the club £60 per week and Mr Last has had enough. He says he wants a stronger first team pool with local youth encouraged into the Under 18s. I can't see the logic in not having some sort of Reserve team, even if in a lower league, because how do out of form first teamers and those returning from injury get a run out? There's much thought that cost-cutting is all well and good but should we not still be aiming for the Football League? Many believe the club's aim, unlike when John Coward was running it, is now to be a mid-table, stable non-league club. This won't attract players or supporters but then I'm a footballer and don't have to run the club. Back in November Mr Last told our shareholders we were losing £200 per week when he took over from John and it's because of this that these measures are being taken but if we have a team capable of winning the League and progressing to a higher status, surely this will bring in additional finances? After all we can still command attendances at home of over 7,000 for the really big league matches, so the fan base is still there.

***

Now towards the end of March we are on a good run of six games without defeat, I spotted an interesting comment in the 'Green 'Un' that this change of fortune has come too late for us to win the League this season. The reporter talks of the difficult away games to come and the fact that we've now played the same number of games as Wimbledon who are currently top but are six points behind. He considers our improvement has come too late but I know the boys are confident we can push on and the crucial games lie ahead, especially over Easter.

Throughout March all sorts of things are happening at the club. An offer for Billy Cassidy has been received from Grimsby Town; however neither the club nor he is interested. Horace Phillp on the Board since 1938 has resigned and the players hear of further ructions in the boardroom. One good thing is that the club is to include a copy of the Football League Review, a glossy and very interesting colour magazine with articles and photos, within the match day programme.

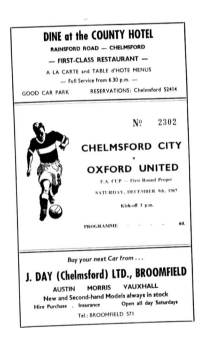
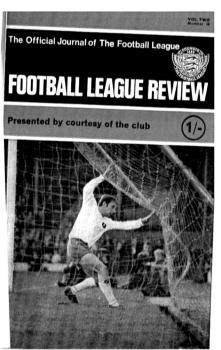

The ordinary black and white programme incorporates the 24-page Football League Review free of charge. A new era begins.

On the playing front we are on the march in March (!) with win after win. However, many fans still say we'll not win the League but the players believe we shall. In all my years here I've never seen such a determined group of players, all pulling in the same direction. The only two teams I believe to also be in contention are Wimbledon and Cambridge United. We remain six points behind Wimbledon with United sandwiched between us but the key is we've yet to play them both, home and away – win those games and we have a great chance. Hereford have been there or thereabouts all season but, not for the first time, are falling away in the second half of the season. We play them on March 16th and win 3-1 but what an honour to be on the same pitch as the great John Charles, their player manager and formerly of Leeds United and Juventus – he's a living legend at both clubs. Clearly past his best he still has a wonderful touch and control but was brilliantly shackled by Terry Eades prompting the great man to compliment Terry at the final whistle.

The supporters are up in arms about the scrapping of the Reserves who continue to dominate their league but it doesn't appear Mr Last will budge this year. Even the Romford manager tells the Chronicle that Romford's worst mistake in recent times was getting rid of their reserve team and so not making use of their ground every week. He suggests clubs should retain these second teams and make up the loss by commercial events within the club such as dances, discos, sportsmen's dinners and even bingo! Len Menhinick urges fans to persuade the Supporters' Club to take up the issue with the Board and it appears they will.

Our biggest league match to date is on March 25th at home to Wimbledon, who have been on a poor run. Over 5,000 are there to see us triumph 3-2 where I manage two (making me the crowd's hero again … at least until the next match) and Peter Shreeves slots home a penalty. The league positions are now: Cambridge United 47 from 34; City 45 from 33; Wimbledon 44 from 33.

This makes the two Easter games against United so vital and the players can't wait, especially as we've now won eight consecutive league games.

***

⚽ 221 ⚽

The busy Easter programme has come and gone and after the win away at Cambridge United, we are favourites to win the Southern League (at last!), having won all eleven league games since February 24th. We can add to that three wins and a draw in Floodlit League matches. My form has been good with eleven goals after my return from being dropped. The crowds have slowly increased with more than 7,500 for the Cambridge United home win on Good Friday, following on from the large crowd against Wimbledon. There were more than 7,800 at Cambridge yesterday including a thousand from Chelmsford.

Wimbledon and United have been amongst the front runners all season but we knew if we could remain not far behind we had a chance of catching them. Winning all three Easter games and with the return match at Wimbledon due at the beginning of May we're in the box seat. With the games coming thick and fast I feel knackered after three important games in four days. I'm sure we can go on and win the title and, having beaten Southend 4-1 in the Essex Professional Cup semi-final in March, we now have a return match in the final against Colchester in May.

The hard, dusty pitches are taking their toll too and most of us have burns to our knees and the outside of our thighs with these stinging like mad when in each game we slide on the ground and shave off the scab that's just formed . Alec Wilson, Bobby Smith and Gordon Pulley have been out injured but what able deputies we have had in Peter Gillott, Micky Block and Roy Walsh. All three were involved yesterday at Cambridge with Roy coming off the bench to score the only goal of the match. Gil was useful to help combat Ian Hutchinson's long throw ins for Cambridge because Hutch can hurl the ball right into your six yard box and this puts you under all sorts of pressure. I've never seen anything like his throws and he's a pretty good player with the ball on the ground and we were told in the bar after the game that Chelsea are interested in signing him at the end of this season.

Billy Cassidy's concussion was the reason for Roy Walsh's introduction. After a nasty clash of heads and lengthy treatment Billy said he was fine and would carry on. It was soon quite apparent all was not right with him as he started running round without purpose and made no sense when we spoke to him, so he was taken off to hospital. He should be fine in a couple of days and OK for Saturday's trip to Weymouth.

With news of us ditching the Reserves it is interesting that Gillott, Block and Walsh have been playing regularly in that team but, like some others, have stepped up to the plate when called upon. Also 17 year old winger Ian Johnston, still at Chelmsford Tech, came on as substitute in Saturday's win at Barnet. This, following the selling of Peter Collins, shows our policy of promoting local youth is also working well. Ian told me on the coach journey that he's off this week to a Festival of Football representing Essex Schools Under 18s along with fellow City Reserve, defender Brian Terry, and three other local lads, Dick Smith, Cliff Hill and Steve Little all from the Grammar School – suddenly the old town is becoming a hotbed of local talent!

With six games to go we top the Southern League: City 51 points from 36; Cambridge 49 from 37; Wimbledon 47 from 36.

Of those six games five are away and include Wimbledon with the one home game against Dover. We believe three wins will do it provided one of those is against Wimbledon, who've been on a recent good run after faltering in February and March.

***

We've just completed nine games in April including two in the Floodlit League. We were a little nervous before Saturday's last home league game having lost away at Weymouth and Margate but the 3-1 win over Dover has settled our nerves. Tomorrow is the crunch game away at Wimbledon. Coach loads will be leaving Chelmsford so we can expect the usual great following to south west London.

***

What a win! 2-1 and the Claret dream is almost a reality. Over 5,000 pack into Plough Lane with the whole of one end City claret. I manage to nick a goal after earlier hitting a post. Peter Leggett did his usual down the wing, squared it to Billy who laid it off to me for an easy finish. Micky Block slams one home and Wimbledon get a late consolation. This leaves us having to win our next match away at Hastings United on Wednesday to bring home the title. I'm so pleased for the club and most particularly for the supporters. It's taken us a long

⚽ 223 ⚽

time to win something meaningful (22 years, apparently) and perhaps the football world might take notice of us at last. It's not done yet, this championship, but already relegated Hastings may not have the stomach for it; let's hope not!

I needn't have worried! We're 1-0 up after five minutes and force nine corners in the first twenty minutes before Micky scores followed by Billy, me and Peter Shreeves so we are 4-0 up at half time and it's all over, surely, and the title is ours. There is only 600 or so at Hastings in their super arena and half those are from Chelmsford. What a shame we're not at home in front of 4,000. Harry has a right go at us afterwards about our poor second half performance which sees Hastings score, but we're too busy celebrating to take much notice and someone does say to Harry: *'Come on, boss, we've just won the bloody league!'*

Old mate George Duncan is playing for them and joins us in the dressing room for a beer and is as excited as we are. That is what City does for you: it's a club like no other and former players rarely lose their love for the place. Many of the fans also join us in the bar and it's late when we all get home and I find it difficult to sleep due to the excitement. For a local boy like me I feel it a bit more; because this is my club and I've had no other and I'm a fan at heart, after all. The final table reads:

City 57 points: Wimbledon 55: Cambridge United 53

Other great news this week is that the Reserves beat West Ham 3-1 to virtually secure the Metropolitan League. This was without Ian Johnston who was playing for England Schoolboys against Wales. This boy could make it but he has a place at university and, like Malcolm Pannell before him, may choose an academic life to that of professional football. More good news for the Reserves is that they are through to the final of their league cup by default.

***

With May coming to an end we finish the season tired yet satisfied at the same time. It would have been nice to have also won the Floodlit League, particularly as we came top. However, the rules say we have to play-off with the team in second place which just happens to be

Romford. We beat them 2-1 at home in the first leg but lose 5-1 at Brooklands with Peter Shreeves wrongly sent off (we hear later that he's been exonerated) amid a poor display. These games followed a fine match against Colchester in the final of the Essex Professional Cup and they edge us 3-2 after extra time.

***

If I look back over the season, it was clearly that great run from the end of February, plus the wins in all four games against our closest rivals for the league title, that counted most. It's about winning the games that matter: you'll lose some along the way but then so will other teams. Keeping a settled team is vital and, as I have said already, this is not the best City team I have played in not by a long chalk, but we gelled. We worked for each other and we had strong leaders on the field with that steely experience, men like Johnny Doc and Johnny Gordon, and we can mix that with the flair of a Leggett, the doggedness of Shreeves and an excellent defence with the best goalkeeper in this league and beyond.

What about the boss? Harry didn't have to do much on the tactical side as we all seemed to know what we had to do. But I do have to say that Peter Harburn helped set up this team and he deserves a lot of credit. One of the players tells Martin Rogers: *'There are times when the boss drove us up the wall!'*

Harry told the Chronicle: *'Overall consistency won us the title.'* And he is right; backed up by players coming into the team from a winning and successful Reserve team – how valuable were the goals from Block and Walsh in those crucial matches? We shall miss that next season when there is no Reserve team.

I'm also pleased for John Coward. He's still a director but is not seen much, perhaps due to his illness, and he deserves this success but it's just a pity it did not come five years earlier when we and not Oxford might have taken Accrington's place in the Football League.

But for now it's time for celebration and we have Friday's open top bus ride to look forward to. The whole club is buoyed ahead of next season and looking forward to carrying on the good work from this but, as I've said already, this team will break up with possibly as many as five or six leaving. Time will tell if they can be replaced enabling us to maintain our current status as the BEST non-league team in the country.

So what of those players who've largely formed this team to make us the best non-league team in the country? This week's Chronicle, having raised its price to 6d, includes a wonderful colour photo of the team with the trophy – the first ever colour in the newspaper – and pays tribute to the team. This is the photo and what the paper says:

Champions: From left to right: Back Row – Lou Costello; Bobby Smith; Owen Medlock; Peter Shreeves; Terry Eades; John Docherty
Front Row – Gordon Pulley; Peter Leggett; Tony Butcher; Billy Cassidy; Johnny Gordon; Micky Block

'**Owen Medlock** *began this term in slightly patchy form then fractured a cheekbone in November but his return to the team at the end of February signalled the start of the great run of league victories, not a coincidence. But now he is retiring – too soon – and we wish him well.*

Full backs **Lou Costello** *and* **Alec Wilson** *showed their experience and professionalism. Lou was due to leave at the end of last season but we're glad he was kept on. Alec lost his place through injury in*

February and the ever-dependable, **Bobby Smith**, was a more than capable deputy.

The half back line of Shreeves, Eades and Docherty showed little or no change all season. Durable skipper **John Docherty**, ever ready to urge on his men, played a quiet, steady part. **Terry Eades** – unsettled at one stage of the season – filled the centre half position with the same consistency of past years. **Peter Shreeves** was an enigma. At times he tested the patience of the fans (a little like Len Phillips in the past) yet on other days he looked a most accomplished attacking player. In one respect he had no peer – as penalty taker of the side, so often an Achilles' heel in the past.

The forward heroes whose goalscoring partnership was the talk of the league were old hand, **Tony Butcher**, playing as well as in any of his dozen years on the City payroll, and **Billy Cassidy** the extrovert Scot who has been an exciting and entertaining player and the darling of the crowd.

At the hub of the midfield was **Johnny Gordon** who took his time to win over the fans but grafted his way through an exacting season, playing in all 42 games, which would have tested the stamina and quality of a younger man.

For much of the season **Peter Leggett** and **Gordon Pulley** were the wing men. Leggett, the Beatle-cut flier, was troubled by injuries in the early stages but on his day could scythe through the best defence. Pulley, a cheerful, clever left-winger finds himself retained but on the transfer list. This decision comes as a surprise to many City followers who rate him one of the best wingers of recent years.

Occasional forward places went to **Roy Walsh** and **Micky Block**. It was Block who finished the season as first choice left winger and scored some absolutely vital goals as did Roy Walsh against Hillingdon and Cambridge United. Both might be leaving us although rumour has it that Block might be offered terms.'

14

SWAN SONG FOR THE RESERVES?

Brian Terry looks back on the Reserves' season when against considerable odds they won the League and Cup. They could, perhaps should, have been runners-up in both but the fates, for once, worked in their favour. It was a remarkable achievement but once more finances were stretched, crowds stayed away and for the second year running it was decided this 67/68 season would be the last for the Reserves with this coming at the time of their greatest triumph.

Well I hoped the season would go well and, quite frankly, I can't believe it can get any better than this! The Double! Even at this rung on the football ladder this is some achievement especially with so many of us local lads bringing the silverware home and with it more than matching anything that has gone before.

To cap all of this, the dream of me playing for the City in the Southern League became a reality. Well almost! Saturday September 2nd 1967 was that great day for me when I donned the famous First Team shirt of City claret and white, albeit with the number 12 on its back. What an honour for a 17 year old local boy, a supporter, now gracing the greatest stage so far in my fledging football life. OK I didn't get on the field to play in a 2-2 draw but it was an experience I shall never forget even if another chance doesn't come along.

On the Friday before the match I'm told I've been selected as substitute for the game at Wellington, missing the Reserves' key game against West Ham at home. It's a long way to Wellington – almost into North Wales – but the first-teamers are a friendly bunch and make me feel welcome. I can see a great spirit amongst them even at this early stage of the season with the usual banter and leg-pulling continuing all the way through the long journey. It's an honour for me to run out with the team even though I'm the one in the tracksuit. The crowd is dotted around this large ground with less than a thousand inside but it's heartening to see a few claret City scarves – what a trek for them. I do enjoy this 'one day in the sun' even though I'm not called upon with no one being injured and I later learn I was taken as cover for Alec Wilson who had a niggle.

***

So what of our season in the Metropolitan League? It was fantastic for me and the other youngsters; helped by the older pros. We were pacesetters in the league all season with the big threat coming from Bury Town who had so many games in hand at the end of the season. Could they win them all and stop us? After all, when we finished our games at the end of April they were six points behind with SIX games still to play and that could be twelve points. Thankfully they ran out of

The Reserves League and Cup winners 1968 but their days are numbered
Back Row: Left to Right: Doug Rollings. Claude Seymour; Fred Kearsley; Don Walker; Wicker Smith; Alec Wilson; Lance Gooch; Dave Pye; Peter Gillott; Brian Terry; Harry Ferrier; Ken Orrin; Bob Last
Front Row: Left to Right: Ian Johnston; Eddie Dilsworth; Martin Rollings; Roy Walsh; Micky Block; Graham Pooley

steam mustering only five points (drawing their last game 1-1 with Cray Wanderers when a win would have given them the title) and, so, we lifted the league trophy by one point: quite an achievement when you look at the opposition in the league! Then we had the League Cup final against Sheppey United after the debacle with Chatham, who played three ineligible players and beat us before being thrown out of the competition.

Mr Ferrier strengthened our team for the two legs adding first teamers Costello, Cassidy and Docherty, which was fair enough given that they'd all played for us at some point in the season. For the second leg the triumphant team was:

Dave Pye; Lou Costello; John Docherty: Lance Gooch; Peter Gillott; Ian Johnston; Eddie Dilsworth; Billy Cassidy; Roy Walsh; Micky Block and me.

Having won the home first leg 2-1 we cruise to an aggregate win to lift the cup and so complete the double for the season.

Before the end of season Owen Medlock and Bobby Smith held a testimonial against an All-Star XI which included Ron Atkinson, Peter Brabrook, John Bond and our own Len Phillips. A decent crowd of 2,300 were there and I was offered the chance to play against and alongside those I had admired previously only from afar. What a thrill for me with the largest crowd I've played in front of. It was 5-5 with referee, Len Menhinick, making some ridiculously generous decisions to either side for penalties. It was all good fun and raised over £400 each for Owen and Bob, such great players for this club and deserving of this decent payday. A sad note after the game was when a tearful Owen told us he was retiring from the game, despite being only 30, to become an insurance salesman. He says he needs to secure the future for his family explaining that he has had some nasty injuries, including a broken cheekbone this season, so didn't wish to have an injury to put him out of the game for good. It's such a shame as he's still good enough to be playing at the top level in the game.

Shortly after this announcement Billy Cassidy tells us he's definitely off to Detroit Cougars. He'll be paid twice what he's getting here and have a house although for the moment his wife and family will remain in the UK. He says he's been told he may be able to return to the City once the Cougars' season ends in the autumn – let's hope so. He's had a purple patch this season striking up such a great partnership with Tony Butcher with them both scoring such a large number of goals. Billy is not the best I've seen at City, a point echoed by Butch, but he's a centre forward, like many before him, who has hit such a rich vein of form at the right time. Good luck to him in Detroit but we all wish it was us on our way there and not him!

***

The celebrations at the Civic Centre were fantastic, especially the pride the crowds felt for us and the warm feelings towards Mr Coward who has given the club so much. How memorable for me and my girlfriend, Eileen, to be on that bus and also for me to attend the Metropolitan League dinner at the Park Lane Hotel, Piccadilly. It was expensive but Mr Coward paid. We met ex England manager Walter Winterbottom who presented the Shield and our medals. Mr Ken Aston was there too and told us about the infamous Chile v Italy match he refereed in the 1962 World Cup when war almost broke out on the pitch; it has become known as the 'Battle of Santiago'. He also spoke, as a World Cup administrator, of trying to persuade Rattin to get off the Wembley pitch after his sending off in that World Cup game against England. These are fond memories that will stay with me forever.

My time at City appeared to be over a few months back but the recent decision to retain the Reserves for the 1968/69 season means I might stay on. Despite the Wellington substitute appearance I will not hold my breath that there is a future in the First Team here. With my schooling at an end I might take up an office job I've been offered in London and pursue a career elsewhere in amateur football. I've already been approached by Enfield from the Isthmian League and may take up their offer at some time in the future. This option would bring in a solid working wage to be supplemented by 'expenses' playing amateur stuff. Despite what the Football Association might say payments beyond expenses do occur in amateur football despite being contrary to FA rules, although this has most certainly not happened at City: whether I might benefit elsewhere remains to be seen.

Some of the amateur players I've played with at Chelmsford, or known through local football, have gone where they might make some money. Take Johnny French, a talented player who could make it as a pro but he has an attitude problem and is drifting from amateur club to amateur club probably to obtain the best money deal he can. I don't blame Johnny in one way, but wish he'd stayed and applied himself here.

Interestingly in a match against Sheppey in March there were NINE amateurs (only receiving expenses) and one pro in Peter Gillott plus semi-pro Dave Pye, both considered to be local as Gil has been here ten years and Dave was born in the town and now combines football with being a teacher at the Tech. Despite our apparent inexperience we won that game and with it the League. Yes, there have been a few more pros playing for the Reserves in other games but, if we stick with this current set up, surely the club can afford to retain the second string, with such small match by match outlay?

Add to the equation the cash from the sale of Peter Collins, Robin Gladwin and Bryan King plus the FA Cup run, surely our coffers are bulging. Could it be that this money is just being used to clear the debts, reported recently in the local press to amount to a five figure sum? Time will tell.

With no professional contract likely at the City and knowing West Ham have looked at me, I'm currently in the middle of a month's trial at Chelsea and only last week played a game for them at Hitchin Town. Incidentally, in defence with me are some really good players and one to watch out for is Stewart Houston. I'm learning so much from him but he plays in my preferred position, so in a way we're competing for that place. Interestingly, the trialists spend most of the afternoons with a football, working on set plays, how to defend and where we should be in certain situations during a game; truly eye-opening and something that clubs like City need to introduce if they're serious about joining the Football League.

Now at the end of this Championship winning season Terry Eades has asked to be put on the transfer list. He knows he has a number of suitors and is almost certain to leave for a decent transfer fee so perhaps the club should cash in now. With this fee added to increased gate money next season now we are League Champions, perhaps we've turned a corner. Of course Harry Ferrier will want to bolster the side offering good money and he has the knack of unearthing talent without having to fork out too much. Perhaps there'll be a compromise by the Board with the cash reducing the debts, funding new players AND maintaining the Reserves – let's hope so.

15

THE COWARD EMPIRE IS NO MORE

Trophies have been won but there is bedlam within the club. Although no longer a director, our 'insider' gives an insight into the shenanigans off the pitch and in particular on the Board. The 'Emperor' has gone and his old empire is in disarray. So, is this the beginning of the end for the club as we have known it? Is the Claret dream over? It seems so after ten exciting and tumultuous years the like of which we may not see again. Here is what happened as the 1967/68 season came to an end as seen by our 'insider'.

Well, we did it eventually. Champions! Well done to the players of both First and Reserve teams. I am so pleased for the likes of Tony Butcher and Peter Gillott who have been with us through the Coward years and to John himself who has given so much but …

John has been sacked from the Board! The news hit me like a thunderbolt. Despite being under stress with his health issues, John has been ousted. Bob Last, the Chairman, has never liked John and he has engineered the dismissal stating John has only been to one meeting in seventeen months and that is in breach of the rules, a fact Last quoted in his letter to John and made known in the Chronicle.

I'm no fan of Last. Before we heard of John's dismissal, Last said the club must compete for the league title for the next three seasons and for him to strengthen the club – perhaps he is being practical and realistic but this is not what the fans or players want to hear – they want to be told we have ambition to go higher up the football ladder. It seems to me that Last wants a Southern League club that breaks even and is solid without stretching itself financially – but this smacks of no ambition and not what our club is about, surely?

Last makes a further stab at the heart of John Coward by being quoted in the Chronicle:

'It is inferred in certain published statements that Mr Coward has poured thousands of pounds into the club. The records of the club do not support those statements.'

That is outrageous. Bob Last knows better than anyone else HOW John put money into the club. Anyone in the town will know that, so I don't have to spell it out. Yes, John's dream about the new stadium has not materialised but it has not been a pipedream. It could have become a reality if the French family, the cricket club and the Council had played ball. Their shortsightedness has left the town bereft of a marvellous facility and not just to benefit the football fraternity. Perhaps it was John's character that upset people – he's not everyone's cup of tea but his heart is in the right place. He has made this club into the best outside the Football League and this should never be forgotten. I fear now the fans will see a downward spiral under Last.

Director Freddie Langton has come out and backed up what I have said, telling the Chronicle:

'The financing from John was through interest-free loans and the club has owed him a lot of money at various times.'

He adds that John also gave employment to many of our professionals who remained part-time.

Now there is more upheaval – Director Claude Seymour has resigned saying:

'The boardroom set up is a farce and when I attended Board meetings certain decisions had already been made outside of our proper discussions.'

It seems to be that the Last faction are exacting their *'pound of flesh'* by getting their own back for when John removed Last and Benge from the Board.

A furious Len Menhinick has written to the Chronicle calling for

John to be reinstated and confirms that substantial funds were constantly available from John during Len's time as Secretary.

With all these comments being thrown about across the press, the Board issues a definitive reply, published in the Chronicle:

'In reply to John Coward's statement in the local press last week that an apology was always sent for (his) non-attendance at Board meetings, he should realise that apologies are always set out in the Company Minutes. Exactly four apologies were received in 17 months; this can be proved. And to put it mildly showed complete lack of respect.

Dealing with the missing thousands of pounds poured into the club John Coward says he has the receipts for same. If this is the case why not produce them together with a statement showing the amount of money refunded to him by the club?

On the other hand has John Coward confused this with the £million plus Sports Arena to which he has given so much publicity, but which in fact was nothing more than a pipedream from beginning to end?

John Coward states that he does not feel that the present Board is good for football in Chelmsford, but it must be remembered that during the five or six years he was in charge neither team won anything worth mentioning. Three managers, Mr Ferrier, Mr Frith and Mr Harburn were sacked; the attendance figures reached an all-time low and a very large sum of money was lost in two years trading alone; the balance sheet revealed a loss of nearly £27,000.

Does John Coward really feel that the Shareholders and the footballing public of Chelmsford want a return to this kind of mismanagement?'

Ouch! What a shame this all is. The greatest season the club has experienced is ruined by this in-fighting. Yes, some of the above is true but the Chelmsford public has wanted ambition, a team to go with that and to have a real tilt at the Football League. With John Coward I always felt our time would come; now I'm not so sure.

Rumours have circulated that the club might go part-time next season. I spoke to Bob Last about this and he said that it had been discussed at a Board meeting but he confirmed this would not happen. He said part-time professionals are expensive. They demand high wages, live away from the town, are only seen on match days and have to be paid for loss of earnings. I understand this and the fact that, with the current employment situation in this country, there are not many employers prepared to find jobs for footballers and give them time off to play in midweek games.

Last has also backed down and settled with Peter Harburn out of court for his dismissal. Peter, to his credit, only ever claimed his loss of basic earnings, some £601, and this is what the club has now settled after arguing the toss for two long years. I am pleased in a way but only John Coward really knows what went on at that Sunday morning meeting. I hear Peter is investing the money into his pub, the 'Bird in Hand'; just across the road from The Stadium.

What of the future? The Bob Last Empire lacks inspiration but we have to live with the fact that we might never be voted into the League unless some club goes bust. Workington are the latest club in crisis and if they do fold surely we would take their place as Southern League champions. However there is a raft of Football League clubs in the North West of England and would this put the improving Wigan Athletic in a better position to be elected? After all being close to so many clubs in that area would mean these clubs would see Wigan as another local derby with increased gate revenue compared with less interest in a game against the City who might only bring along a smattering of supporters. Apparently Workington are trying to manage on gates of less than 1,000 whereas our lowest league gate this season was 1,518 against Burton with the highest 7,514 against Cambridge United. Some difference; but it cuts no mustard with the League clubs – they will continue to vote Workington, Bradford Park Avenue, Hartlepools and the like back in every year. Hope and rumour abounds that the 92 League clubs might increase to 100 with a regional fourth and fifth division. We've heard it all before and I bet it doesn't happen. What we need is a football pyramid where one or two teams are automatically promoted into the Fourth Division by right at the expense of the bottom two teams in that division. This would mean junior teams and more established professional clubs, like City, would have a goal. Surely it must be good for football in general to allow a club to rise from park obscurity to the Football League?

The 'Soccer Star' has recently carried a two-page article about City and discusses this very point, detailing City's professional set up, achievements and right to be in the Football League. I imagine Martin Rogers might be behind this article as he used to write for this regular magazine before he joined the Essex Chronicle. Let us hope someone influential at the League headquarters reads it!

What future is there at the club? I'm worried – very worried – and quite frankly fear the worst.

EPILOGUE

The ultimate irony! In 1968 we win the Southern League making us the best non-league team in the country with this coming right at the end of our journey through the glory years of the Clarets. But what if we had achieved this feat when Gateshead dropped out of the Football League in 1960 with Peterborough United taking their place? What if we had won it in the year when Accrington Stanley folded and Oxford United were given their place as Southern league champions in 1962? What if …..?

The ten years from 1958 to 1968 were tumultuous for the City ending with the Holy Grail of the Southern League Championship in 1968 and not forgetting our Reserve team lifting the Metropolitan League and Cup titles against very strong opposition.

Neither team had what we would call 'star names'; they had come and gone in the early 60s. John Coward's considerable financial support had gone too, along with more than two thousand regular supporters despite the burgeoning population in the town. 1968 was about the pinnacle of the City success matched in 1972 and from that period the club began its downward spiral to virtual oblivion.

Our once majestic ground – a proper football ground – would eventually go. Stout hearted Chelmsford people and supporters like Claude Seymour and Doug Fawcett would do their best as Chairmen of the club they loved, but the chancers, the asset strippers, the property developers and non-football people would oversee the club's fall from the top table of the non-league.

Now in the second decade of the 21st century the club is back in the hands of Chelmsford people – fans. Other long-term supporters help in the running of the club; ex-players are involved too. Since 1987 non-league clubs do not have to rely on breaking into the 'old boys' club' by securing votes at a League AGM, there is now a pathway to the Promised Land of the Football League. The City remain one removed from that in our 75th year but we can do it – we will do it, but it will be tough. Tony Butcher says Chelmsford, at last a proper city, deserves a League football club and he's right. We have a very generous Chairman in Mansell Wallace. He has already poured money into the club he has supported since he was in short trousers and we fans should salute what he has done and continues to do, but his generosity is not a bottomless pit of funds. We need to be in the Blue Square Premier and Mansell deserves the financial rewards ultimate promotion to the Football League would bring, something John Coward dreamt of and funded in the 1960s.

But what if John's dream had been fulfilled? He was no multi-millionaire like Dave Whelan at Wigan Athletic, but what if we had 'done a Wigan' with John's financial support, or even a Wimbledon, a team we bettered in 1968?

What if in 1963 with Mason, Smillie, Isherwood, Hatsell et al we had walked away with the Southern League and reached the Fourth Round of the FA Cup beating, say, Newcastle United on the way like Hereford United were to do in the early 1970s?

With attendances from 1963 at the predicted 10,000 once we were in the League, our income and John's cash could have allowed the development of The Stadium in New Writtle Street. Imagine it now – an all-seater stadium that holds 25,000. A hotel (part of John's dream) situated between the football ground and the cricket ground on the site of the old French's yard. With the County Cricket Club not even playing at what is now the County Ground in the 1960s and themselves in dire financial straits, John Coward might have been able to go into partnership with them and develop the whole site; even moving into the old hospital grounds, buying up properties like those in Hayes

242

Close and making a combined Premier League stadium and possible International Cricket venue – just think what that would have done and would now be doing for Chelmsford!

Our football club might have led the way. Instead the County Cricket Club were eventually saved by a generous loan from Warwickshire CCC saving them from oblivion in the early 70s and allowing the development of what had been the Chelmsford Cricket Club's ground for more than a hundred years.

Imagine the City being where Wigan are today or to have shared a journey like that of Wimbledon. A journey for them that started at the same time as we were winning those league titles in 1968 and 1972. We would settle, surely, for a Cambridge United – back now a league above us but they too enjoyed an adventure like Wimbledon.

All this was not to be. John Coward was a great man and gave the club some of its most exciting times – those floodlit friendlies, the titanic struggles with arch enemy Romford, top players coming from Division One (the Premier League of its day) to play for us, THE CITY!

What times they were but poor John was struck down with serious illness – some say it was the stress of it all – before he could see it through. No one knows for sure, but he must have been mightily disappointed that his vision, his dream, was never fulfilled – but there was no one who deserved it more. Did he, on reflection when it all came to an end, look back on those decisions to sign Bobby Mason, Dennis Hatsell, Harry Taylor and others and regret what he did? Other clubs did the same as us and we were, after all, not breaking any rules, but along the way we might have upset a few people with the power to decide our future. Some clubs put in the same position as City with a ban, like Yeovil Town and Cambridge United, bounced back and have made the Football League along with many others. None of those or the likes of Wigan or Wimbledon had any more than us but perhaps they were in the right place at the right time to get voted into the League. Perhaps in the end it all comes down to luck.

It is galling to long term supporters, some like me stretching back into the 1950s, to see us usurped by the likes of Braintree (no offence to them and good luck to them) but I'm with Butch – our newly anointed city deserves what league football would bring. It would be a lift for our city and for those dedicated supporters, the youngsters who only know of our recent success or we old-timers, to hope 'Living the Claret Dream' does eventually become a reality.

Up the City Wheel 'Em In

Steve Little 2013 – celebrating 75 years of the Chelmsford City FC

APPENDIX

THE DREAM TEAM

Looking back at the most exciting decade of City's history to date, many supporters would enjoy speculating on what would have been our best team drawing from all those who played between 1958 and 1968. Two men are in a unique position to judge and comment on that. As football correspondent for the Essex Chronicle, Martin Rogers saw most of the matches and stalwart Tony Butcher played in most of them.

Martin has kindly put together the following thoughts and has been allowed to add in some substitutes. Tony, of course too modest to include himself, has a slightly different view on 'selection' and his 'team' has a few surprises.

To round things off some contributors to this book have added their twopenneth and I have taken the liberty of my all-time eleven drawing from the choices and comments of everyone.

Here is what Martin has to say:

It sounds like a simple request, but the reality of picking a 'best team for the decade' turned out to be anything but.

Managers and coaches, however small or large the squad of possible selections at their disposal, like to prepare for the best case scenario; ultimately many learn to go with what they've got come game time rather than spend all week devising tactics and formations only for injury, illness or other intervention to undo all their best-laid plans.

There's no need for such pragmatism here though, as our squad of 16 players drawn from a decade rich in character and talent can all be assumed to be fit, healthy and at the peak of their powers.

In any era, it's a fortunate team boss who can base his selection around a solid spine. That presents as good a place as any to start, with Owen Medlock my first and last choice between the posts, Terry Eades an obvious candidate at the heart of the defence, and Bill Cassidy a standout to lead the attack.

From day one, City have had some distinguished centre forwards and Cassidy's contribution, admittedly, was one short and sweet season – but what a season. The club's first league championship in 22 years owed much to the scoring efforts and effervescent character of the exuberant Scotsman.

Medlock and Eades, by contrast, were two of the game's quiet men, reassuringly self-contained, sound and solid achievers. Safe and organised, not a showman nor particularly imposing in stature (despite the nickname 'Big'Un' bestowed upon him by Peter Gillott) the sure-handed Medlock nevertheless inspired confidence.

Eades, one of the all-time outstanding local products, quickly grew into his role and seamlessly replaced the long-serving and hugely loved Derek Tiffin. It was all but inevitable that he would gravitate to higher things, going on to play 248 games for Cambridge United and to help smooth their entry into League football.

Tony Butcher, another local boy made good, is the logical choice to operate in tandem with Cassidy. His record (560 games, 286 goals) is unsurpassed and likely to remain so. It's a happy coincidence that the pair complemented each other to such telling effect in that title-winning year of 1967-68.

The period contained other notable strikers, for example the maverick Arthur Adey who rarely seemed to be short of trouble or goals, for that matter. Later came big, strong Bud Houghton, another voracious scorer who really looked the part – if there had been no Bill Cassidy then Bud would have been a shoe-in.

In between times FA Cup winner Tommy Wilson made his presence felt, with subtlety and style. Just as Medlock and Houghton had known championship success at Oxford United, so too did Wilson and old-fashioned half-back Sammy Salt at Cambridge City before Billy Frith spirited both into the Chelmsford ranks.

As a crafty creator and battle-hardened campaigner Wilson was one of the best, and Len Phillips, once an England international, remained a supremely artful midfielder even in his elder statesman years. But the thrillingly talented Bobby Mason gets my vote ahead of them, if only for the enormous impact his signing made in the summer of '62.

Kidnapped from Wolves at the age of 26 and a man of stature in one of the country's most consistently successful clubs, his arrival and departure provided an achingly accurate cameo of Chelmsford's lofty but flawed ambitions in a period high on expectation yet ultimately laced with disappointment.

With his muscular physique and authoritative air the crew-cut Salt arguably was the pre-eminent performer of his type in the period under review, a sort of non-league Paddy Crerand, ferocious when it came to winning the ball, all vision and authority when it came to distributing it, especially over long distances.

At the back, Lou Costello, deceptively leisurely but tellingly effective, was another astute football brain, his experience honed by years on the League circuit – many of them in the colours of Southend United. One-time West Ham hopeful Terry Hayward also appealed as a candidate for the number 2 shirt; in the end though, I settled for the streetwise and usually elegant Costello.

Teams loaded with crowd-pleasing personalities invariably need some foot soldiers to win them possession. When it came to getting the ball and imposing his will the indomitable Gillott (376 appearances) was old school, a pro's pro and a presence running through the heart of the side like a vein of colour in a stick of rock.

Peter was one of Harry Ferrier's first recruits, a genial but uncompromisingly hard man hewn from the Barnsley coalface, to be followed four years later by Billy Frith's inspired acquisition of Bobby Smith from the same source. Bob, by contrast, was wiry and nippy, a defender with pace, and versatile enough to contribute effectively and creatively in midfield.

In some ways the self-effacing 443-gamer was too capable in too many positions for his own good, being the player successive managers relied upon to plug a gap or slip into a role instead of being left to quietly ply his trade in one spot for successive campaigns.

There was nothing subdued about Tony Nicholas, my choice for the left wing spot. From teen prodigy at Chelsea, to record signing at Brighton, he was another of Mason's hugely heralded class of '62 and, as it turned out, the longest stayer of that intake. Always effervescent and rarely settling for the ordinary when something spectacular would do, he was still good enough to go back into the League four seasons later.

Since we can indulge ourselves with the luxury of two wide men, a further trove of riches presents itself for consideration on the opposite flank. Wes Maughan was for a while one of the most effective of stealth bombers with a keen eye for goal; Peter Leggett, all Beatle hair and gangling gait, had as swift a pair of heels ever glimpsed at New Writtle Street.

Harry Taylor, once of Newcastle United, narrowly slips into my side ahead of those well-appreciated entertainers. Taylor, it might be recalled, was another of those players transfer-listed by a top club and purloined for nothing by Ferrier a couple of years before the furore caused by the signing of Mason, Nicholas and co.

In the first of his two seasons Taylor was one of the standouts in the competition, usually wearing the No.9 shirt only to frequent the flanks to great effect on occasion, as he had done for most of his time at St. James's Park. Speedy and resourceful, he was a tough little nut, a quality which just shades the artistry of his rivals.

Here then, is a line-up which combines the virtues of looking good, always a prerequisite for the connoisseurs (with a nice 4-2-4 formation to make it work), and the ability to get down to the nitty-gritty when circumstances demand.

There were times during this decade, as with many others, in which style and substance were not always in tune with each other. City frequently flattered to deceive, days of delight too often punctuated with the reality that the Southern League in those times also required players to get down and dirty.

It's probably no coincidence, then, to find seven of the starting eleven in this fantasy team to represent the period under review actually featured – most of them large – in the 1967-68 championship line-up. When the going got tough, the tough got going, the ingredients meshed and the boys brought home a title for the first time in 22 years.

My team for the 1958-68 decade:

Owen Medlock;
Lou Costello, Terry Eades, Bobby Smith, Peter Gillott;
Sammy Salt, Bobby Mason;
Harry Taylor, Tony Butcher, Billy Cassidy, Tony Nicholas.
Substitutes from: Alan Collier, John Docherty, Wes Maughan, Bud Houghton, Tommy Wilson.

***

Tony Butcher comments as follows having excluded himself:

I would be extremely happy to play in this team and that's for sure! Martin mentions Arthur Adey and I would put him in alongside 'King Billy' Cassidy – Arthur was a unique talent, but perhaps this was wasted by his lack of discipline, particularly off the field and yet he was good enough to attract interest from Arsenal in the late 50s, so I was not the only one who rated him highly.

I would have Len Phillips edging out Sammy Salt only on the basis of his greater experience and I would want Len as my captain. Leggett for Harry Taylor is a marginal choice as it was the other way for Martin.

Bobby Mason was a fabulous footballer but we only saw him at his zenith for a short while and, whilst he latterly took us apart when playing against us for Poole Town, his second spell at the club was rather disappointing. I would put Denis Hatsell in his place as I feel he contributed more to the club in his time with us, particularly when the chips were down. I agree with Tony Nicholas and, for me, he just edges out Geoff Walker who I thought would have graced any City team which he certainly did in the years up to 1961. Peter Gillott has often said that Geoff was the best winger he played with as his first touch in trying to control Peter's over and under hit passes was second to none! So, my team in 4-4-2 is:

Medlock;
Costello, Eades, Smith, Gillott;
Leggett, Phillips (Capt), Hatsell, Nicholas;
Cassidy, Adey

***

Len Menhinick can rightly judge the players from these golden years from his unique position as Secretary and Director. He has selected a side that he says will actually win something made up of those who were not necessarily the best footballers that played in the era we are looking at, but players who, when the chips were down, you would want in the claret and white. This is typical Len under whose management I played post 1968 at Old Chelmsfordians – he had no 'fancy dans' in his teams!

Medlock;
Hayward, Hopkins, Tiffin, Gillott;
Leggett, Smith, Phillips, Docherty;
Houghton, Butcher
Subs: Collier, Costello, Salt, Smillie, Cassidy

***

Terry Ketley and his brother, Rob, not surprisingly disagree, as brothers often do, with Terry preferring Alan Collier in goal, somewhat surprisingly, and also includes Tommy Wilson and Stewart Imlach, the former Forest duo. Whereas Rob does not fancy Tony Butcher in his team at all and, instead, has Moyse and Houghton spearheading the attack with Shreeves in midfield.

Mick Butcher, younger brother of Tony and a player at the club in the early 1960s, goes with:

Medlock;
Hayward, Collins, Eades, Gillott;
Phillips, Mason;
Leggett, Cassidy, Butcher, Nicholas

He is the only correspondent to select Peter Collins, who of course went on to greater things but was very young and still early in his career when at City. Long-time supporter Steve Cawley selects Robin Gladwin at left back instead of Peter Gillott. Robin, of course, was a late developer and went on to play at Norwich – so he is a good shout for that position! Steve, like the Ketleys, is a fan of Ron Smillie and interestingly would have Wes Maughan on the right wing instead of Leggett.

***

It is very interesting to look through the variety of choices and to see how views differ. As I said at the beginning of this amble through such a vast list of quality players, Martin Rogers and Tony Butcher are best placed to provide the definitive choice but then we all like to have a contrary view – that, after all, is the nature of this glorious game!

With this in mind I shall use my editorial privilege and try to draw all these views into the one team with five substitutes.

Medlock, Butcher, Eades, Smith, Gillott, Nicholas and Leggett seem to be automatic 'shoe ins' for the starting eleven leaving four to find. The right back is a straight choice between Costello and Hayward. Costello had some success at centre forward and once even played in goal (rather erratically, as it turned out, after Medlock was carried off!), so he provides an attacking option should we need to chase a game. For me Lou edges out Terry who is rewarded with a place on the bench. So far then we have the 4-4-2 line up looking like this:

Medlock;
Costello, Eades, Smith, Gillott;
Leggett, ? , ? , Nicholas;
Butcher, ?

Tony Butcher chose Billy Cassidy and he should know the best striker pairing he played in! Personally, I thought Tony linked very well with Tommy Wilson with Tony acting as the Alan Shearer like spearhead and Wilson the Teddy Sheringham link man. Bud Houghton like

Cassidy was the spearhead in each of their prolific seasons with Tony playing off both. I shall have to go with Cassidy and have Wilson on the bench, so as to change our system if we have to.

In central midfield we have the remaining two places to fill. Ideally, we need someone there to control the game, to hold up the ball and not waste it and to sweep in front of the defensive line. Salt, Phillips and Shreeves could all fill that one position and perhaps we could use two of them but I would prefer the other remaining midfield position to go to a more attack minded player to score some goals. I will have to go with Len Phillips in that holding role in view of his greater experience and leadership and for being the one person to change the way we played in his time with the club.

So, with Alan Collier, an able deputy for Medlock, also securing his place on the bench, currently alongside Hayward and Wilson, we need the attacking central midfielder and two substitutes.

For midfield Mason, Hatsell and Smillie are the popular candidates with an outsider being Johnny Gordon who played brilliantly and in every game of the 67/68 championship winning season, but perhaps he was not so much a goalscorer as the other three. Hatsell could also play as a centre forward as well as in midfield and Smillie could play on the wing; so both would provide switching alternatives in any game. However, I side with Martin Rogers in that Bobby Mason was the catalyst and defining player of this golden era for the club and alongside Phillips presents a midfield of pure class. With this choice Hatsell and Smillie take their place on the bench leaving the team as:

Medlock;
Costello, Eades, Smith, Gillott;
Leggett, Phillips (Capt), Mason, Nicholas;
Butcher, Cassidy
Substitutes: Collier, Hayward, Hatsell, Smillie, Wilson

So there we have it – a team to match anything before or since the golden years of the Claret Dream.